BRIDGING

CAMPUS AND

COMMUNITY

Events, Excerpts and Expectations

For Strengthening America's

Collaborative Competence

A Professional Memoir

PAUL A. MILLER

ISBN: 149498475X
ISBN 13: 9781494984755

TABLE OF CONTENTS

$\mathcal{P}$ R E F A C E

NOBODY IS OBLIGED to read what another may write, but I came to the notion that a life's calling is a story worth telling. One also reaches an age when to speak of the past grows pleasant, especially after ninety-seven years. This summing up of my career also includes personal and family events, all in light of the twentieth century.

As the twentieth century unfolded, American colleges and universities responded ever more quickly to societal needs and pressures. My life and career spanned much of that century. A large part focused on adult and continuing education as one agent of the monumental change in the influence of American colleges and universities. How this change agent came to enhance the offerings of myriad academies is a saga worth more understanding, telling, and retelling. My own reflections, which spring from my efforts as an administrator to fashion academic outreach through adult and continuing education, form the thread that weaves this story together.

My life story throws into relief America's change from an agrarian to an urban industrial society. Now taking place on a global scale, this shift is further embedded in an information and electronic era of change and development. These two transformations joined to initiate and launch the technological revolution of the twenty-first century. Woven into this revolution are the missions of county (agricultural) agents and the Cooperative Extension Service to which they belong; land-grant colleges and universities; and other outreach services of state, regional, and federal governments. This collaborative system is little understood by citizens in urban, suburban, and exurban societies—yet it is one of the most inventive of America's worldwide efforts.

Moreover, this arrangement—the collaboration of universities, several levels of government, and private and public support groups—joined in common cause to play key parts in the political, economic, and informational movements of the twentieth century. Also associated therein are challenges defined as mounting crises for the twenty-first century, especially those related to technological, ecological, environmental, and social transformations. This account selects certain events that I personally experienced in some seventy-five years of professional life; it also explores models of facilitation for helping devise new solutions for ongoing and new challenges.

My initial professional post was that of the county agricultural agent. My life's pathway continued from there, directed by several related assignments. Some tasks found me serving other county agents and the universities that sponsored them. All bore the imprint of my first assignment of helping rural people accept change and use knowledge to shape it. Agents of change, however, must accommodate the very changes they promote! Thus, this account selects events from my career and excerpts from my writings that such events stimulated me to compose. All are observations on certain societal changes and adjustments that fell upon my life's agenda from boyhood onward.

Overlapping and leaping forward from such adjustments is the digital and multimedia revolution, now termed the electronic era. Challenges facing colleges and universities in the next fifty years are likely to be even greater than those of the past when student enrollments and costs, governmental support and public demands, all accelerated. Academic institutions must evermore engage with society and with each other, a demand now stretching from individual homes and local enterprises to an acceleration of global forces.

New needs abound both on and off the campuses; new models and missions spring up. A growing confusion suggests that the traditional esteem in which the public holds universities is being challenged. But the seeds for recovery of a new acceptance and service were planted in years passed: some sprouted and lived; some died; others were spurned. The attempt herein identifies certain portions of that background.

Moreover, new institutional alliances now spring up in a globalizing age! They need address the growing gap between rich and poor, improve health among those who still await modern medicine, and work to overcome humankind's disposition not only to employ science and technology beneficially, but also to wreak violence upon itself, the human habitat, and the earth's nature as a whole.

We have yet to live successfully and peacefully with the consequences of human knowledge. However creative our social and economic institutions become, they must learn to better link together and connect with families, workplaces, schools, neighborhoods, religious institutions, and the many other such groupings that join to form the civic context. This quest for a more intimate linkage among primary institutions governed the choice of events and writings that make up these memoirs.

$\mathcal{M}$ E T H O D

THE EVENTS, ROUGHLY in chronological order, sum up key career-related experiences during some eighty years of my life. Linked to them are some one hundred forty excerpts, brief selections drawn from the full body of my writings, with an emphasis on the outreach functions of universities with which I had firsthand experience. The excerpts are taken only from my complete papers, monographs, and books that were either published and/or formally delivered to audiences. None are taken from informal notes. Neither have they been edited, except for minor clarification. Nor has the gender usage been changed, thus reflecting the times in which they were written or given. The places and dates of delivery are given for the unpublished material; the published selections are cited and highlighted in customary fashion. Importantly, the excerpts from my writings also join and probe the history of the changes occurring along the course of an intellectual journey through most of the twentieth century.

While the events describe mostly professional situations, they also include personal and family happenings. Devotion to career does not develop without being reconciled with more intimate domains. The challenges, gains, and, yes, the tragedies, all coalesce and penetrate one's profession to shape and give it direction. The book includes brief and candid references to events that had decisive impacts upon both my life and professional pursuits.

This work touches upon several fields for which there are canons of high scholarly quality, for example, biography, social change, technologic innovation, human development, public and educational administration, economics, and political science. Yet this collection aims for no authority in any such categories; rather, it is an assembly of career experiences within a defined but important context, and personal analysis and reflection upon them.

The selections from the larger body of my writings in adult and continuing education, plus other professional papers, are located in the West Virginia and Regional Collections, West Virginia University, Morgantown, West Virginia. A similar but more limited collection, including those papers from which the chosen excerpts herein were taken, resides in the archives of the Wallace Memorial Library, Rochester Institute of Technology, Rochester, New York.

The following account consists of nine chapters. Chapter one defines the county agent system and how I was led into it; chapter two describes related and graduate studies and assignments at Michigan State University, which shaped the whole of my career; chapter three sums up a briefer period at West Virginia University, my alma mater, though held as the centerpiece of that career; chapter four summarizes how my primary concern of academic outreach widened while serving in the US Department of Health, Education, and Welfare; chapter five highlights this theme while I served as the leader of planning for a new academic institution in the University of North Carolina System, one geared especially to public service and continuing education in Charlotte, North Carolina; chapter six carries these experiences into an urban setting and a private university and, ultimately, our home in Rochester, New York; chapter seven summarizes a transition in the Rochester period that includes certain national and international assignments, plus the return to a professorship; chapter eight sums up relevant and continuing involvements in partial retirement at the University of Missouri-Columbia; and the ninth and final chapter, an epilogue, providing relevant glances backward and forward.

$\mathscr{A}$CKNOWLEDGMENTS

Two persons are importantly acknowledged: I dedicate this account to them.

CATHERINE, MY FIRST wife of twenty-five years, until her untimely death in 1964, lovingly, faithfully, and effectively supported me in the grounding of an occupation. My professional posts demanded incessant days of travel and nights for preparation, duties that extensive fieldwork cannot avoid. Catherine patiently nurtured the whole family at home and in its pursuits beyond, yet reserved loyalty, affection, and endurance to care for the absent but loved one. This is one of the most heroic functions in American society, and she faithfully practiced it throughout the foundations of my professional life.

Francena came into my life for some forty-five years before her death in 2010. Prepared in a similar field, she joined me in an array of mutual interests in family, community, and profession. She remained faithful to her own notable career of human service, yet never faltered in her enthusiasm and support of the track I was on when we met and married, even as it undermined her own. No aspect of my life and work escaped her character, love, intelligence, loyalty, and toil; I am much the better for it in every way. The same may be said also for this account, which received her early reviews and suggestions.

Also, a large number of beloved members of my extended families, friends, colleagues, supervisors, students, college trustees, and civic leaders too numerous to be all remembered much less openly thanked, helped me enjoy what was more of a calling than a job. They sacrificed for me, taught me, shared with me, corrected me, and stood by me in one trial after another. Some of these people will be introduced later. Such values and actions rank high in academe, and I am grateful that they challenged me to practice them myself.

Paul A. Miller
Montrose, Colorado

WEST VIRGINIA

BECOMING A COUNTY AGRICULTURAL AGENT

THE COUNTY AGENT: ORIGINS AND SYSTEMS

MY FIRST PROFESSIONAL job, as assistant county (agricultural) agent in West Virginia's Ritchie County, began on July 1, 1939. But not until 1955, when I became state director of the Cooperative Extension Service at Michigan State University, the employing agency of county agents in Michigan, did I begin to understand this uniquely American innovation. Other agricultural students were likely no better informed. Our knowledge of the county agent's history was limited to a few key events: the founding of public land-grant universities, the later creation of an agricultural experiment station (AES) in each state, and the eventual establishment of county agents by congressional action in 1914.

This lack of understanding was due to our emphasis on vocational and technical agriculture. We were fieldworkers, not students of history or theories of complex organizations, even those of our employer. By 1955, however, an agricultural revolution, in which county agents were

assuming critically important leadership, would fall within broader technological and industrial revolutions. And this impressive change would
quicken and challenge the county agents themselves!

The intellectual challenge of the Cooperative Extension Service was
present from my boyhood onward and throughout my entire career. The
challenge is not only to trace but also to understand how county agents
entered into the more than three thousand counties across the American
landscape and proceeded to foster a technological revolution in world history. They would do so by the basic employment of science-based knowledge in food production. This effort led America from a rural past into an
urban future and, ever further, into global expansion. County agents invented a model of informal education to be emulated at home, guided into
courthouses, legislative halls and university laboratories, congressional
and White House offices, and eventually adapted and adopted throughout
the world.

The story of county agricultural agents as they led this revolution of
social and economic change is rooted in an elaborate history of organizations and institutions not easy to describe or understand. Importantly, the
story runs parallel with much of American history in the nineteenth and
throughout the twentieth centuries, and continues now into the twenty-
first century. County agents were at work before the US Congress established them in law with the passage of the Smith-Lever Act of 1914.

As president of Iowa State College, Seaman A. Knapp strove from
1905 onward with his dream of placing an agent of positive social change
in the rural countryside. Knapp held that ideal county agents "must be
practical farmers." He would say, "No use in sending a carpenter to tell
a tailor how to make a coat, even if he is pretty well read up on coats: the
tailor won't follow!" The county agent helped bring public opinion into
harmony and then made forceful by support of the press and by the cooperation of farmers, merchants, and bankers. Knapp's preferred method
for county agents was through demonstration: showing how calves grow

better with their horns removed; placing a strip of fertilized pasture at the bend of the road for all passersby to see the difference; helping children grow better corn than their parents, and thus help teach the latter; converting the fabric of sugar sacks into household draperies; and teaching farmers how to plow fields in a way that reduces the erosive damage of the sudden thunderstorm.

The Smith-Lever Act gave official acceptance to Knapp's teaching and preaching, thus adding another federal entity for the land-grant institutions to develop and manage. The Act defined its aim as to "aid in diffusing among the people of the United States useful and practical information on subjects relating to agriculture and home economics and to encourage application of the same." Both the legislation and the actions were anchored in earlier and historic endeavors. The Morrill Act of 1862, authored by US Senator Justin Morrill of Vermont, authorized a new kind of public "land-grant" university in each state, with public service as its trademark. This response answered new pressures to expand science and share it with the then leading enterprise of farming. To further strengthen this response, Congress passed the Hatch Act of 1887, and sponsored an agricultural experiment station as another division of each land-grant institution.

Such official steps were preceded by earlier and not fully rural forces seething in pre–Civil War times. They can be traced back to the ferment about free public schools, the addition of science to classical studies, and the demand to guarantee education rights to women. Experimental institutions of the early nineteenth century were also in the background. These include the Gardiner Lyceum in Maine, the Agricultural Seminary in Connecticut, and the 1824 forerunner and proposed model of a land-grant college, the Rensselaer Institute of Troy, New York. Also involved was the labor movement of that time: a New York cabinetmaker, Harrison Howard, urged a "people's college" in central New York State. Later, with the turn into the twentieth century, the Progressive movement added other influences, notably the American Country Life Association and its founding president, Kenyon Butterfield.

The Smith-Lever Act of 1914 gave legitimacy to Knapp's quiet demonstrations in the countryside. New organizations came into place as sponsors and supporters of the first county agents. The US Department of Agriculture, established along with the land-grant colleges in 1862, grew to resemble a national agricultural university and joined with the colleges to support the agricultural experiment stations (AESs). In 1890, a second congressional act regularized federal funding of the colleges, their county agents and experiment stations, and established several land-grant institutions to serve Negro students.

An elaborate cooperative enterprise then grew to provide the county agent the means to promote rural change and create an institution within an institution—the Cooperative Extension Service (CES). The CES would not only link research, teaching, and demonstration; it would also form a collaborative system of the federal, state, and county governments with the colleges. First, however, the idea had to win the approval of the local people before this new force could begin placing agents among them—agents determined to enhance if not change traditional ways of farming. The sponsors of the earliest county agents were committees of farmers and local business leaders. Eventually named farm bureaus, these committees created coalitions at state and national levels; in time, they evolved into the American Farm Bureau Federation. Other organizations formed and joined as partners, including the Grange and later, the Farmers Union. Thus was a field organization born to stimulate radical change in the lives of farmers and their rural communities and to react to social pressure and local needs. The county agent served to link the problems of farm, home, and community to the knowledge of the campus and other sources. Moreover, three other roles were invented to stand at a county agent's side: the volunteer planner, the campus specialist, and the state director.

Normally laypersons, the volunteer planners had an understanding of local needs and resources. They were usually successful farmers and civic leaders. They produced work plans based on knowledge of local conditions, what changes local people might accept, and potential "early adopters." Adept at bringing common sense into play, these volunteers knew the centers of both opposition and support. They did not overlook advancing their own enterprises and opportunities for members of their families, but they were reliably loyal to the grassroots, the idea of the family farm, and the need for local control.

Campus (or extension) specialists were advanced in a special subject and had offices on the campus with or close by the research worker. The specialists delivered knowledge to the county agent and others involved, and carried back to the researcher the need for analysis of special problems. Such exchanges were enhanced by visits to the field, meetings with farmers and their groups, and by the use of available media. The specialists served as the bridge between laboratory and family farm, remained in touch with new developments, and, when useful, collaborated with other specialists.

The state Cooperative Extension Service director led efforts to fashion and monitor workable linkages between county and state governments and the US Department of Agriculture and related federal agencies, with the land-grant college or university as the center of this cooperating arrangement. The state director also was concerned with funding and program issues that defined the system's uniqueness and brought citizen ire to bear if support was threatened. Moreover, these officials also designed and expedited cooperative agreements with regional and national groups.

Local people gave the movement much of its energy and grassroots philosophy, but agreements among county, state, and federal governments made it legitimate. Each of these levels had administrative, technical, and legislative sectors. Agreements tied all levels and sectors together and gave the movement competence and legitimacy, secured the needed finances, and defended the movement when challenged. Importantly, democratic creeds and local controls could also be defended, despite the movement's aim to change the very nature of farming.

County level administration and technical competence centered on the county agent and related technical agencies. County government normally provided local operating expenses and, occasionally, a portion of wages. The Farm Bureaus and other rural organizations backed up these local arrangements. As agriculture accepted and applied more advanced technology, interests formed in support of specific commodities, such as dairy products, livestock products, wool, cotton, tobacco, and wheat.

Administration at the state level evolved with delegation normally from the president of the land-grant institution through the dean of agriculture to the state extension director. Technical power resided in the state AES, academic departments, and several state agencies (e.g., state departments of agriculture and the growth of federal farm-related agencies, especially during the 1930s. State legislatures provided appropriations, mainly for the campus specialists, but also, in time, for a portion of local salaries.

Federal administration fell to the US Department of Agriculture, shaped by cooperative agreements with the land-grant institutions. The USDA also created technical backup sectors, such as the Agricultural Research Center at Beltsville, Maryland. The Smith-Lever Act provided for congressional appropriations to the USDA. These, in turn, went to the colleges by means of grants by formula and memoranda of agreement. National offices of farm organizations also sprang up, along with commodity groups and advisory councils. These groups entered their own interests into the public process for securing resources to undergird the overall effort. They also supported the county agent system in its mission to help rural people accept and adjust to technical change.

Thus, three levels of government, each with administrative, technical, and legislative sectors, formed into a cooperative whole. That they could do so was not due alone to law and agreements; they also held in common the agrarian ideal that democracy performs best when decisions are made at local levels. The power held by this arrangement, in which the county agent was a central figure, consisted of three elements: technical knowledge, the harbinger of progress for the twentieth century; the capacity of rural people to employ their disproportionately large representation in state legislative bodies; and an equal skill to forge coalitions among organizations, among levels of government, and between such agricultural regions as the American South and the Midwest.

The Cooperative Extension Service, and the role of the county agent within it, became a technological and institutional innovation unparalleled in the United States or elsewhere. This meta-idea in education and social change galvanized the unprecedented technological progress of American agriculture, and the model was increasingly emulated throughout the world.

THE START OF A JOURNEY

THE NARROW VALLEYS of West Virginia hide behind Appalachian undulations as far as the eye can see. Deeply cleaved, they allow only a road, sufficient level space for a house, outbuildings, and a stream to invade them. In one such gash cutting through the hills of the state's northern panhandle, Middle Run flows into the nearby Ohio River. In 1928, my father brought my mother, an only sister, and me to a small farm along Middle Run. I was eleven years old. The move achieved my father's dream of having his own farm. After hardscrabble farming with his father in southeastern Ohio, and the death of his young wife and baby, he migrated to the small city and commercial pottery center of East Liverpool, Ohio. There he became an industrial worker, but he could not forget the lure of the seasonal turns of the countryside and the farmer's challenges when greeting them.

My father, tallish and thin, had taken only partially to industrial life. His hands, hardened and thickly veined, and differing from a fair and smooth-skinned face, would not escape notice. With some six grades of formal schooling, he was an avid reader of newspapers. He was zealously devoted to the Democratic Party and the labor movement, and unflinchingly patriotic. The whole family joined in his annual ride to the courthouse to pay his taxes. The trip enabled my father to lecture us on good citizenship. Harry Ausborn Miller was a storyteller! At the top of his repertoire were humorous tales of subsistence farming; they never failed to disclose some principle of honesty, loyalty, and hard work.

My father, rather slow to discipline his children, could burst suddenly into frightful anger, only to have it collapse into pleas for forgiveness. Such anger might explode when a farm tool took the blame for a mishap, prompting him to throw it as far as possible, then asking me to retrieve it. On one such occasion, when I was sixteen, I refused to obey, stimulating more anger; he loudly reminded me of a father's authority...and then broke into laughter and set off to find the tool himself. The episode became a story of his presence when his younger son became a man.

Not long after his migration from country to city at the start of the twentieth century, my father met and married Mary Elizabeth Stewart. Similarly limited in formal education, my mother-to-be had also entered industrial life as young as it was possible, finding work at the potteries. She had been born in nearby Van Port, Pennsylvania, where her father, with more interest in religion than money, eked out a living for his wife and four children as a shoe cobbler and lay preacher. Like him, while relenting some with the years, my mother held tenaciously to a strong religiosity. Her olive skin, deep-set brown eyes, and prominently high cheekbones cascaded over with black hair were all set in the sturdy frame and bearing of one not at all tolerant of lassitude or nonsense. She clung to the cause of temperance, stored my grandfather's library on the evils of alcohol in my bedroom; she refused to overlook her husband's occasional saloon stop after work, which soon prompted him to choose the life of a teetotaler.

My mother was as outgoing in relationships as my father was shy—apart, that is, from his storytelling. She knew and called by name all whom she met on the village streets. My father told his stories to underscore principles; my mother defined and oversaw the household rules for carrying them out: never go into public without scrubbed faces, hands, and clothing; keep your sleeping quarters mercilessly neat and ready for inspection; and take on no job that you did not expect to finish. Attending church was surely a sacred venture, and all the more important when you might feign illness. Hers was the message that sloppy and inconsistent behavior, not the absence of money, defined you as poor.

Once in East Liverpool and married, the couple settled in its East End, a working-class neighborhood strewn along Pennsylvania Avenue and peopled by pottery and steel mill workers of various ethnic and racial backgrounds. In 1910 and three years after the birth of my only brother, Bernie, my father, much with his own hands, built a small cottage on Harker Avenue. From there, he could walk to the plant and work as a pottery kiln placer. This job demanded a skill for climbing tall ladders to the top of brick kilns with a container (itself of some weight) of unfired dishware on his head. He would carry deepened scalp indentations thereafter throughout his life. I was born in the small house on March 22, 1917. My sister Ethel followed in 1919.

My clearest memories of eleven years spent in that urban working-class neighborhood are of my father's stories of life on his boyhood farm. My mother, native to the local region, tolerated my father's sadness for departing that farm with good humor, and mildly dismissed his tales of the countryside. But we children were regaled as he would tell and retell his favorites. That not all of them passed the standard of truth was of no matter. What did matter, when his illustrations and mimicry turned to the farming sections of Sears, Roebuck and Co. catalogs, were the way they sparked our vivid imaginations of farm life, fields, barns, tools, and animals.

Our lives began to change in 1926 with the building of a modernized pottery plant across the Ohio River at Newell, West Virginia. When daily bridge tolls added a new and permanent financial demand, the search for a way to escape this cost rekindled my father's dream. So it came to pass that he purchased the small farm on Middle Run, a mile from the equally small village of Chester, and five miles from Newell and the plant. What we found in 1928 was an angular and worn farmhouse in need of repair, a small workshop building, an outdoor privy ten yards to the rear, and a barn and pig lot across the narrow road. All were backed by sixteen acres of almost vertical pasture, a narrow garden plot, a small vineyard, and a weedy orchard of apple, peach, and plum trees.

A new kind of family life began. Part remained tied to my father's pottery shop; another turned to a miniature version of the life he glorified. The winding road along Middle Run separated the small farms and homes of a mixed population of natives and newcomers. All were linked to nearby potteries, steel mills, and small farming enterprises. Gardens grew beside the narrow creek and small orchards on the hills. A few families, my own included, kept a milk cow or two, a couple of hogs to butcher at Thanksgiving time, some grain growing to partially feed the animals, and flocks of chickens and other fowl sufficient for household use and minor sales.

My father and I had arrived at a choice site, and I accepted easily his early knock on my bedroom door to begin the day's chores. While my mother would gradually adjust to the new life of expanded chores and reduced conveniences, her initial enthusiasm was shaky. My convivial sister Ethel never fully warmed to the greater isolation and such symbols as the privy behind the house. My older brother, Bernie, just married and no longer in the household, remained on the Ohio side of the river with his wife, Mildred, and four sons to follow. He would give decades of support to the move of the family, including his unusual skill with tools and their repair.

Thus began a new chapter on a small part-time farm as well as an experience with what was happening then to many farm and rural youth as they grew into adulthood. The 1930s found rural youth facing evermore stringent requirements for becoming farmers, including the need for more land and higher capital investment. These factors, plus the serious downturns posed by the Great Depression, greatly reduced prospects for youth to earn a living on a farm, and greatly increased the need for many to seek industrial work instead or to combine it with part-time farming.

Years later, given the experience of intervening years, I wrote of the transitional challenges that faced rural youth whether they remained or departed to seek new opportunities. One such reference came as an address to close a White House–sponsored National Conference on Rural Youth at Stillwater, Oklahoma, September 25, 1958. Its theme described the difficult adjustments often confronted in shifting from rural to urban life as in the three points below.

Rural youth are too often caught in the forces that tend to constrain rural communities from making rapid adjustments to a larger-scaled geographical and social life, which do little to reduce the gulf between technological maturity and institutional immaturity, and even make for an ambiguity in what it means to be a rural American.

First, rural young people acquire skills—and the work habits to go with them—that may not relate to aptitude or aspiration, may not be realistic in terms of the structure of employment in or out of the rural community, and may frequently be oriented to the disappearing end of the occupational hierarchy.

Second, while certain distinct strengths are often cultivated in rural children and nurtured by realities of family, community, and kinship, the rural milieu can sometimes hinder growth as well. The range and quality of visual and verbal impressions, in and out of school, may limit rural children's knowledge about professional and personal alternatives, reduce their ability to deal with abstractions and concepts, and emphasize an inward-facing disposition toward change.

Third, rural children are increasingly destined to make major moves along any or all of three mobility pathways: the axis of *physical* mobility, which may remove and even isolate them from familiar geographies and communities; the axis of *social* mobility, which may lead them to discover new social circles, activities, and standards of success and achievement; and the axis of mobility, in which the move to more densely populated urban environments—the transition to being a "small fish in a big pond"—may lead to increasing depersonalization of relationships, and an increase in the number of superficial connections.

THE ROOTS OF A CALLING

THE INFLUENCE OF my family on me grew with the 1928 move to the farm. My parents held the aim of advancing the children beyond their own station. Importantly, despite his own travail in the Depression years, my brother Bernie, ten years older, remained the wisest of mentors. His early childhood had provided fewer opportunities than mine: formal education beyond high school seemed out of the question for him. But he never failed to exude pride in my chosen pathway, which grew to be quite different from his vocation as an industrial machinist of definitive skill and support. His emphasis upon hard work and honest dealings made him a remarkable human being. He became first among my role models and nothing less than a clearly moral influence on my growing up and throughout adulthood, even to the present day. Thus did my brother Bernie, along with his wife Mildred and their four sons (James, Robert, Terry, and Jerry), continue happily as a beloved family and supporters of me and mine.

The move also opened the door to my earliest inclinations to become a county extension agent, and more dimly, to be part of an academic institution. That moment came when I learned of 4-H work from youthful friends and was invited to join a 4-H club at the one-room school of a nearby community. This odyssey began at my initial meeting in that school, when I. B. Boggs, the beloved state 4-H leader, told the story of Henry A. Wallace of Iowa, who had greatly improved the growing of corn as a youth. From that moment through many years to follow, a small number of men and women of West Virginia University influenced the shape of my interests and intentions. When I was only twelve, such leaders introduced the idea of a university to me, even the importance of its outreach to Middle Run.

Chief among these leaders was the local county agricultural agent. Walter C. Gumbel arrived in Hancock County about two years before my family, just after graduating from The Pennsylvania State University. He plunged into its rural life, taking special interest in youth and their projects. I learned to shorten his name to "Gumbel," as adults had fondly chosen to do. Tall and slender, and a long, square-cut face, Gumbel was as wiry in body as he was disciplined by purpose. Exhibiting a genuine kindness, he soon won wide and affectionate support of young and old alike. Gumbel would join my brother as a lead role model.

His interests in me, as in other youth, created a widening circle of experiences for me beyond Middle Run. When I was fifteen, he arranged a month-long summer fellowship at West Virginia University's Nature Training School at Oglebay Park near Wheeling. The adventure continued with me serving as a youth delegate to Washington, DC, and a conference of the American Country Life Association. Gumbel spoke with my parents about college, insisting that I become the first of my family line to have that opportunity. Above all, he helped my parents and me to understand college attendance as more than an impossible dream.

Another helpmate and model entered here as well. Davy Evans, in his early twenties, had arrived from Wales, Great Britain, to live with a nearby aunt and seek factory work in America. His friendship widened my horizons, and introduced me to Welsh history and music. He was also relentless in his insistence that I understand the importance of attending college. Eventually Davy returned to Wales with his bride, another young immigrant from that country, but we met again in Wales some fifty years later, shortly before his death. It was then that I learned how he had met quietly with Gumbel all those many years before and how together they had conspired on how best to spring me into college.

Meanwhile, the years in high school in nearby Newell also made their mark. I fell under the spell of two exemplary teachers who gave me an early love of books and study. Naomi Bowmaster taught English and classics, and defined for me the importance of Latin. Frederick Miller mentored me in mathematics and science. They and others, especially the staff of the nearby Carnegie Public Library, led me to important books about human service that connected life in the countryside to larger spheres. Among these were Paul DeKruif's *Microbe Hunters*, dramatizing scientific research and service, Sinclair Lewis's *Arrowsmith*, and Somerset Maugham's *Of Human Bondage*. Also included were short stories with idealistic plots, amply available in the cheap pulp magazines of the Depression period.

My high school career closed in 1935. While the times and family financial capability did not warrant it, I was determined to enroll in agriculture at West Virginia University (WVU) in the fall. My parents were prepared to give support up to and even beyond their limits. I had accumulated a small savings from selling broilers thru door-to-door sales, the result of a 4-H project. The decisive resolution, however, came in the form of Bernal R. Weimer, professor of biology and later provost at nearby Bethany College; having been apprised of my high school scholastic record and distinction as the 1935 graduating class valedictorian, appeared at our door and offered a tuition scholarship and a campus job.

My family and I seized this opportunity, although it sidetracked my desire to follow the model of Gumbel and become a county agent. But I went off to a happy and productive first year at Bethany College, electing biology as a major and Dr. Weimer as a mentor. Following a solid first year of studies and campus landscape work, I was invited in that summer of 1936 to remain on campus for a continuation of the latter. It was then, however, that my resolve to become a county agent returned and strengthened. Dr. Weimer seemed greatly disturbed, pointing out positive options for the future by remaining at Bethany and, with some heat, that he was aware of my ambition to become another Gumbel!

Nevertheless, without consulting family or gaining further advice from Bethanians, that fall I transferred to the College of Agriculture at WVU! To no small degree, my courage for this step was sparked when two fellow 4-H members, then sophomores at WVU, invited me to share a small basement apartment in Morgantown. One of them, William Conkle, later married my sister and remained a lifelong friend and colleague. The other, Lester Miller, also became a county agent.

However, with the impact of the Great Depression, with more college job seekers than available jobs, the fall semester of 1936 grew into a financial crisis. While saved in part by janitorial chores in the chemistry laboratories and an inexpensive meal plan in one of the numerous boarding houses of that time, I realized by the Christmas holidays that enrolling for the next semester appeared impossible. Discussions followed with my parents. We assessed local job opportunities, especially one for routine testing work in the laboratory of a nearby steel mill, but the crisis was solved when my father quietly placed a check before me at the dining table, one sufficient to enable a return to WVU in January 1937. Despite traditional values hardened against such a step, he had mortgaged the farm!

Once I returned to WVU, new and surprising opportunities to make my own way developed. One was to serve as a student assistant in the biochemistry laboratories. Another, part of an invitation to join the Sigma Nu fraternity, was the job of making beds and helping prepare and serve meals. My list of mentors grew rapidly to include professors William MacLachlan in biochemistry; L. M. Peairs of entomology; Robert

Dustman in agricultural chemistry; and John Longwell in animal husbandry. I grew better acquainted with the Cooperative Extension Service
and its state director, J. O. Knapp. Due to my growing belief that my
limited experience on a small part-time farm would defeat selection as a
county agent, I broadened my studies to include such other specialties as
biochemistry, veterinary and human medicine, and animal nutrition.

I met several county agents in my initial year at WVU, thanks in part
to Walter Gumbel, who had become the university's extension soil con-
servationist. The county agents I saw daily in the university's corridors
appealed as people of professional independence, the hallmarks of outdoor activity stamped on their faces, their comportment typifying the
bearing of those with substantial responsibilities. My knowledge of their
lives and work grew rapidly. They remained focused on practical fieldwork
with demonstration as their method. But the technological revolution in
farming practice and the farm policy reforms of Washington's New Deal
were being felt. New extension duties were mounting rapidly. In sum, to
a second-year student of agriculture, the county agent's mission suggested
both prestige and adventure. Those early county agents were pioneers in
every sense of the world. I remained pleased to have experienced a lasting
shred of that seeming adventure. This was enough to help me compose its
nature in later years when the descriptors at that earlier time had begun
to change:

Source: "The Evolution of Extension." *Extension Service Review*, March
(1959).

The first chapter of the Cooperative Extension Service
[was] reasoned from the demonstration method of
Seaman A. Knapp. The county agent was at work
with the thought and elementary practice of the rural
family [and] the technique was the collection of ideas,

admonitions, courage, and artifacts which filled his experience of a simpler world of farming and the saddlebags of his mounts or the recesses of dimly remembered Model T-Fords. That county agent lacked visual aids, the assistance of campus specialists, memoranda of instruction, ready encouragement, passable roads, and dependable tenure. He did not lack interest in inclement weather, bristling dogs, candy for backcountry children, and growing and guarded supports and loyalties.

Meanwhile, I participated joyfully in the community of students, faculty, staff, and other workers in the classrooms and on the farms of WVU's College of Agriculture. As students, we had accepted the often-sacrificial assistance of our families. We suffered occasional mishaps in our studies, and unfortunately—to our future loss—avoided courses in the social sciences and humanities, considering them impractical and irrelevant to our professional goals. Our job prospects were optimistic with the growing presence of New Deal agricultural agencies. Although mindful of the war clouds rising over Europe, most of us would return to a farm or join an agency in West Virginia once we graduated, ensuring lifelong contacts with the college. We relished the association with farmers, leaders, and groups who gathered there on a daily basis. We proudly considered that the concept of the land-grant system centered in the innovative network of agricultural colleges rather than in the land-grant university as a whole.

I began work as an assistant county agricultural agent on July 1, 1939, in Ritchie County, West Virginia. That destination had been quickly determined just before graduation. Concerned in the prior months that too little farm experience would deny an invitation to join the Cooperative Extension Service, I had been pursuing other options: a graduate assistantship in agricultural chemistry at the University of Wisconsin, enrollment in WVU's School of Medicine, and a position with the Farmers Home

Administration, one of the new agencies. But such initiatives vanished when J. O. Knapp, the state extension director, called me into his office and urged me to go to Ritchie County. My boyhood dream was reborn, and I accepted on the spot!

Ben Morgan, the Ritchie County agricultural agent, supervised my apprenticeship, joining the ranks of other mentors who had unforgettably influenced my early life. The duties were threefold: strengthen 4-H youth work; be an understudy of Morgan in his notable livestock program; and assist Ritchie County and three adjacent counties with a new national planning effort. This combination found me on duty by day and most evenings as well.

It was pleasing to take up the 4-H portion, for it built on my own experience. Emphasis was given to the formation of new clubs in the more isolated parts of the county. This unforgettable experience brought me face-to-face with Appalachian youth. I hope that in today's urban world we do not forget the saga of how farm children no longer needed in agriculture made their way out of backcountry regions to find different lives. I was privileged to be one such example of how 4-H clubs have inspired youth to conceive futures built on disciplined effort and leadership skills. That the concept was developed and made to work so brilliantly was due not only to a hierarchy of professional leaders within and related to the land-grant colleges and universities; of equal importance were the local 4-H volunteers who to this day serve as leaders, root the organization in community life, and provide the voluntary guidance that has become legendary. In my own case, one Mrs. William Oyster served memorably in this capacity. I will always remember sitting with her on a porch swing following my military service, and hearing her approval of my plans to further my educational adventure.

As one of many anecdotes that spring from my years of direct experiences with 4-H clubs, as a member and staff worker, the following two paragraphs recall a precious memory indeed. Upon request, I contributed the account of it to a book of anecdotes related to extension work and prepared in 1950 by Clinton Ballard, then state extension director in Michigan.

Leatherbark Creek runs through the far northeast corner of West Virginia's Ritchie County. In 1939, a narrow and rutted road curved alongside it, finally lapsing into little more than wheel tracks to a tiny hamlet of a few houses and a one-room school. It was there that I met Denzil Mather. Perhaps fifteen years old, he had joined other youth and me in forming a 4-H club. When the time came to choose a project, the hallmark of 4-H membership, Denzil insisted upon sheep husbandry, especially bringing a lamb to yearling status. With upper Leatherbark clearly unsuitable for a lamb project, it seemed necessary to discourage Denzil in favor of another emphasis, but he would not be defeated; I finally relented and persuaded a service club to provide the lamb and sponsor the boy's efforts. Denzil lived with his grandparents in a slab-sided shack of a house, and I gave them all instructions on the proper care of the lamb, especially feeding the animal on a fixed schedule.

I returned to Leatherbark several weeks later, and was surprised to see how the lamb had blossomed. I learned from the grandfather that Denzil had fed it by settings on an old alarm clock! By county fair time, Denzil's lamb had grown into a remarkable yearling ewe, enabling it to win first prize at the county fair and qualifying it for the state competitions. It was at those competitions that an extraordinary event brought the spectators to their feet for round after round of applause. Bringing a nervous sheep into the show ring generally calls for firm grips at throat and tail, but not in Denzil's case: he urged his ewe, named "Patty," into the show ring using only body language and voice signals, guiding her into the lineup of animals without placing a hand upon her. All present, schooled in the ways of sheep, understood that only deep bonds of affection formed through the animal's care could account for such a performance. The ewe led in its class, the Leatherbark people were animated with local pride, and Denzil—with a glimpse of new possibilities—went off later, first to the military and then to a career of his own

As to the second task, my apprenticeship with Ben Morgan continued until March 1941. He was the consummate county agricultural agent. Given to an impeccable garb of polished field boots and breeches, Morgan carried with him the confidence of one who loves his job. He was tough-minded, frank, and direct almost to a fault; he was fearless of difficulty, whether in choice of program or taming an angry steer. We became companions on memorable journeys marked by friendly arguments along winter's almost-impassable roads in his Model A Ford car. Morgan focused keenly on livestock production and marketing. Very soon, we agreed that my orientation went more to organization. But despite the not-so-subtle contrasts in outlook and practice, Morgan never failed to demonstrate that, whatever the task, genuine human service was done shoulder-to-shoulder with people, not at an office desk. My exposure to Morgan's example only strengthened my resolve to be a county agent.

As my new job took form in the early months of 1940, I became drawn to the importance of the newly expanded presence of Washington and the federal government in the domains of county agents. A new technical era for agricultural production and marketing had been born in the New Deal of President Franklin Roosevelt, and county agents found themselves in the middle of it! An early article of mine, from which the following excerpt is taken, may suggest the dynamism of that new evolution:

Source: "The Evolution of Extension." *Extension Service Review*, March (1959).

The second chapter [of the county agent] reasoned from the agricultural events of the "thirties," essentially in the linkage of government to farming. Within county agent offices, there appeared more white shirts; committees behind closed doors; specialists from headquarters; and mountainous memoranda from somewhere. New steel desks and men with agricultural diplomas streamed into county seat towns to execute fresh mediations of government. The county agent helped to establish through interpretation this grassroots cartel of experts, dollars, fertilizers, and parity prices [but soon] such groupings of official agricultural organizations fragmented, and each agency proceeded along preferred and policy-driven ways. [The county agent's] experience in organization was improved and access was opened to community services other than his own. Soon to come were issues forming the educational challenges of the third chapter: balancing technological and nontechnological innovations, the relationship of farming and government, the circumstances of who is to participate, and what are the measures of how best to understand the farm, the family, the community, and the region, all as an interrelated whole.

Catherine Spiker and I were married in 1940, the most important event in an altogether happy experience in Ritchie County. She was the youngest daughter of Jacob and Gay Spiker. They headed an extended family, having seven children and parenting two others after a local tragedy. They managed a small but productive livestock farm, and toiled throughout their lives to enhance the quality and prosperity of rural life. They would normally be the first to volunteer, whether in the formal circles of Extension work and the church, or in the care of neighbors who were ill or otherwise in crisis. The Spikers gave me the most rigorous inspection and questioning that a possible son-in-law might ever expect, but I would survive and win approval! For the balance of their lives, they would become as beloved parents to me rather than in-laws, an experience of a family whose members still form and provide a cherished set of relationships with me and mine.

Catherine, or Kitty as she was known to all, was a secretary in the new office of one of the earliest of the New Deal agencies, the Agricultural Adjustment Administration, which at that time was administered as part of the county agent's office. Our early acquaintance soon included her entire family; her love for her family was deeply felt. She possessed an understanding of rural living and agrarian issues. Her intelligence and charm, along with such competencies, contributed at once to my resolve to become a full-fledged county agent. Her siblings—one a county agent nearby and my friend at WVU, a younger brother beginning to farm, and others as teachers in the rural schools—also supported this direction for the new couple. Catherine and I were concerned about the turmoil in Europe, but not enough to interrupt our belief that we had found the correct direction for a life together.

My third major task challenged me greatly and, unknowingly then, set me to thinking in new ways about rural life. The Mt. Weather Agreement of July 8, 1938, established a coordinated system of county-based land-use planning. This action aimed to improve cooperation among the new agencies concerned with agriculture, respond to such disasters as the "dust bowl," and launch a nationwide inventory and plan for the nation's natural resources. The meaning given to "land use," however, was as broad as the entire community. Not only were the physical and commercial properties of land taken into account; issues of education, health, transportation, communication, and marketing were also included. The legislation directed each state to form committees of lay and professional people at state, county, and community levels. Their mission was to study problems, decide on goals of agriculture and rural life in differing land-use areas, recommend solutions, and define who should act upon them.

My job was to help form and assist the committees in Ritchie and three other adjoining counties. The competence required went far beyond land, crops, cattle, and farmers. New concepts—which I could not truly define for many years—came into play. I was confronted with a host of other subjects and processes quite outside my experience and training: community organization, human motivation and development, agency rivalry, and trust (and the lack of it) among professionals. I grew even more puzzled when the program was abandoned some three years later due to pre-World War II distractions, agency competition, and political conflicts as land-use recommendations moved into practice and activated special interests.

REACHING THE DREAM

Catherine and I moved to Summersville, county seat of West Virginia's Nicholas County, on March 1, 1941. I had earned a promotion. I began work as the county agricultural agent in an office with two other professional workers, one to serve the program in home economics and the other to administer the local efforts of the federal Agricultural Adjustment Administration (AAA). These colleagues, supporting staff, and I occupied two courthouse offices overlooking the main street of Summersville, one of two small towns in Nicholas County. This county, among the state's largest, joined potato cultivation to cattle and sheep farming. Although its coal reserves were sufficient to challenge farming, Nicholas, rather distant from a larger city, was fully an agricultural county.

The assignments in Ritchie County had given me a new vision of the county agent's role. The galaxy of new federal agricultural agencies (e.g., the Agricultural Adjustment Administration, Soil Conservation Service, and the Farm and Home Administration) required collaboration of the county agent, thus reducing the time given to farmers on their own farms. These tasks, along with the changing nature of my interests, led me to my initial emphasis: to establish a cooperative marketing organization for potatoes, similar to one recently formed for wool marketing. Potato growers, with few means to stay abreast of marketing trends, too frequently found themselves the victims of outside buyers.

A second emphasis grew out of the likely threat of coal production to the natural resources of the area, especially soils, water, and forests. Building on the earlier effort in county land-use planning, I directed my interest to conservation, while also maintaining my more traditional duties such as crop and livestock production and 4-H efforts with rural youth. But the new federal efforts, such as those sponsored by the Soil Conservation Service, Agricultural Adjustment Administration, and the Farmers Home Administration, all turned to additional challenges of identifying, training, and working with volunteers. Such assignments grew increasingly satisfying to me, and such assignments grew more numerous.

A philosophy took root in my outlook of the importance of sound planning and action in reference to the roles and functions of volunteer leaders. I came early to an interest in how county agents were challenged to choose between devising methods by which they might "trap" the citizens' volunteer energies for selfish program purposes, or, instead, by which they could help them develop personal, group, and community understanding and skills. I learned that volunteer leaders cannot be incidental to program goals, be standardized in recognition, or be taken for granted. Moreover, they will expect a certain amount of adventure in their service as volunteers, and will desert more readily if they are diverted into predictable channels and unvarying circles of procedure.

Does participation in extension programs lead to further participation in community, state, and national responsibilities? The participation, development, and recognition of volunteer leaders are not incidental features but full and primary objectives of extension programs. My memories as a county agricultural agent of Nicholas County center on the fellowship with volunteers. The example following was another anecdote prepared for the book by Michigan's state extension director Clinton Ballard. And, some seventy years later, it still remains both fresh and indicative of the importance of volunteers in social change.

Oscar O'Dell, an efficient owner and manager of a medium-sized farm, was among the core of helpful volunteers in Nicholas County. Gaunt and weathered, he appeared unannounced at the office one Saturday morning to help me through a crisis sufficient to seriously interrupt my role as a competent county agent. At the moment of his arrival, I had no idea of how to meet the crisis! The county's cooperative wool marketing association, of which O'Dell was a member, was reeling from an unexpected snag. The cooperative had agreed earlier on a price for its wool with a New England textile firm. However, before the wool was pooled, graded, and delivered, the market price moved above the price of the agreement: some farmers were tempted to sell immediately at the higher price in the open market, thus breaking the contract with the firm. This problem became a crisis when the firm in New England suffered a labor strike and indicated a delay in paying the wool growers the agreed-upon price. With a rising price on the open market and above the one in the contract, the promise of a delayed payment, and the wool still in hand, more members of the cooperative threatened to bolt and break the contract outright. Such a step would have divided the members and endangered the reputation of the local organization. An alarm spread throughout the county, and in came Oscar O'Dell. His first words were, "Young man, I think you are in trouble!" He proposed to arrange his own funds at a local bank so that those threatening to break the contract could be paid if the firm's payments to the local participants failed to arrive. His plan worked; he saved the day.

Volunteers carried the day more than once during my stay in Nicholas County. The cooperative marketing association for potatoes was organized on a legal basis, with an elected board and appropriate officers. By the 1941 potato harvest season, the association was located in a small rented building with grading and washing equipment installed and quality control mechanisms in place. Of great importance, and not without argument, was the advertising nomenclature to be used by the association. My part, for which I was poorly prepared, was attempting to overcome the suspicion of those growers who felt that the association would eliminate their freedom to buy and sell as they pleased. Others could not accept the rules that guaranteed a quality product. The itinerant private buyers felt threatened by this collaborative mode, and had to be persuaded that the step would improve the local economy; if such persuasion failed, members had to simply ignore their opposition. Yet somehow, thanks to much assistance from volunteers, from March to September the tasks were sufficiently complete to open for business.

The second emphasis, an attention to natural resource conservation, grew from evident needs and interests discovered in Nicholas County. With good lowland and highland soils, large forested areas and lumbering enterprises, and a landscape more level than most West Virginia counties, the area deserved better planning. Moreover, a sudden expansion of the coal industry could permanently affect soil, water, and other resources. Also important was the emphasis on soil and water conservation districts, then encouraged by the US Soil Conservation Service. This new form of local governance came into being by the vote of landowners and enabled natural resources to be assessed, planned, and acted upon. Land-use regulations could also be established by vote, a controversial provision that would be later eliminated.

Such factors converged to make conservation a major focus of my stay in Nicholas County. Another reason was the presence of Walter Gumbel, a principal leader of the District movement in West Virginia. My boyhood model and mentor was back in my life! We joined with representatives of two adjoining counties to study, plan, and secure the Elk River Soil Conservation District, one of the earliest districts in the nation to include an entire watershed rather than a single county. These events gave purpose to career-long interests in conservation and environmental issues. And later, with Gumbel as the founding editor of the

Journal of Soil and Water Conservation, the same events would stimulate my first published articles.

Source: "A Cultural Basis for Education in Conservation." *Journal of Soil and Water Conservation* 3 (1948): 13–16.

> One worthy objective of educational programs concerned with soil and water conservation is that the stewardship of land and other resources becomes a humanly natural "value" of the people. Experience demonstrates that the completion of a farm conservation plan does not always guarantee that application of the practices will be made….This discrepancy between planning and action is fed by breakdowns in the educational process, meaning that somewhere along the line, conservation as a "value" was not fully accepted. The acceptance of conservation in such a positive manner would mean that local group sanctions would apply, tending to informally enforce, as a prestige factor, the application of proper conservation measures. Conserving soil and other natural resources would then become a cultural trait.

Source: "A Social Phase to the Conservation Task." *Journal of Soil and Water Conservation* 7 (1952): 238–242.

> Neighbor group conservation planning, discussed and applied in recent years [provides] an opportunity for cooperators to look at their own farms and at their conservation behavior from the position of every other member of the group…. There is little enduring learning without verbal interaction, or just plain talking. A verbal

environment helps the participating farmer to combine and re-combine ideas about conservation into patterns which not only fit his/her farm but those of the neighbors, and those of the community at large…. A constant attention to developing true conservationists, girded by deepened values and the beliefs in applications…will render it unnecessary that the ends of conservation be promoted by arbitrary rewards, subsidies, and agrarian narrowness.

Not all was pleasant in the Nicholas County stay! The cooperative marketing projects never failed to garner conflict, whether from disagreements within or the outright opposition from those outside who saw them as threats to private initiative. The conservation program faced agency competition, as when the AAA became independent of the county agent's jurisdiction. The interest in land-use planning, for example, so disturbed some logging enterprises that I was challenged to a debate on the courthouse lawn—a debate to which, thankfully, their representatives failed to arrive! My emphasis on volunteer groups took time and disturbed those who preferred a county agent more given to farm visits and direct service. Meanwhile, it grew increasingly clear that I found greater pleasure in working with farm groups than in attending to specific issues of plant and animal husbandry. Also, the old dream of campus work began to reappear while making the rounds in Nicholas County.

The 4-H youth program continued as a major plank in the Nicholas program. One important task was to find the site for a future county camp. To gather information on site selection, I spent the weekend of December 6–8, 1941, at an adjacent county 4-H camp. Neither the camp nor the automobiles present possessed a radio, so it was not until my return home that I learned of the Pearl Harbor tragedy. New directions for Catherine and me began immediately, as they did for countless others.

Food production for the war effort soon rose to the top of the agenda. Military draftees grouped frequently on the corner below my office window in the courthouse, and then entered a bus to quietly depart. My identification as a varsity boxer at WVU led to an invitation to join the navy's physical education program. But for a county agent, food production needs came first, so I declined. Yet, with Catherine, I began a study of other military options, weighing the conflicts of marriage, family, and the likelihood that food production assignments would excuse me from serving as a soldier. But the men kept disappearing from the corner below... so in May 1942, I enlisted in the army air corps, intent on becoming an aerial navigator.

The decision was grave to me and my family, a sense shared by all men and women of my generation. We knew instinctively that World War II would be a defining moment in our personal lives and generation. How we decided our place of service at that time was sure to shape our whole lives. Despite the legitimate pulls of job and family, joining those departing more frequently from below my window became necessary. Catherine and the respective families sadly supported my decision, understanding that their lives would also be changed and defined for the future.

A COUNTY AGENT IN TRANSITION

THE SUMMER MONTHS of 1942 were given over busily to victory gardens, other mobilization tasks, aiding the university in finding my replacement, and becoming ready for the call to military duty. Finally it came: I was to report to Nashville in October 1942. Sadly, Catherine and I were confronted with personal tragedy in this period with the premature birth and deaths of twin daughters. My request for a brief delay in the reporting date was denied, and Catherine returned to her family home in Ritchie County. I was off to Nashville, classified a navigator, and sent to Monroe, Louisiana, for months of training and commissioning. After months of watching others depart, it had become my turn; with tears streaming from our eyes, my father-in-law drove me to the bus designated to take me to war.

By the luck—literally—of the draw, following my training in Monroe, I was withdrawn with five others from a contingent on its way to air force service in the South Pacific. I was assigned instead to Washington, DC, to study the navigational problems of the South Atlantic Ocean, and to prepare to become a navigator on the new major wintertime route to deliver aircraft, military personnel, and supplies to England, Italy, and other war zones. The tasks to follow included delivering planes, personnel, and supplies in the Ferry Command and, later, the Air Transport Command of the US Air Force. Finally, from March to December 1945, duty placed me near Dakar in French West Africa. My task there as an aerial navigator was to assist the rapid transport home to the United States of soldiers, following victory soon to come in Europe, along the western coast of Africa and across the Atlantic Ocean to Brazil.

When not flying, I took to the fields and villages. Various books on tropical agriculture came into my possession. New concepts therein linked up with the former projects in Ritchie and Nicholas counties: human culture, social change, social class, and economic development. Somewhere, I think in Africa, some works in anthropology appeared. I read them with relish, especially during the period while I was stationed on the edge of the Sahara Desert near Dakar. The long Atlantic crossings back and forth between Dakar and Natal, Brazil during that period allowed breaks from navigational duties for serious reading. Sensing that the war was moving to a close, I began to look to the future in earnest. This interest rose to high priority with the birth of a daughter, Paula, in June 1945, thus sharpening the anticipation of returning home to join the family and make plans for a new life.

I reviewed some of my previously considered options—further study in medicine, agricultural chemistry, or veterinary medicine. Rural extension work in two counties had included close ties to rural newspapers, so my imagination turned occasionally to owning and publishing one. But the new interest in the rural social sciences held firm despite the lack of preparation. My wartime reading had introduced me to Carleton Coon, a noted Harvard anthropologist. While in Africa, I wrote him of my experience and reading. He returned a quick and courteous letter, and urged that I investigate a fresh and creative emphasis upon the rural social sciences in a new department of sociology and anthropology then under way at Michigan State College.

The army air corps released me at Andrews Field in Washington, DC, on December 12, 1945. When I returned home to Ritchie County, where Catherine and I, along with members of both our families, discussed our future. Should we act upon the military leave and the legal right to return to Nicholas County? Might we attempt to purchase a local weekly newspaper that was then for sale? Still interested in Carleton Coon's suggestion, I took a hurried trip to Michigan State College. There I learned that despite my lack of background, a probationary admission was possible. The decision came quickly. Director J. O. Knapp and District Extension Supervisor Russell H. Gist of West Virginia University both supported my plan to go off to Michigan State for one year, but with certain provisions: I would retain the right to continue as a county agent; I would abandon any claim to the previous job in Nicholas County, but count on a similar opening once we returned. Our modest savings during the war, joined with the equally modest allowances of the GI Bill (the Servicemen's Readjustment Act of 1944), made this new adventure possible.

On January 2, 1946, I moved into a rented room in East Lansing, Michigan. The housing crisis for returning veterans meant that Catherine and the new baby, Paula, had to remain in West Virginia until something adequate was found. We knew nobody in Michigan except a friendly relative of Catherine. I was twenty-nine, and had had no formal study in the social sciences, and uncertainty weighed on me as I stood in the admission lines. Had our decision been too hasty? If so, at least I was not alone; I was but one among a horde of veterans with similar feelings. I was assured by the yellow half-sheet in my pocket, written by WVU's Extension Director Knapp, noting that on or before January 1, 1947, a year later, we would discuss future plans.

My graduate study in sociology and anthropology began. As I was closer in age to the younger faculty than to the few other graduate students, I soon felt at home. Since the department gave emphasis to rural life, my stint as a county agent won early recognition, which partly explains why three people took early and special interest in my graduate studies.

The first was Charles P. Loomis, the chair of the department. He valued and quizzed me on the county agent's job. He invited me to his seminars on the theory of rural social systems and helped me as I floundered much of the way with what seemed (to the then-neophyte) the impenetrable writing of Talcott Parsons, Harvard's famed scholar on social systems. Loomis, a lean, vibrant, and hard-driving son of the Southwest, seemed at first glance more the cowboy he had once been than the scholar (prepared at Harvard and Heidelberg) of creative theories of rural society. I held him in awe as a scholar and rather as an older brother when, for example, he floated the idea of turning the upper floor of his garage into a tiny apartment for my family. He invited me repeatedly to faculty seminars to hear papers and observe the discussion. Sensing that my interest lay at the border of university and community, he suggested such timely readings as Harold Allen's *Come Over Into Macedonia: The Story of a Ten-Year Adventure in Uplifting a War-Torn People*, which tells the story of how Greek settlers, once free of Turkish rule, had become established in northern Greece. Loomis remained a friend and colleague for decades and to the end of his life.

The second was Dr. Solon Kimball, who took curious interest in my self-directed reading of cultural anthropology during the war. He helped me confront an evident lack of background. Until he departed later for a distinguished chair in anthropology at Columbia University, Kimball worked with me on a memorable year of classic readings. These ranged from J. G. Frazer's anthropological overview, *The Golden Bough*, to the esoteric *Meaning of Meaning* by C. K. Ogden and I. A. Richards. My initial semesters of weekly discussions with Kimball on book after book, followed by headaches and aspirin, taught me to read and understand with greater intention. Knowing him and his work added to an enduring interest in anthropological methods. Until his death, Kimball continued to be my friend, advisor, and colleague. And on a much later day, I would be asked to submit a chapter in his honor to a noted book on the state of applied anthropology in America.

The third, professor Paul Honigsheim, seemed a most unlikely helpmate for someone whose background differed so much. Yet his eventual approval gave me self-confidence and advanced the idea that I might serve in academe. A noted student of Max Weber, the famed European sociologist and social philosopher, Honigsheim had escaped Hitler's Germany and arrived by a circuitous route at Michigan State College. I enrolled in his three successive semester seminars on the History of Social Thought. His macrocosmic competence in social history, his utter devotion to scholarship, and his own studies in the sociologies of music and religion amazed us all. Struggling through his seminars emphasized how much we lose out on when we avoid the humanities in our undergraduate years. In my case, the poignancy of that loss would never end.

On the basis of his three-semester sequence of seminars, Honigsheim challenged each student to prepare a major paper, many the equal of a master's thesis. I chose Blaise Pascal's transition from mathematics to philosophy, stimulated by his role in the Jansenist Movement, a protest related to French Catholicism in the seventeenth century. With my choice, I had wandered unknowingly into a subject related to Honigsheim's own doctoral studies at Heidelberg University, which fact was revealed when he appeared unexpectedly at my oral examination to say as much and to speak well of my paper. Perhaps more than any other single event,

Honigsheim's approval at that milestone event was enough to tip forward my earlier and growing preoccupation with the idea of a taking up a doctoral program.

I had almost completed the requirements for a master of arts degree at the close of 1946. This was also the time of the fateful decision, as agreed upon with Director Knapp. Would we return to West Virginia? The question grew in importance during the summer and fall of 1946 while I was engaged in fieldwork: first the mapping of social structure in Michigan's Livingston County, which yielded a master's thesis; and, second, a study of perceptions and uses of health agencies in Van Buren County. The latter study introduced me to its sponsor, the W. K. Kellogg Foundation, a relationship that has endured importantly for the whole of my life and career. A monograph, the write-up of the Van Buren studies, placed me for the first time among authors of printed professional bulletins.

Catherine and Paula arrived in Michigan in March 1946. We resided first in an apartment over a drugstore in the nearby village of Okemos. Consisting of one large room, this tiny studio apartment had a kitchen in one corner and a closeted but tiny bathroom in another; we placed a curtain across a third corner for the baby's bedroom. However, in July we purchased and moved into a small one-bedroom cottage. For the remainder of 1946, the haunting questions were clear. Should I return to West Virginia and its extension service? Or should I continue at Michigan State College and begin doctoral studies? There were good arguments for each option. West Virginia held strong memories and promised family and professional linkages. Continuing as a county agent, though with new views of the tasks, remained desirable. However, even with limited income and despite years of study ahead, hopes for campus life would win. Finally, in December 1946, I wrote to Director Knapp to inform him of our decision to remain in East Lansing. I thanked him for his generous offer, and relieved him of further obligation.

On January 1, 1947, my career as a county agricultural agent seemed over. But the ideal upon which it rested—to serve in a college or university—remained alive, if without form. That uncertainty began to clear in March when dean of the Department of Agriculture Robert Baldwin, Extension Director Clinton Ballard, and Dr. Loomis called me into conference to discuss a proposition: Once my master's degree was completed, I could begin work as Michigan State's first extension rural sociologist and continue also with doctoral studies. This position of university outreach would relate directly to aiding and enhancing what county agricultural agents do. And additional academic options, given the certain toil that lay ahead, might become possible. My new assignment began on July 1, 1947.

A transition begun in boyhood at age eleven was complete!

II

$\mathcal{M}$ICHIGAN $\mathcal{S}$TATE $\mathcal{U}$NIVERSITY

$\mathcal{B}$RIDGING $\mathcal{C}$AMPUS AND $\mathcal{C}$OMMUNITY

THE EXTENSION SPECIALIST
AND ADMINISTRATOR

THE NEWLY CREATED job as extension rural sociologist had to be defined, for I would be the first to hold the position at Michigan State College (later Michigan State University, or MSU). The Department of Sociology and Anthropology was part of the School of Arts and Sciences; other extension specialists normally practiced in departments of the School of Agriculture. Rural sociology extension emerged from such early interests as community recreation. But in the 1930s and 1940s the "social" sciences quickened on building a stronger base of science. County agents and other fieldworkers would expect a rural sociologist to demonstrate how to apply science-based knowledge for solving local problems. The success of anchoring agricultural production in the natural sciences had already been tested and verified. Such an application of the social sciences remained unclear, and, in some views, unlikely.

As described in the first chapter, the Cooperative Extension Service brings county, state, and federal entities into a common effort that is largely planned, coordinated, and led in the land-grant universities. Serving in West Virginia had given me experience with the local roles of the county agent. One such role was to consult and join with campus-based extension specialists and enlist their support as providers of research-based knowledge; another was to help them define local problems requiring new or further study. The mechanisms for such tasks, which required data based on the natural and physical sciences, had developed from the outset of the Cooperative Extension Service. Such could not be said for the social sciences: their testing and fuller evaluation had yet to arrive!

However, performing these tasks with knowledge born of the physical sciences was based on long research traditions. That the social sciences would come to serve similarly in the 1940s and beyond demanded a new history of how best to employ them in finding solutions to local problems of a more economic and social nature. Of course, to do so also required an understanding of the core functions of an extension specialist's role, as the following excerpt, after some years of experience, suggests:

Source: "The Commonwealth of Extension Education." Paper presented at the Annual Extension Conference at the University of Missouri-Columbia, Columbia, MO, October 20, 1958.

The first obligation of the extension specialist is embodied in the title. He [sic] *is a specialist who is* supposed to know something and to know it better than others in a given extension program. The first obligation is to stay that way.

The second function is teaching. The county agent designs the public framework for informal education and evaluates the educational sequences that follow. The extension specialist serves in these sequences to inject the appropriate and available knowledge and demonstrate inspired teaching.

The third function is leadership. This requires specialists who know what they are talking about and are deliberate about it. A stature of intellectual honesty discriminates between what is known and what is not, between the exact and the inexact, and between viewpoint and documentation.

Of key importance to my new post was to draw upon the research base of the Department of Sociology and Anthropology, in which I would reside. One immediate opportunity lay in the research program focused on rural health. Another took up how local social organization helps shape program administration. My interest in the latter topic drew upon my earlier work as a county agent. Moreover, the reading program with Professor Solon Kimball (as noted in the previous chapter) revealed how an anthropologist views field administration; indeed, his case studies stimulated me to design a course to help county agents analyze social group behavior and thus learn how better to respond. This effort would eventually evolve into a graduate course for the campus. But the first area of real application, with science-based knowledge available, was rural health.

Several senior researchers in the department were engaged in major research on rural health. Noting my decision to initiate the extension effort in this field, they invited me to join some of the projects. This invitation also opened the door to my doctoral program. As the research program expanded and the outreach effort began, the rural health emphasis mushroomed sufficiently to add a second extension specialist, David G. Steinicke. He helped create and conduct the new effort. Following our colleagueship, Steinicke became a professor of distinction in health policy at the University of Michigan.

The research program in rural health included several themes. All grew from a major study known as the *Michigan Health Survey*. This work employed a validated instrument by which the symptoms as revealed by informants themselves would accurately indicate their need for medical attention. A statewide sample of a thousand rural and urban families provided comparative data of health needs in Michigan. Analysis led to recommendations for the organization of local health resources and how communities might improve health and medical care. Professors Charles R. Hoffer, Edgar A. Schuler, Charles P. Loomis, Duane L. Gibson, and John F. Thaden were the senior researchers. They invited me to participate in the research effort and as one of the authors of *Health Needs and Health Care in Michigan: A Report of a Statewide Survey.*[1]

Such initial activity in rural health research and extension opened new doors. The national interest in hospital construction and other health needs in the late 1940s led to the opportunity to serve on a rural technical panel of a national commission on the health needs of the nation, including an appearance before a congressional committee studying rural hospitals. I was invited to join the US Public Health Service and survey the health needs of Indonesia, and informed of major posts available with a new Health Information Foundation as well as the American Medical Association. I respectfully declined all such options. I was grateful for the notice, but especially for other unforeseen benefits.

For example, they brought Frank Peck to my office! As president of the Farm Foundation in Chicago, Peck was interested in the capacities of rural

---

1   Charles Russell Hoffer et al., *Health Needs and Health Care in Michigan: A Report of a Statewide Survey*, vol. 365 (Michigan State College, Agricultural Experiment Station, Section of Sociology and Anthropology, 1950).

areas and small cities to meet their own health needs and in particular the relevant roles of leadership. He invited a proposal. The resulting project added a major research project in the department, became a resource to the extension program, and provided a major effort from which I could develop my doctoral dissertation. Proposals to reach such aims were accepted by MSU and the Farm Foundation and work began in early 1948.

Given such personal and professional interests, our family roots deepened in Michigan life. Our small cottage, purchased in 1946 while I was a graduate student, was exchanged in 1949 for a larger house. Our new neighbors included colleagues in the department. One was John Useem, an anthropologist who, following Kimball's departure, agreed to head my doctoral committee. Others and their respective families included Duane Gibson, Allan Beegle, and Wilbur Brookover. All strove to advance my graduate study on a part-time basis, and to backstop my new tasks as an extension specialist. While the initial emphasis fell on rural health, these new colleagues were sympathetic to the other tasks of an extension rural sociologist. Anthropologist Useem especially guided me on how best to devise and apply fieldwork. This built upon my interest in social organization and administration. He and his wife Ruth, also an anthropologist, mounted distinguished careers of global importance and continued as mentors and friends until their deaths, a period of more than fifty years.

Our family lives were also bolstered in that formative period by the arrival of James O. Miller, a nephew. The oldest of four sons of my brother Bernie (whose great impact on me is cited in the initial chapter) was exiting from military service and chose Michigan State for his college work. He would graduate with honors, move into public education, and then into academic life. Following graduate study and several administrative posts, Jim began a career leading to deanships and a college presidency. Our similar pathways enabled a lifelong fellowship of special strength to follow to the present day.

But now I return to the research on health matters and further graduate study. The Farm Foundation study rested on a synthesis of rural health, social organization, and administration. The proposal focused on comparative decision-making processes and styles leading to a rural/small town hospital and/or other health-related programs. The rather extensive effort sprang from recognition of an impressive increase in the construction and organization of new institutions and programs in the late 1940s, especially in communities with fewer than ten thousand residents: about four hundred hospitals, more than 115 new public health departments, and nearly one hundred medical prepayment plans.

The research began by first surveying such efforts with carefully constructed questionnaires that were designed to capture detailed and comparative contrasts of steps taken to plan, build, or otherwise form health institutions. Data were gathered from 218 hospitals, 51 public health departments, and 18 prepayment plans. From these, researchers chose five hospital building projects from as many states. Analysis of the questionnaire data enabled such choices as best representing all the efforts in five major regions of the United States. With pseudonyms, field studies would follow and focus on *Midstate* (Indiana); *Norwest* (Wyoming); *Noreast* (New York); *Farwest* (California); and *Southeast* (Alabama). Research teams for each community study consisted of at least two members. I served as team leader in Indiana, New York, and Alabama.

Designed with the perspectives of applied anthropology, the field studies (each commonly requiring three to four weeks of on-site effort) had two aims: explore and compose the decision-making stages and leadership patterns, and contrast these processes in the respective regions. Since the size of community and the subject hospitals were rather identical, comparisons of leadership and decision-making styles enabled definitive comparisons of how best to assist such communities with building new hospitals and devising public health departments or prepayment health plans. The study's results would ensure that planning assistance to such communities could be more carefully planned, targeted, accomplished, and evaluated.

Two key components of the doctoral research helped provide the methodologies for the ongoing work of an extension specialist and create an outlook on methods of planning and administration. The first component was to comprehend processes of decision-making, such as choosing from optional courses of action, recognizing that decisions require measures of legitimacy by those whom they affect, deciding appropriate action steps, and forecasting the likely consequences. The second component suggested how to build testable models of authority and influence as the two major qualities of community leadership capable of shaping decision-making. I discussed such definitions and their applications at length in my later book devoted to the research as a whole. An excerpt follows:

Source: *Community Health Action: A Study of Community Contrast.* East Lansing, MI: Michigan State College Press, 1953.

> The capacity of *authority* is that body of rights and privileges belonging to certain roles in the community…as that of "office" [based] on *election or appointment, family position,* the prestige of a kinship group and/or *socioeconomic status.* The capacity of *influence* is primarily that collection of public perceptions brought by the decision-maker to the community action project: participant's *wealth*; perceived *morality*; felt *obligation*; *organizational skill*; *skill with symbols*; relevant *subject matter competence*; *access* to relevant community institutions; and the extent to which one, based on community history, has become a *legendary personality* capable of creating and entering avenues of action leading to change.

As noted above, the research aimed also to identify the differences, if any, in regional leadership styles and relevant modes of social organization and administration. Using questionnaire and field data, only subtle differences appeared in the Midwest, Northwest and Far West regions of the United States. However, sharp contrasts appeared between the Southeast and Northeast regions as summarized in the following excerpt.

Source: "The Process of Decision-Making within the Context of Community Organization." *Rural Sociology* 17 (June 1952).

To understand decision-making and small community action in the Southeast, one is forced to veer toward an inquiry into community structure and offices of constituted authority; while in the Northeast more attention to the social psychological components of influence is required. Although both sets of decision-makers had strong positional attachments, it appears...that the Northeast communities functioned in decision-making more squarely on the basis of social property, e.g., of resources and proficiencies vested in persons of influence; while the Southeast communities were characterized by a structural setting in which positional elements led to roles of authority. Decision-making in the Southeast community revolved around two structural axes: a vertical hierarchy moving downward from the probate judge, and a county-wide horizontal, informal political organization operated by a small number of large landowners and storekeepers. This informal organization functioned, in part, through a politically acute farm organization. In the Northeast community, the inner circle of decision-making consisted of four men, linked together by past events, who, through extensive influence due to diverse reciprocal obligations and positive community imagery, greatly influenced prestigious and associational life.

From 1948 into the early 1950s, the Farm Foundation project joined with other efforts in rural health. During the same period, preliminary training events were under way for county agents in social organization and administration. In no small way, they drew upon such experiences and data as that discussed above. My remaining a part-time graduate student seemed not to detract from a growing colleagueship with seasoned members of the department, as exemplified by the privilege to chair the departmental research committee for the Farm Foundation study. Loomis, assisted by such others as listed above, missed no opportunity to push the extension effort forward and to make me feel at home in the department. Occasionally, when unable to meet with the departmental chairs in the School of Agriculture, he would ask me to go in his place. The period was never to be surpassed in the quality and steadfastness of common endeavor with colleagues as also friends and supporters.

These interactions added and sharpened values about working with people. They built handily on the early guidance shared with me in West Virginia by county agent Walter Gumbel, other state extension leaders, and county agent Ben Morgan, under whom my apprenticeship as an extension agent began. How lay people and professionals relate to each other grew in importance. But more than relationships was involved. Other, and often puzzling, questions arose. Whose knowledge really counts? How do we come to know what we know? How does the indigenous knowledge of farm people mesh with that of the professional?

Thus, my interest in "participatory research" developed before it was so named, and greater opportunities appeared to experience it. One example found me serving briefly with Carl C. Taylor, an eminent and much-admired rural sociologist, under the auspices of the US Soil Conservation Service and the tutelage of Melville H. Cohee, director of its midwest region. We explored several midwest sites to learn how informal rural leaders influence conservation. Similar approaches were applied in cooperation with health and other community leaders, given a growing interest with "community self-surveys" as a device to bring civic and professional representatives into a common effort. Of great importance was to work with lay leaders in presenting not only a method for such surveys, but also to fashion ideas that would enable citizens to follow with purposive actions.

Source: "Community Self-Survey: A Social Scientist's Viewpoint." *American Journal of Public Health* 43 (July 1953).

> We must appraise the community self-survey of health...in terms of its usefulness in carrying a concern for an increasingly adequate health environment into the "life-streams" of the people [and] to shift the focus from the individual to the family, the community, the county, and other units.... The community self-survey works in this direction because of two tenets of educational theory: there can be little education without activity, and there can be little education unless those involved are in situations that help them view the problems peculiar to them, as well as the problems...from the vantage point of others.... The device of the community self-survey of health, beyond its requirement that the people, themselves, become working members of the health team, will work in the direction of attitude change and re-education. The least that may be said, when it is crucial to seek a two-way flow of communication between the professions and the people at various levels of public life, the self-survey can raise a platform upon which lay people may ply their labors shoulder to shoulder in common cause.

One challenge in "participatory research" was to stimulate interest of technically prepared county extension agents in such methods. To gain such perceptions might best begin in both college experience coupled with on the job training at the outset of an extension appointment. This did not intend to undercut the preparation and practice of professional subject matter, but rather to enlarge the practice of linking professional and lay clients in common planning and action. Believing that basic training needed to change, I took advantage of the opportunity as chair of a subcommittee to reflect on preparing future extension workers:

Source: *An Undergraduate Education Program for Extension Work: A Planning Guide.* Report prepared and published by the Subcommittee on Pre-Service Training by the National Association of State Universities and Land-Grant Colleges (1953).

There is danger of students confusing immediate and short-term aims with the ultimate and more important objectives of helping people themselves through education to solve the many inter-related and continually expanded problems that affect their lives…. An introduction to educational philosophy is needed, rather than countless courses on method. It is not so much through such courses but through the total curriculum that the student gains a basic knowledge of and skill with human relationships and a belief in the educational process…. Teaching in the social sciences should result in an understanding of the basic principles of human growth and the developmental needs of youth. Undergraduate work should give extension agents the ability to adjust their teaching to changing home and community situations, to accept the values of persons whose background, environment and goals may not coincide with their own.

STATE EXTENSION DIRECTOR

I COMPLETED MY doctoral program in the spring of 1953. Although offers for other positions appeared, none overcame my intention to remain at Michigan State. The tasks of the extension specialist and the collegial welcome to applied research and occasional teaching proved to be a satisfying mixture. However, certain health challenges faced by my wife, Catherine, and our desire to have another child made the continuous travel in field-work less desirable. The hope of more campus work came with promotion to full professor of sociology and anthropology in early 1954.

Such speculation was thrown into turmoil on a single afternoon in October 1954. In the morning of that day and with the ring of the telephone, I found myself speaking to John A. Hannah, Michigan State's president. His question was direct and brief: "Could you be at my office at 3:00 p.m.?" Mr. Hannah was revered both on and off the campus. He was already destined to be one of the century's greatest university leaders, as well as an official in Washington. Other than the occasional greeting at a faculty reception, I had spoken with him but once; he had advised me not to accept an Indonesia project with the US Public Health Service, saying, simply, "Miller, Michigan State will have enough international work whenever you want it."

After a hurried visit home for a fresh shirt and suit, I appeared at the appointed hour. Not one to mince words, Hannah leaned forward and looked me straight in the eye. And, more informally this time, he said, "Paul, I want you to report to the Extension Service next week as its deputy director, and meet as soon as you can with Woody (Director Durward Varner) about your responsibilities." Hannah further spoke on how the sweeping changes in agriculture and rural life demanded the views of social scientists. He emphasized that Varner, an agricultural economist, desired me to assist him in the new post. I was stunned, believing that Hannah's invitation likely dealt with a committee assignment.

Striving for composure, I responded quickly—and negatively! I hurried on to explain that with the completion of graduate study and recent promotions, I desired to try my hand at more scholarship on the integration and dissemination of knowledge. I pointed out how happy my lot had been in the department, and that, beyond the brief and early duties of a county agricultural agent, my administrative experience was minimal. I next gave a quick review of what I had in mind, especially to trace the outcomes in the five regional communities where hospitals had been built. What I did not share was the desire for a more stable family life, our hopes for a second child, and my continuing concern about Catherine's health.

My protests were to no avail. Hannah applauded my agenda and indicated that some elements might be done as part of his proposal, and then pressed on. "Paul, go over there and spend five years doing the best you can; after that, return to the department and we won't bother you again," he said. "There are jobs in Extension that Michigan State needs to have done. I want you to take them on. So does Woody!" I surrendered!

Durward B. "Woody" Varner had served as state extension director but a short time. His leadership, formerly in farm policy, had galvanized the organization on the campus, and among the some four hundred professional employees of the Cooperative Extension Service throughout Michigan. Varner had widened the scope of the extension program and directed attention to urban needs, especially in consumer education. He was a young, assertive innovator, and was supported by new initiatives in program planning and rural development led by C. M. Ferguson, director of the Federal Extension Service.

Varner initially assigned me two major tasks: one was to advance the new national initiatives through my working relationships with county agents; the other was to draw on my interest in social organization and administration and explore how to improve the structure and function of the Cooperative Extension Service.

The new appointment would put into practice what I had been moved to write and publish about. The combination of administration and writing was also encouraged, not only by Varner and my colleagues in sociology and anthropology, where my professorship remained, but uniquely by Herbert A. Berg, Extension's assistant director. With a profound competence for Extension work and its history, Berg insisted that I carry on these dual roles. At that time, one of rapid change in rural community life, a thorough review of extension philosophy was in order.

Changes in the role of the county extension agent was then but one indication of new problems and opportunities confronting the Cooperative Extension Service. The terms *program* and *program planning* were much used in conversation, but less often used in practice. The term "program" was one of the most used notions to describe a state of affairs within Extension activities, yet its repetitive use often produced confused meanings of direction, balance, design, and vitality. At the outset of my new administrative post, I grew intent to bring debate to bear on what was meant by the word. As the following note suggests, challenging the meaning of "program" was important during my stay in Extension work, and I often wrote on the topic:

Source: "Basic Philosophies and Principles of Extension Work." *Extension Service Review* (November 1955).

An Extension program may be divided four ways.... First, it must provide for enough time and talent for establishing contact with the people. The people must learn what services are available and be in position to recommend how these services may best contribute to their needs. Second, it will provide for the time and means to do something about those who indicate a positive interest. To call forth this interest places upon Extension workers the ultimate responsibility of providing a process by which representatives of the people at large may make their own judgments. Three, [it] will be a provision to provide time to be spent with people to encourage adoption of ideas and practices. Positive interest will not be secured if Extension workers cannot be close enough to the people whom they serve to bring to them modern research and technology in such a way as to improve their decision-making skill. The fourth way will provide for sufficient follow-up in order to assist in the application of ideas and practices once they are adopted.

I served as deputy director for just five months! In February 1955, Varner was selected as vice president for off-campus education, a new post that would include leading an effort to rename Michigan State College as a university. Immediate skepticism grew of the relevance of me and rural sociology and anthropology, especially among some farm and commodity groups, when my name was advanced as his likely successor, but Hannah and Dr. Thomas K. Cowden, dean of the College of Agriculture, stood by their recommendation. I entered one of the most challenging and stimulating chapters in my career in March 1995 when I began my new role as state extension director.

This was a time for genuine innovation in university outreach. A rapid rise of emphasis upon both adult continuing education and the Cooperative Extension Service was under way. The federal office and national director C. M. Ferguson recognized that enormous change was on the way in both rural and urban life. The clienteles were changing. Growth and greater prestige now characterized the land-grant universities. Michigan State was widely recognized as a leading American university; it had just built the

Kellogg Residential Center for Continuing Education. Director Varner (later the founding president of Oakland University and president of the University of Nebraska), had created a readiness for fresh ideas, despite the brevity of his tenure.

Several new personalities came into my life. None was more stimulating than Thomas K. Cowden, dean of the Department of Agriculture and my superior officer. Our working relationships were productive yet unique. We held rather different views of how the agricultural colleges and Extension should face the turbulence in rural society! Cowden, an agricultural economist and dean, focused more on the changes under way in commercial agriculture and rural institutions. My view added new populations to the traditional ones. My enthusiasm for extending the model of cooperative extension into new fields was known. As it turned out, Cowden and I accepted the likelihood that, for our tenures, the emphasis would fall between the two views.

We spoke frequently of our duet as dialectic but capable of keeping each of us alert. As Cowden smiled and said as we gathered in his office one late afternoon to discuss the day's high points, "Paul, I suspect that folks in the hallway on the other side of the wall are making bets on how long you will last!" Our respect and trust of each other grew, as did the joy of serving together. Cowden would properly brake my exuberance for reform when it might risk unwise use of resources. But he also gave me more room for experimentation than one might have expected—for example, the exploratory location of marketing specialists in two labor union centers! I learned also of the gentleness and affection for farm people that hid behind his frequently stern exterior (as when a 4-H boy's lamb died at a campus show and Cowden instructed the animal husbandry department head to find the best lamb possible as a gift to the distressed boy).

Thus, through the new post, I added many others to my small family of colleagues in extension work, sociology, and anthropology. When

Arnold Kettunen, Michigan State's long-term and famed state leader of 4-H work retired, I chose Russell G. Mawby, then twenty-eight years old, to succeed him. While his youth was starkly contrasted with the maturity and prestige of the predecessor, Mawby—as I predicted for the skeptics— soon became a national leader in youth programs. He eventually went on to a distinguished international career as chief executive officer of the W. K. Kellogg Foundation. We remain lifelong friends and colleagues at this writing.

Joining the team as associate director for program planning and development was George Axinn, also in his twenties, and with a rare capacity for learning and innovation. He would go on to distinguish himself in rural development throughout the world on behalf of Michigan State, including service as India representative of the United Nation's Food and Agriculture Organization.

John Stone, county agricultural agent in Livingston County, Michigan, and a helpmate on my research for my master's degree, joined as director of extension training. He later became Dean of Extension at South Dakota State University. Others of the central staff, among them Harold Foster, Albert Griffith, and Casper Lott, were notable among the key leaders and advocates.

Such representatives, some quite young and new while others were veterans in the extension world, were ready and able to work with the new state director in updating an already accomplished Extension Service. Certain authentic differences of opinion, reaching throughout Michigan State, the Office of the Dean, and the College of Agriculture, were expected and due, given the sweeping changes then under way in production agriculture and rural life. My responsibilities as state extension director called for careful study of the organization and of the county agricultural agent model with which this memoir began. Throughout a demanding but stimulating period, assessing how best to employ a large statewide organization within the rapidly changing Michigan countryside remained a paramount interest. Of course, for the new director, sharing such views and behaviors as those following seemed quite urgent.

Source: "On a Commonwealth of Extension Education." *Extension Service Review* (1958).

The chief functions of the state extension director are in discovering the objectives of extension education and then collecting and ordering the resources to achieve them. The first calls for a high order of comprehension; the second calls for a high order of character. The real drain on the extension administrator is on his fortitude for continually seeing that objectives are discussed and recast and then in arranging the resources to achieve them…. The formulations of policy in extension education flow more from collaborative understanding of situations than it does from the orders of administrative office. This understanding requires a never-ending discussion if not lively debate throughout the entire system. To arrange this debate is an essential aim of administrative office.

The state extension director daily encounters the risk of losing appreciation for the intellectual restlessness of the academic community. There is no greater strain than marshalling resources that are possessed by specialists, each with a tight brand of personal interest. The administrative temptation is to standardize…. But the objective is not containment by the categories and machinery of administration; instead, it is in shaping the specialties into always new patterns of educational resources and back-up.

In 1955, the year of my appointment, the various state Cooperative Extension Services were in a special and perhaps unusual collaboration with each other and with the Federal Extension Service. Two themes stood out: "Farm and Home Development" and "Program Projection." Each theme was to be articulated within the context of a particular state and county. Both aimed to improve understanding of the swift changes under way in rural society, especially due to the division of production and marketing into specialized commodity managements and the mounting migration of people from rural to urban society. In addition, the enlarged scope of program and the expansion of new clienteles were recognized. The approach in Michigan sought to derive new principles from an old philosophy. My task was to help find the levers to action, workable objectives, clearer definition of the audiences to be served, and the subject matter these audiences would require. We spoke of such redefinitions in the Michigan case: modernize Extension's organization; strengthen communication skills; give greater weight to changes under way in family and farm enterprises; and stress the requisite changes in staff training as well.

My initial two years in the new post included a steady stream of visits to the eighty-three county extension offices in Michigan and to becoming familiar with the organization of campus resources. Opportunities for consultation outside the state also appeared. The time seemed critical for the Cooperative Extension Service throughout the nation and encouraged a frank sharing of views. Perhaps of greatest importance was the attempt to understand Michigan itself, including its contrasts in both urban and rural change, the concerns one felt when trying to comprehend the cultures of Greater Detroit and the Upper Peninsula, and how Michigan State's extension services might respond and adapt in multiple ways. Summarizing such differences and trying to reconcile Michigan's complexity and relevant educational responses prompted much personal strain when preparing to address

the annual state Extension conferences. The following excerpt is sug-
gestive of that strain:

Source: "The Extension Enterprise: Today's Activities for Tomorrow's
Goals." Address presented at the Michigan Annual Extension
Conference, East Lansing, MI, October 29, 1956.

My outline today presents tasks [that] grow from the needs
and trends of Michigan life. These tasks result from (1)
the industrial revolution in farming, (2) the dependence
and relatedness of agriculture to the total economy as
expressed in part by the marketing system, (3) the complex
connections between natural resources and their potentials
in Michigan, and (4) the underlying challenge of enriching
the minds and hearts of the people whom we serve.

We must recognize that there will be no let-up in
Michigan's industrial growth and decentralization, no
slacking off of the movement from country to city,
no lessening of the consuming public at our doorstep,
no change in the multitude of rural workers who travel
our highways to and from the industrial centers, and no
lessening of the new rural community peopled by dahlia
growers, rabbit keepers, and do-it-yourself enthusiasts.
There are still to be more septic tanks, not less; more
strained tax loads, not less; more issues of providing
human services, not less; more adaptations to local governments, not less…. We must help with the design of a
satisfying community in which the resources of land, of
water, of capital, and of people will be in a productive
and satisfying balance. We should help people inventory,

assess, and act on the state's basic resources...encourage
county-by-county study for developmental opportunities; and lead a crusade for bringing to all people a general awareness and interest in the vast natural resources
of Michigan....

We would take on a bold venture in Cooperative Extension
Work—the growth of people into able leaders. The prime
responsibility is to establish such situations as to provide
for the development of people so that they may better
decide the issues of family, farm, community, state, and
nation. The Extension career [that] you and I will look
backward to someday...will be measured in terms of what
happened to the people with whom it was our good fortune to cooperate.... Let us not forget also that our work
with youth and women is a bridge of service to people of
both country and city; of every race, creed, and religion; of
every age, and of differing social and economic positions.

Such ideas did not win universal acceptance! Some saw them as a too
rapid shift to professionalism and the loss of direct consultation and service.
I was not altogether of one mind. Amid such planning statements, it was
possible for me to exclaim, and to be remembered for it, that county agents
should be so much a part of the life of the people that they could "enter the
back door of farm homes and make a sandwich when nobody was at home!"
Of course, the staff detected such uncertainties and reminded me of them,
sometimes in startling form (as with the circulation of a cartoon depicting a
leader sitting backward on a log headed downstream to an awesome waterfall,
but shouting, "What we need around here is more long-range planning!").
Other scenes were equally communicative! At one annual conference, the skit performed, while of dubious dramatic quality, carried the

message that hardy county agents have little if any fear of administrators! The skit portrays a single lonely farmer showing up at the county agent's office with a chicken under his arm. He wants to know, as he has heard can be done, how to determine whether or not the chicken should be kept. Our county agent, dressed like the farmer, and found in a quite seedy office, moves forthwith to demonstrate the art of chicken culling. Year by year the scenes follow. Other farmers, each with a chicken and a similar question, keep showing up at the county agent's office. But there all seems in a state of change. Paper is piled everywhere. Agents in business suits sit with telephones lifted from shiny steel desks, but the chicken culling specialist never seems to be present. Eventually the farmer is tactfully reminded not to return with the chicken, sent off instead with several bulletins, and exhorted to listen to the county agent's radio broadcast. Not surprisingly, he ponders on the way home why he is still without an answer.

As history turned out, the skit failed in accuracy, for farmers *did* change their questions. But, in addition to friendly laughter at the director's expense, the skit was also symptomatic of the changes in rural society in the 1950s. Such changes would bring challenge after challenge of how best to assist the client with new technical and institutional complexities.

These client needs also raised the issue of how best to organize the Cooperative Extension Service. The traditional organization around major functions (e.g., agriculture, home economics, and 4-H youth programs) failed to address the growth of other technical specialties in response to unique geographical needs. Other issues were also present. The growing stock of technical knowledge had begun to overrun more traditional approaches; regionalization of some services seemed essential.

Following study and debate of such issues, and with less than full consensus, a new administrative organization came into place. This called for two major changes: designate a member of each county staff as the "county extension director," and create five regional offices and directors.

At the same time, in addition to transforming conditions in the nature of Michigan as a state, changes in the social and economic life were introducing new concepts, new centers of specialized knowledge, and needed versatility in matching knowledge, whether that of science or experience, to new taxonomies springing from social and economic change.

Source: "The County Agent's Job." *Better Farming Methods,* July 1957.

Changing conditions are forcing a frank appraisal of the county agent's job. My following considerations are submitted as future directions to guide the new kind of county agent....Tomorrow's county agent will need to adjust to an expanding university....the Extension system, which supports the county agent, must substitute competition of ideas for departmental competition....The county agent's program will become more fact and less fiction, for the county agent can expect to find laymen who will be more expert than he about some subjects or areas of interest.....The county agent will return to the farm and home with a new set of tools—the concepts of management....the county agent in tomorrow's agriculture will master educational logistics—the fitting of technical, natural, and human resources into patterns of problem-solution....Tomorrow's county agent will be a partner in shaping the agricultural-industrial region in a day of use, conservation, and development of resources....The county agent will recognize the more broadly defined agricultural industry through marketing and public affairs education....Tomorrow's county agents will have to exhibit more leadership at the "high-range"—government, politics, economics, science....

This new road is more swift, more hazardous, and less well marked; and for those who are on it, the qualifications are tougher.

There were also other consequences of change in the 1950s. What scope should be given the program of Cooperative Extension? Who should be included within the served populations? How far should extension work go in mobilizing the resources of the entire land-grant university? Michigan as a state was clearly a laboratory to test these questions. They were of great interest to me, perhaps the highlight as state director.

What the Smith-Lever Act of 1914 implied as legal grew in importance. That legislation defined its objective as "to aid in diffusing among the people of the United States useful and practical information on subjects relating to agriculture and home economics, and to encourage the application of the same." A wider scope was defined in 1948 by a joint statement of the US Department of Agriculture and the Association of Land-Grant Colleges and Universities. President Hannah of Michigan State had chaired the joint committee. This action recognized mounting interdependence of rural and urban society, and opened the door to new programs and clients.

But in the mid-1950s, the changes in the countryside remained short of a thorough review. In 1956, the Extension Committee on Organization and Policy of the National Association of State Universities and Land-Grant Colleges appointed a subcommittee on Extension Scope and Responsibility. It consisted of six state leaders and two representatives of the Federal Extension Service; I was asked to serve as its chairman. Published in April 1957, the resulting report was entitled "The Cooperative Extension Service: A Statement of Scope and Responsibility."

Soon known as "the Scope Report" throughout the land-grant system, it was adopted by the respective bodies of the Association. Interestingly, one of the early opponents of widened scope, Director James Burch of Missouri, first moved its adoption; his successor, Dr. Brice Ratchford, who also led the process of implementing the Scope Report, would first apply it in Missouri. Of lasting importance to me was a brief leave of absence to write the report in the Washington office of C. M. Ferguson, director of the Federal Extension Service. My summary statement of this work is cited next:

Source: "The Scope Report." (Washington, DC: National Association State Universities and Land-Grant Colleges, 1957).

If we accept the principle that Extension's responsibilities are to farm families first, but not to them alone, then a major operational problem of Extension is how to allocate its time and resources so that the highest priority needs of those other than farm people are given attention. Because of the diversity of economic and population patterns throughout the nation, this allocation of Extension resources necessarily must be determined within each state, and to a large degree, within each county.... Care must be exercised by Extension and the people it serves that problems of major importance at any given time are given priority.

It is apparent that for the present and the years immediately ahead, there are several areas of program emphasis [that] should be receiving high-priority attention by the Extension Service. Although the degree of emphasis with respect to each of these areas may vary from one county or one state to another, the total effort of Extension work in the United States should fully recognize efficiency in [these areas]: agricultural production; efficiency in marketing, distribution, and utilization; the conservation, development, and use of natural resources; management on the farm and in the home; family living; youth development; leadership development; community and resource development; and public affairs. The Scope Report generally advised that Extension can and should cooperate with local people, other public agencies, and lay organizations in efforts to improve agriculture, promote non-farm employment opportunities, strengthen community services and institutions, and in other ways encourage the optimum development and utilization of all local resources.

I had planned a stimulating study leave for the fall of 1956, serving also to ponder issues to be taken up later in preparing the Scope Report, with a stay at the University of Wisconsin. But a downturn of Catherine's health after the birth of our second child, Thomas, required that we remain in East Lansing. Three months of study and writing in the Michigan State University Library followed. Importantly included was a serious reading of *Proceedings of the National Association of State Universities and Land-Grant Colleges*, a history of the organization from the outset of its origin. During this period, Douglas Ensminger, a notable figure among rural sociologists and the Ford Foundation representative in India, visited on the chance of my availability to join him in that pursuit. I declined.

New learning grew in that period, especially a widening acquaintance with other state extension directors. A core group had emerged to consider extension challenges in an innovative manner. They taught me much about needed reforms in the outreach of land-grant universities in a range of situations. Among those of special importance were directors Ernest Nesius of Kentucky, Brice Ratchford of North Carolina and later of Missouri, Henry Algren of Wisconsin, Marvin Anderson of Iowa, C. A. Vines of Arkansas, G. E. Lord of Maine, and Henry Hansen of Connecticut. C. M. Ferguson remained open to stateside innovations, as did his colleagues, Gladys Gallup and P. V. Kepner, among others. These associations and my own assignments combined to stimulate thinking about a future model of the Extension system. While the program focus had become the initial focus, there followed, as the excerpts below suggest, my statements of concern about the nature of competence to be required for a changing world.

Source: "A Director's Viewpoint for 1958." Address presented at the Michigan Annual Extension Conference, East Lansing, MI, October 28, 1957.

The great problem today of the Extension movement in the United States is not how to work longer, but how to work intelligently; not how to scatter broadside, but how to pinpoint our targets and to hit them; not how to hire more people, but how to produce greater impact with those we have; how certainly to work in ever greater freedom, but not to drift into chaos; and not only to be an excellent agency, but indeed and rather, a devoted and imaginative leader.... My belief is that the world is catching up with the Extension Service. More and more people have farsighted visions and some of us do not; more and more people read and some of us do not; more and more people have felt the first flush of leadership but some of us have not; and more and more people are willing to dare and some of us do not.... The immediate future of our Extension Service will be better insured by a stress on quality of personnel and performance rather than on quantity. We need a deepened and more positive professional ethic in Extension work...

Source: "Adjustment Needed in Extension Thinking and Organization." Address presented at the Annual Meeting of the American and Canadian Farm Economics Associations, CAN, August 1959). Also published in the *Journal of Farm Economics* XII (1959).

The most useful [extension] orientation is that of management. This orientation is not necessarily farm management or home management or any other discipline in which management may happen to be a central feature. The management orientation here is an outlook or point of view toward problem-solving, and deliberately assumes interdisciplinary arrangements of more traditional subject matter....

This orientation centers about three pivotal applications of extension work. The first is the farm family, and we term the process as decision-making. The second is the neighborhood, community, and region, and we term the process as planning. The third is at governmental levels, and we term the process as policy-making. The model requires investigation of ever-expanding situations, and is bound together by these: the procedures of management; the focusing of attention on the circumstances found in given situations; discovering the problems [that] the circumstances yield to achieving objectives as expressions of goals and values; identifying the alternative solutions [that] are available; the varying requirements of the solutions, or resources and techniques; judging, if not measuring, the probable consequences of the alternative solutions; and confronting the probable responsibilities [that] particular alternatives will exact if chosen.

Chairing the Scope Committee was both intense and stimulating. My travel about the country increased, especially to speak at state extension conferences. In 1958–1959 came opportunities to chair both the Cooperative Extension Section and the Division of Agriculture of the National Association of State Universities and Land-Grant Colleges. I was presented with opportunities to consider other posts but did not pursuee them; these included one of special interest, the Deanship of Agriculture at West Virginia University. My extramural activities also expanded in Michigan. For example, I chaired the Farm-City Relations Committee of the Michigan Farm Bureau, became a member on the Citizens Advisory Council of the Michigan Department of Health, and served as a trustee of the Michigan Health Council. Unfortunately, however, all required more time away from home. My aversion to travel strengthened...as did my desire to return to the Department of Sociology and Anthropology!

Such assignments, within and without the immediate precinct of Extension, widened my thinking about the outreach function of an entire university. Cooperative Extension, while ever broadening its mission, still mainly oriented its efforts to rural society. Meanwhile, "general extension" activities, broadly invigorated at Michigan State by the newly founded residential W. K. Kellogg Center for Continuing Education, were also expanding in scope and variety. Thus, I began to model intellectually how the future university might comprehend, organize, and administer such functions. Mounting in the late 1950s, such ideas would influence my professional interests in the years to come.

Source: "Adjustment Needed in Extension Thinking and Organization." Address presented at the Annual Meeting of the American and

Canadian Farm Economics Associations, CAN, August 1959). Also published in the *Journal of Farm Economics* XII (1959).

[There is] a whole series of perplexing [issues], among which are the following: the functional and organizational relationship of extension to the rapidly growing general extension movement; the [limiting] administrative attachments of the state extension director to the agricultural colleges; the possibility of rounding out the Extension Service in some areas as the single field arm of the land-grant university; the usefulness of the county as a principal administrative device in contrast to district or commodity areas; [and] the nature of the preparation and assignment of county workers and their organizational ties to the campus.

These widening reflections led me for the first time into the classic literature of the university form, especially such historic works as Cardinal John Henry Newman's the *Idea of the University* (1859); Karl Jaspers's *The Idea of the University (1946)*; and José Ortega y Gasset's *The Mission of the University (1944)*. Among my new mentors was John F. A. Taylor of Michigan State's Department of Philosophy: "The civilized and civilizing risk [that] the society assumes in creating the university is that it is creating its own critic.... The university also has the knowledge...that as it builds society, it builds itself; that as it tears society's vitals, it tears its own" (*The Masks of Society*, 1966, p. 227). Accordingly, my papers and speaking engagements turned to confronting the logic and methodologies of how a widened university outreach might be set in motion:

Source: "The University Idea and Off-Campus Education." Paper presented at the National Seminar on Adult Education Leadership, Michigan State University, East Lansing, MI, June 17, 1959.

The new community is not less than an intricate network of services and agencies in its own right; and builds with other communities into local, regional, and national webs of particular agencies engaged in disseminating particular services. Within these webs each agency develops agents of change, requires a clientele for the dissemination, and sponsors the counsel and the not unusual motive of promoting the demand for more.... The agency rises to special need. It faces to a special range of issues, and, therefore, to a special range of people who confront such issue.... The agency discovers its legitimacy in being construed for a particular function, and perpetuates this legitimacy by identifying a clientele and capturing support. The endless strategy of the agency is to articulate its purpose with those of its clientele.... The university is established on different grounds.... The university became a remarkable idea in that the nature of its usefulness is not wholly defined by the society [that] created it, a responsibility that to great degree it must take on for itself. The root meaning of the university is that it is a universe or method of inquiry.... There can be no denial of placing the university in the service of society. But the concept of service is not to be confused with the process of rendering services. The elusive quest of the university is to discover the alchemy [that] transforms the rendering of services into the ultimate continuity of learning in society.

The impact of the technological revolution on rural society was in full swing by 1959. The trend noted responses made and promised, but institutional innovation and change still lagged. The younger Extension directors felt the need to broaden the scope of programs. County agents in urban counties felt the same way. But these reactions met resistance to changes that the innovators sought. Not unexpectedly, general farm organizations and agricultural commodity groups would not accept radical moves. The agricultural colleges, supported by funds earmarked by rural representatives in state legislatures, hesitated to back the innovators. My stance surely went beyond what Dean Cowden and the general outlook of the College of Agriculture could support. But the opportunity was sufficient to sprinkle pilot projects across the state: consumer education, family nutrition, urban-related 4-H projects for young people, and natural resources management. All included linkages to urban institutions. In addition, I was free to write of the changes and the needed responses, including my own take on them, as below.

The American landscape was also undergoing radical change in the late 1950s. Moreover, events of the Cold War, and such new congressional enactments as the National Education Defense Act, moved American universities into a new alignment with the federal government, the strength of which renewed concern with multiplying challenges of an accelerating transformation at the grassroots. A measure of discontinuity between past plans and new program pressures provoked widespread reviews and sometimes undermined outreach reforms in academe.

Source: "Up From the Farm." *Challenge* 7, no. 6 (1959): 48–51.

> The problem of values is one that is becoming more and more acute in the United States. It is inevitable in a country characterized by mobility of such proportions…. The new Chicagoan, still ignorant of the sophistications of city dress and manners, is quick to become acquainted with the easy joys of the installment purchase system. No one tells him that he is a poorer man in other ways

than he was back home, where he had a fraction of the disposable income. He once believed in a congeries of intangibles that have vanished in the city lights…. It is in this area of values that the rural and urban Americans find themselves joined in a community of discontent.

Source: "The Role of Institutions and Organizations in Community Development." Paper presented at the Annual Conference of the American Country Life Association, Carbondale, IL, July 13, 1959.

The provincialism of old-style grassroots thinking won't work. Rural and urban Americans have created bigness and complexity. Both must now confront and learn to live with bigness and solve its consequences. Technologic innovation goes unrewarded without nontechnologic innovation. [Both must continue] with reasonable observance of symbols and philosophies but not with the perpetuation of myths; with attention to individual and organizational learning but within the span of the real world's circumstances; with a loyalty to historic commitments but with an awareness that destinations do not necessarily fall on single highways; with renewed attention to the agricultural community while acknowledging that the problems of the countryside are larger than simply residence and style of livelihood.

As the most intense learning period of my career, this first chapter of administrative duty would soon end. Michigan's large Cooperative Extension Service was spread throughout several different socio-economic regions. In the 1950s, rural life traditions were being overthrown. By the close of the decade, American society had clearly become more urban and industrial. Science and technology had emerged as ruling themes. My interests broadened to include economics, political science, urbanization, university philosophy and organization. Still wedded to rural sociology, my respect for county agents had grown apace.

BECOMING PROVOST

WHAT HAPPENED TO me in March 1954 happened again in March 1959! President Hannah called me to his office, announced that Vice President Varner was moving to Oakland, Michigan, to create a new university and that the university wanted me to accept the vacated post to oversee off-campus programs. I restated my desire to return to the department, but Hannah cut me short. He exclaimed how I could continue the reforms of Cooperative Extension, explore further inter-institutional alliances, and grow more acquainted with the multiplying programs of the Kellogg Center for Continuing Education. He assured me that a return to the department, if that remained my wish, would happen in due course. And without giving me much chance for further comment, he took my arm and briskly marched me two doors down the hall to my new office. I went to work there on March 1, 1959. Dean Cowden expressed skepticism about the new post, muttering, "Why do we create all these deans and vice presidents who supervise neither people nor money?"

Perhaps now the incessant travel would diminish. Thirteen years had passed since my arrival as a probationary graduate student engaged in field-work by day and study by night, and then as an administrator. Given her patience and support throughout those years, and despite periods of uncertain health, Catherine was no less than a genuine heroine. She served as a steadfast mother to our daughter, Paula, and Thomas, our new son, maintained the relationships with beloved families in West Virginia, and managed household and social obligations. She never forgot those years when I disappeared to study and write on weekends, returned from an out-in-the-state speech at midnight, and prepared for a meeting at breakfast. Those absences, as a husband and father, fed my mounting guilt that I supposed a return to the department would prove an antidote. Still unanswered was how, if at all, the new post as vice president for Off-Campus Education would yield such a correction. Thus, and again, a new chapter began.

In terms of overseeing off-campus education, little was accomplished in the new post. With Michigan State legally and newly renamed a "university," and with burgeoning enrollments and programs, President Hannah appointed a Committee on the Future of the University in the spring of 1959. Ten of the eleven members were faculty. Hannah asked me to become the remaining member, representing administration. All members were given leave from other duties and assigned special offices and meeting rooms. Newly arrived as a professor of education, Dr. Ernest Selby, a noted educational philosopher at Columbia University, served as chair. Dr. Floyd Reeves, after a long and distinguished career at the University of Chicago, and then resident consultant to John Hannah, was chief of staff. This group formed an extraordinary fellowship for the study of higher education and Michigan State's place in it. The effort consumed all members of the committee with full-time service for some eight months.

To be expected, my first assignments on the committee dealt with the outreach functions of Michigan State University. Close attention was paid the Kellogg Center for Continuing Education; I acquired the acquaintance and a long friendship to come with Dr. Howard Neville, who had succeeded Edgar L. Harden as its director. But other tasks of the committee also found their way to me, such as reviewing the collegial structure of Michigan State University and student learning in the residence halls. Quite special relationships blossomed within the committee and with individuals and groups throughout the campus. Of special importance to me were joint projects with another member, Dr. Richard Byerrum, professor of chemistry.

I was soon aware that my role as the single administrator on the committee, and one whose past work and contacts were largely off campus, had made me less known to the campus. Thus, it came as no surprise that faculty and other campus groups would seek ways to learn of my perspectives. As the committee geared up for its work, requests came to me to explore certain issues that seemed vital to the process then being initiated. Below are excerpts from my responses to two such requests, one to recognize a central principle in Michigan State's founding, and another to reflect on a university's inherent structure:

Source: "What is a University? A Panel Discussion with John Barron, John F. A. Taylor, and Paul A. Miller, Michigan State University." *College of Education Quarterly* (1959).

We are well aware that this University is firmly rooted in the seven-hundred-year-old tradition of universities in the western world. In consequence, we tend quite often to think that a university hardly needs definition at this late date. There are others (paraphrasing the poet), that a "university must not mean, but be"; that we should do less talking about our nature and our goals, and spend more time pursuing them. There is a good deal of truth as well as justification in these positions. Indeed, I will agree that a university is not a place, but a spirit; a university is not an "institution", but a mode of association, a "gemeinschaft." [Michigan State University] is the first institution in which scientific agriculture was taught, but Joseph Williams in his inaugural address as our first president remarked of the student who matriculated, "Morally, physically, intellectually, he must be a man before he can be a farmer."…. There may have been some question why farm boys beginning their education in a literal wilderness should be receiving such a heavy dose of the liberal arts, but the liberal arts were taught nevertheless.

Source: "A Vignette on the University." Speech presented at the Michigan State University Men's Club, September 29, 1959.

The trustees face both to the world and to the university and shape requisite aims through the necessary process of discovering and responding to the areas of agreement and the areas of disagreement between society and university. They must legally employ the first and defend the necessity of the second.

Faculty members give the university its style, without which the enterprise will serve the convention of an agency rather than the drama of the university. The expressions of the faculty through the media of the student intellect, scholarly publication, and the colloquium deliver the content of the house and how this content is to be organized, which is its meaning and truth….

The students bring to the university the element of freshness. One consequence of rigor and discipline is still more rigor and discipline: the devotee is confronted with other intellects [that] are still uncommitted. A denial comes easily to us at the end of an unyielding day, but ignorance, immaturity, and naiveté are the gifts of the student and they test the university's resilience….

Research and scholarship bring the most delicate of treasures and an unbounded, uncompromised exaltation in the creation of knowledge. This creation delicately engenders the atmosphere of dignity within the university, and…binds to the community all those whose credentials present an open passion for pursuit of the truth.

The administrator interprets the inner logic of the university in order to secure and arrange the means [and] remains a guardian over accommodations to centers of persuasion, whether organizational, curricular, or societal, and defends the codes by which the academic community lives, nurturing the truthful even when unpopular.

Through the spring and summer months of 1959 the Committee on the Future of the University would instruct me further. I grew more familiar with the measures taken in Michigan and elsewhere for enhancing cooperation among academic institutions. I took up an interest in the consortium movement and statewide systems of higher education. Joining other committee members in writing the report, my sections reflected mainly on outreach functions, including organic linkages with other institutions, how best to organize the arts and sciences, and the mission of student residence halls. The committee's report was due in early 1960, and I would turn to off-campus education.

In late September 1959, I traveled to North Carolina State University at Raleigh to address the Annual Cooperative Extension Conference. As I stepped from the speaker's podium, a message from President Hannah awaited: give him an immediate call. He informed me of a special board meeting in the afternoon of the next day, to be preceded by a meeting of the officers at which I should be present. Once I returned, another note summoned me to a luncheon prior to these sessions. However, when I arrived it was immediately clear that no one else would be attending!

As was his custom, Hannah came quickly to the point. "Paul, Tom Hamilton (Michigan State's first vice president for Academic Affairs) will reveal today that he is going to Albany as president of the State University of New York. I have consulted with Melby, Reeves, and others on the campus, and I want to combine your job with Tom's, give it the title of provost, and have you do it!"

Once my shock subsided, again and honestly I protested that my experience was much too narrow and short-lived, that I was unknown outside the agriculture and extension divisions, and that I was hoping to return soon to the department and begin building a scholarly portfolio. Once again, Hannah countered quickly. "You have been learning about Michigan State in recent months. You have taken up issues in the Committee of the Future that we must deal with, and more people know this than you might expect. I've checked enough to think that the campus will welcome your appointment. I want to recommend it to the board this afternoon." Then he continued—and I shall not forget his almost exact words—"Paul, pick up the telephone there and tell Kitty you have a new job." And so I did. For the third time, I had lost another appeal, which I believe was as genuinely meant as former ones, to resume the pathway I had begun in Sociology and Anthropology some twelve years before.

On October 1, 1959, action took over from planning! The new office included the small staff recruited by Thomas Hamilton. He was much admired as an academic leader for having helped elevate Michigan State's academic standing. Another was Paul Dressel, a foremost specialist in institutional research and already a helpful mentor. Another helpmate was John Wilson, director of a new Honors College, although he was destined to soon join Hamilton in New York. My first step was to invite Richard Byerrum, a close associate in the Committee on the Future, to serve as assistant provost. Similar titles went also to Howard Neville to lead in continuing education, and Paul Dressel to further emphasize research on the programmatic and budget essentials of the institution.

The new post generated a flood of reading and study, part on the philosophy of universities and part on the pragmatics of Michigan State, then a large and complex institution of more than twenty-five thousand students. While my earlier interests and competence centered on the link-ages of campus and community, strictly academic challenges now headed the agenda. Continuing my evening graduate seminar on social organiza-tion and administration also seemed worthwhile. Also, with Neville at my side, the then-maturing Kellogg Center for Continuing Education in the state capital of Lansing had become a statewide crossroads of public life and educational activity. The Center also beckoned me into an ever wider and new array of academic and public gatherings. My intellectual preparations, and coincidentally my capacities for them, mounted rapidly. The following excerpt from an address to an audience at the Kellogg Center, one representing a field of interest in my college days, illustrates one example of sudden preparations then beginning to challenge my competence.

Source: "Veterinary Medicine in the Post-Modern World: A Layman's View." Paper presented at the National Postgraduate Conference for Veterinarians, East Lansing, MI, January 20, 1960.

[T]he layman is accustomed to believing that human medicine has been for hundreds of years the profession in which science, art, and careful education have been one, while believing that animal medicine has made use of scientific methods only in recent years. Both branches of medicine are in some ways ancient and in some ways modern. Four thousand years ago, the code of the Babylonian King Hammurabi set forth regula-tions for those who treated the diseases of animals. Yet the American Veterinary Medical Association is still to celebrate its centennial. The oldest school of veterinary medicine, Alfort in France, has such a recent founding as in 1762; and one-third of the veterinary medical schools in the United States have been established since World War II. Although human medicine organized its schools much earlier, in such Italian universities as Bologna and Salerno in the twelfth century, it was such recent events as the famed Flexner Report in 1910 [that] revolutionized medical education and gave human medicine its present educational and scientific character.

Coping with new knowledge and related duties did not, however, reduce my interest in rural life and the agricultural colleges; indeed, I now view these topics in a wider perspective. Along with the new duties of provost, my studies continued of the outreach functions of the land-grant universities. More careful study followed on how rural society had managed to perpetuate its social, economic, and political values. Rooted in the ancient Greek, Roman, English, and early American concepts of agrarian democracy, these values nurtured the idea that democracy, and individual freedom and private property, were best embodied in the theory of the family farm. A "rural commitment" had emerged to glorify farming as a way of life, and later charge, as did the agrarian revolts of the late nineteenth century, that family farming, viewed as a seedbed of democracy, was being undermined by the spread of urbanization.

Viewing such contentions from a central job in a major university raised the question of how its rural commitment was being eroded by a technological revolution led by the agricultural colleges! A new paradox seemed apparent: the outreach model devised specifically in the agricultural colleges had yet to sufficiently accommodate such changes. Perhaps a chief challenge seemed evident with the agrarian idea being increasingly absorbed into the ever more urban, industrial, and international age. Such crosscutting strongly implied that the competent leader in agriculture would increasingly need an updated education in order to accommodate such a future. The following excerpt, from my address to a major conference on such issues, probed the new and mounting challenges to practitioners in agricultural and rural fields.

Source: "Philosophy and Objectives of Higher Education in Agriculture." Address delivered at the National Conference on Curriculum Development, Fort Collins, CO, July 18, 1960.

A basic essential is a view that higher education in agriculture be a projection of technological humanism rather than technical vocationalism. This assumes the importance of considering agriculture as a humane topic rather than only a vocational skill. This orientation should make agriculture more attractive to quality students and prepare them for leadership at those levels of intellectual abstraction the field of agriculture so desperately needs. A new interest must be discovered that plans a curriculum [that] relevantly integrates the liberal subjects (the sciences and the arts included) into a technological core of producing and distributing food and fiber and the human organization which accomplishes it. [Underlying all this] for the future of the agricultural college is the premise that the production, distribution, and consumption of food and fiber is the largest and most vital industry in any society. But it must now be considered understood that the agrarian commitment is being displaced by a new technological edifice.

My tasks as provost were genuinely joyful. Days filled with meetings, large and small, with faculty and administrators were, in sum, occasions of stimulation and personal learning. But conflicts and their tensions were part of the job, and mediation was ever in demand. A major issue over whose philosophy of engineering education would win (in a time of national disagreement on the subject) led eventually to a difficult dismissal of a department head to reach a settlement. The committee planning for a new school of medicine at Michigan State, which I chaired, provoked a brief disagreement with my esteemed associate, Dean Cowden of Agriculture, over the recommended consolidation of three biochemistry units then present. Reduced legislative appropriations at the turn of the 1960s required difficult eliminations of entire units, and forever etched in my memory was a face-to-face meeting for such an action with the director and staff of the Highway Traffic Safety Research Center. Hannah gave much day-by-day operating responsibility to the provost. One pivotal task was to plan, negotiate, and approve academic budgets, and to reconcile them with the several categories of funding origins. Such an experience would stand me in good stead when later assignments elsewhere arrived.

Despite my relative inexperience, Hannah patiently defined and granted me, as he did his other subordinates, more room to make mistakes than I often expected and likely deserved. End-of-the-day conversations with him not only brought encouragement, but also one memorable aphorism after another. His gems included these: "Never fail to get the best financial officer possible, one who enables you to go to bed knowing that tomorrow not one penny can be questioned" and "All else being equal, pick the younger people; they have more energy, take greater risks, and, if they fail, the gift of more time to recoup the loss in another post." Best of all, perhaps, Hannah, also an extension specialist in his early career, never failed to encourage my interest in the outreach function of the university; I suspect that interest figured substantially in my appointments.

He grew ever stronger as a role model for all those who worked closely with him. I will never forget his Monday breakfast meetings with the officers. Always the first to arrive and impatiently tapping the table with his fingers, Hannah would then astound us with what he was reading and what it implied for Michigan State. What was billed as a staff meeting often became a seminar on higher education. A spur to my learning also occurred when Hannah, frequently absent for national and international assignments (e.g., as the initial chair of the US Civil Rights Commission), asked me to serve in his place.

Happily, what had happened in the Cooperative Extension Service was also possible in the provost's office—enlisting younger colleagues in common endeavor. Richard Byerrum, as assistant provost, served with distinction, and later became Dean of the College of Natural Sciences. Our customary day began by meeting at a street corner near our homes, walking onward to the campus, and reflecting on the day's plan; we might also return similarly and dissect the day's results. Paul Dressel, a person of quiet but strong conviction and intelligence, converted me to the necessity of institutional research data for academic decision-making. He acquainted me with a youthful Stanley Ikenberry, who would join me later in new circumstances and, in time, become a national leader in higher education as president of the University of Illinois. Dressel remained a loyal mentor throughout with introductions of five-year plans and teachings about zero-sum budgeting (i.e., don't just argue about additions to last year's budget; rebuild it each year from ground zero!).

Howard Neville gave unusual leadership of continuing education not only to Michigan State, but to the nation as a whole. Later a Michigan State provost, he continued a brilliant career as president successively of two universities before his untimely death in 1981. The daily routine of provost's duties, and how it took up all aspects of campus and related public events, would include a busy schedule of local presentations to a range of groups. Importantly, soon to be realized, was the steady inclusion of a central theme in my interests to be shared: the connections of the university idea to society at large. Moreover, my reading also expanded into more classical treatments of the meaning of the university in and to society. Such discussions, plus brief writings in *Open Letters from the Provost*, a regular newsletter to the Michigan State faculty and staff, enabled a campus-wide discussion to mount on matters of proper concern. I had also to withstand the critical reactions to such efforts, not to mention those of grammatical correction (e.g., "Please, use more active verbs!"). Two excerpts below illustrate such conversations; the first is from a local address, and the next taken from the one of the provost's "letters" to the faculty.

Source: "The University in the Post-Modern Community." Address delivered at the National Continuing Education Seminar, East Lansing, MI, February 23, 1960.

Whatever universities do in the years ahead will likely show in the kind of society attempted or achieved by the people whose lives they touched. T. S. Elliot once suggested that our education is not so much the generator of our culture as it is the offspring. If there is more than truth in the statement of Eliot, then it will not matter much in the years ahead what we do, for few people will know or care. If, on the other hand, we attempt to help people, on and off the campus, to a new vision of themselves and society, then, regardless of our failures, the years ahead will be worthwhile ones. Running the risk of failures is one of the useful plights of universities. I continue to find comfort and confidence in the words of the German philosopher Karl Jaspers: "It is not by the record of disappointments by which a university may be judged, but, rather, by the nature of the aims and the spirit and steadfastness which is directed toward their achievement."

Source: *The Provost's Letters*. Michigan State, East Lansing, MI, October 7, 1960.

For some this university is too big; for others, too small. For some it is too poor; for others, rich enough to do better. Some believe our university to be vital and dynamic; others that it is too shallow. Some would create from it a research institute; still others would make it an academy. Some organize their affections with nostalgic reaction to the Red Cedar [River] and Spartan Field, but others wish we might emulate the university at Berkeley. All of us know that duplication and empire building within a university are wrong, but many of us accelerate these processes anyhow. It may be necessary that such differences of opinion make up modern academic life, and those of who stay around may learn to take it and even to like it. Yet I wonder what it does for our students? Have we fallen into C. P. Snow's "gulf of incomprehension?" If so, have the students noticed?

Throughout my stay at Michigan State, an international interest animated the campus. When President Truman signed the Point Four Program into law in 1949 (to assist the poor nations in social and economic development), John Hannah, then president of the National Association of State Universities and Land-grant Colleges, called the White House and offered the services of public universities. Moreover, thanks to Hannah's leadership and a general campus readiness, Michigan State, in the next decade, was numbered among the leaders of that response. By 1959, more than two hundred of the faculty had experienced international assignments, by contracts with the Agency for International Development and other sponsors, in Africa, Asia, and

Latin America. Glen Taggart, a rural sociologist in the US Department of Agriculture's international divisions, had come at the turn of the 1950s to assist Loomis (and become one of the closest friends and colleagues in my life and career). He first led in internationalizing the US Department of Agriculture. In the mid-1950s, Taggart became Dean of the Office of International Programs at Michigan State, likely the first appointment of its kind.

My Michigan State duties, while involved with the international expansion, had failed to provide even a short-term project abroad. Knowing of this interest, Taggart and Hannah facilitated my appointment as vice chairman of a Joint Commission on Higher Agricultural Education in Colombia, South America. Supported by the presidents of Colombia and the United States, this Commission of five leaders from Colombia and three from the United States was funded by the W. K. Kellogg Foundation in partnership with staff support of the Ford and Rockefeller Foundations. Arthur Weber, dean of the College of Agriculture at Kansas State University was originally appointed chairman, but when he resigned due to poor health shortly after the Commission convened, the chairmanship fell to me.

To complete the project and write the report, the Miller family spent the summer of 1960 in Bogotá. The Commission's charge was to review higher agricultural education in Colombia's development. The National University of Colombia (Educación Agrícola Superior en Colombia) published a monograph in April 1961 in both English and Spanish languages. Our major recommendation was to create the Colombian Institute of Agriculture (ICA). This new institution, while part of the national government, would possess a large measure of independence to organize, coordinate, administer Columbia's rural research and extension functions, and collaborate with academic centers. I will always remember that I was in Colombia to help celebrate ICA's new campus on the day President John F. Kennedy was assassinated in November 1963.

Upon our return to Michigan State for the fall quarter of 1960, I began work on a project addressed by the Committee on the Future that dealt with Michigan State's residence halls. Already a large sector and growing rapidly by reason of need and Hannah's creative use of bonding powers, exploding enrollments after World War II had required huge capital investments. Despite more refined and attractive architectural features, they still imitated the traditional "dormitory" model of an earlier and simpler day. Little attention was paid to their place in the total learning environment. President Hannah gave steady support and his own ideas to addressing this shortcoming.

Residence hall reform at Michigan State had been taken up at length by the Committee on the Future, and became one of the most radical projects of my tenure as provost. The university enrollment had grown to be among the largest in academe, and would still expand. The number of students choosing to live on campus was also sure to grow. So the Committee on the Future turned to the issue of "bigness" and what might best be instituted for the purpose of student learning and comfort:

Source: *The Provost's Letters.* Michigan State, East Lansing, MI, March 15, 1961.

> Although learning is said to be our aim, we seem to have an unusual genius for arranging the university to inhibit it. While the university grows larger, the compartments within in it seem to me to become relatively smaller. Small groups of specialists locate themselves in the various corners of the campus for the purpose of a specialized communion. In other corners, but with little relation to the first, the classrooms and laboratories are found. The residence halls are found on the periphery, large blocks of them devoted to eating, sleeping, and maintaining a

non-academic culture. Thus, thousands of people are called upon to move in restless tides across the campus. Their reason for doing so is to discover each other. This strikes me as remarkably inconvenient; it is costly in time, energy, and even money.... What I am thinking over is a plan [that] would combine the best features of the residential college and the comprehensive university. Realizing that so many of our students reside on the campus, together with the belief that many of the elements necessary to learning should join rather than separate, I envisage several undergraduate colleges designed as learning-residence-faculty centers. Here a student would take a part of the curriculum, as well as being led into association with the research-graduate units of the University.

Campus support gathered for such an exploration. Michigan State's Brody Hall was remodeled in the summer of 1961 with this philosophy in mind. Moreover, the design of several "living-learning centers" came off the drafting tables. Each of these "colleges" would house students whose majors fell under a specific theme, such as international affairs, natural sciences, or social sciences. Faculty in related fields, but not of single disciplines, and interested in testing the teacher-scholar concept, would have office there. Designed to foster a learning environment, the structures also included classrooms and seminar rooms.

This was only one of three significantly new steps at the time. The others concerned how best to organize a new medical curriculum and achieve a better structure for the College of Arts and Sciences, both also considerations of the Committee on the Future. The provost's office addressed them in 1960–61.

Forming a medical school rose in the natural evolution of Michigan State as a comprehensive public university. A planning committee with representatives from the related disciplines and the College of Veterinary Medicine was formed. Hannah appointed the provost to chair it, thus providing me with a most unusual experience in planning. I visited other medical schools, either established or being planned, including the stellar experiences of visiting Dartmouth, the University of Florida, and the University of Kentucky. The Michigan State plan incorporated a radical principle: an interdisciplinary approach by means of a Biomedical Institute. Thus, students, after completing a common preclinical course of study in the basic sciences, could choose among tracks leading to a PhD in one of the biological disciplines, an MD or a DVM. This plan went forward and has influenced Michigan State's approach to medical education since its inception, including another much later option, that of osteopathic medicine.

The third project of lasting result, to reorganize the College of Arts and Sciences, was given careful consideration by the Committee on the Future. A full account of the reasoning is unnecessary. In short, the forces at work were unique to Michigan State as the first land-grant university, and one with a rising reputation for public service on a worldwide basis. Also unique, and intended to feature general education, was a Basic College, formed alongside the College of Arts and Sciences. Moreover, the rapid growth of faculty and student numbers in the latter had become disproportionate in size, influence, and unwieldiness relative to other major divisions. These and other factors pointed to the need for better balance. After lengthy campus-wide debates, official campus bodies elected to divide the College of Arts and Sciences into three colleges: Humanities, Natural Sciences, and Social Sciences. The trustees received the proposal in early 1962.

During the summer of 1961, my aim of returning to the Department of Sociology and Anthropology arose again. While no other post could have matched the pleasure and stimulation of serving as provost for three years, I had to choose carefully between an academic pathway (with the need to emphasize teaching and research) or remaining in administration. Given my continuing interest and continuing appointment in the department, the uncertain health of Catherine, the equally uncertain appeals to both of us of the public demands, and the needs of two children, we leaned toward eliminating administration as an option. We proved this to ourselves by declining invitations I received to become a candidate for presidential posts, especially one from West Virginia University in the spring of 1961.

A continuing interest in my seminar on social organization and administration grew more intense as well as the traditional concern with cooperative extension, adult, and continuing education. My speaking engagements turned again to these themes as my decision strengthened to move back to the department. Three years as provost, with the principal task of reflecting on the university as a total system, motivated me to look more and more at the outreach of the total university form. Certain principles grew from considerations of the outreach function as the responsibility of the whole university. Selected from a relevant paper are key points for the future of university outreach.

Source: "Higher Education in the New Community." Address presented at the Conference on the Search of the Century, Texas A&M University, College Station, TX, July 25, 1961.

Extension or continuing or adult education, or off-campus services, should be recognized for what they are: a voluntary, dispersed, nonconforming education [that] stretches as far and as deep as the life of the mind may elect.... The extension function is most capable of imagination, experimentation and choice, for it is a promise for human learning at the crossroads of maturity.

Intelligent conversation should take place about what the university intends for the issues of contemporary life. Our patrons should also be invited to join the forum. By such means, the community may discover its aspirations through the university and the university discovers its mission through the community.

There are obscure parts of scholarly enterprise [that] might be guided into the community. The scholar's workplace is usually choked with the published results of scholarship. Somewhere in our communities to be served are those thoughtful persons who would be honored and enriched to receive a reprint.

Universities are colonizers of communities of the mind. The target is the intellect, whether occupied in the laboratory of Chemistry 101 or in the feedlots of Texas ranchers. The university must be able to begin the colonization anywhere...helping people come to know the wholeness of issues and how to engage in the definition of problems and the formulations of solutions.

Family decision-making on the future was challenged in late summer of 1961 when the board chairman of West Virginia University appeared unannounced at my office door! Forrest H. Kirkpatrick had been Dean of Students during my sole year at Bethany College in West Virginia, and he was among those who had contributed to my presence there and lamented my departure. His mission to East Lansing was to reopen discussion about my earlier refusal to be considered for the presidency of West Virginia University. So Catherine and I turned once again to key factors of reconsideration: our personal needs and interests, the lives of the children, our families and other kinfolk resident in West Virginia, our affections for WVU, and our happiness and loyalties at Michigan State. We consulted with colleagues, especially President Hannah ("too few resources there; commit yourself to Michigan State") and Dean Cowden ("why not give it a try; at worst, you can return here").

We finally agreed to an informal discussion with the Board of Governors of WVU, which, in turn, led to two more formal meetings. Both meetings were in Pittsburgh; we made no visit whatsoever to Morgantown for even a single encounter with faculty and staff, a practice soon and properly to become inconceivable. Nevertheless, on a Sunday morning in September 1961, I received an offer to become the university's fifteenth president. I accepted. The family returned to East Lansing, the board went to Morgantown and, at a general meeting of the faculty, announced the appointment. With the MSU provost's duties to be put in order, and to complete my fall semester seminar, the starting date settled on February 1, 1962.

My desire to return to the faculty had been sidetracked, but not abandoned. The appointment also included a professorship in sociology. Chairman Kirkpatrick and I carefully discussed my uncertainties, especially of how the family would accommodate the challenges. We agreed that I should aim for an initial assignment of five years, after which the board and the Millers would evaluate the personal and professional factors, and, if that seemed best, I would be free to take up the professorship. Thus, for the time being, our emotions for serving West Virginia people won us over to a new chapter of undetermined length.

Many poignancies remain memorable, some rooted in Michigan and others in West Virginia. For example, in the period after declining the invitation to be a candidate and before the visit of Forrest Kirkpatrick to East Lansing, my father entered a hospital in July 1961 with a terminal illness. On my final visit with him, my father, always hoping for our return to West Virginia, pointed out that he knew that WVU was searching for a president and that I should work for it. Not disclosing my initial decline of candidacy, I repeated how happy we were in our service to Michigan State University and that we intended to remain there. He died shortly after, not knowing that his long hope for a son and his family to return "home" would come to pass.

Along with putting the provost's office in order in the remaining months of 1961, a special scholarly effort loomed that year—the annual conference of the National Association of State Universities and Land-Grant Colleges would celebrate the centennial birthday of the land-grant institutions. I was asked to prepare a paper on the past, present, and future of the agricultural colleges to be included among several papers to express the centennial theme. The processes of the move to WVU overlapped my need to plan and write the paper. Not unnaturally, the paper gave opportunity to summarize my intellectual evolution over some sixteen years at Michigan State University: research and extension in the land-grant mode; changes and challenges in how institutions are organized and administered; the growth of international linkages and development; and mounting concern with the university as an idea and as a form. Moreover, as the paper took shape, it also held promise as a guide to the tasks that were sure to come at West Virginia University. The paper was perhaps the most important one of the East Lansing years.

The paper's chief argument highlighted the agricultural colleges as an innovative development organization, worthy of emulation throughout the world. The paper examined the major reasons for this uniqueness: its central location in an integrated planning and action system at local, state, regional, national, and international levels; how this system responds to national purpose; its proficiencies in organization; and the manner of its useful access to other social, economic, and political institutions.

The paper also discussed how the agricultural colleges were challenged and even threatened by the consequences of their leadership: the impact of industrialism upon agriculture; the dispersion of expertise among new agencies; the redefinition of national goals in urban and international terms; the decline in rural power by reason of governance institutions no longer dominated by rural interests; and exploding urbanization then stimulating steady and ever larger migrations from rural to urban communities.

The paper stands as perhaps the most fully considered one of my career! After all, the agricultural colleges had fundamentally led me into a stimulating professional life, one sufficiently apt as to provide reflections at the centennial recognition of such institutions. In short, the paper explored certain issues of accommodation for the agricultural colleges of the land-grant universities: accommodating their subject matters to the agricultural and industrial revolutions then under way, fashioning more permanent linkages to international development, and assuring adequacy of their intellectual perspectives within higher education as a whole. The following excerpt suggests the central theses of this paper, which concluded my sixteen-year stint at Michigan State University and helped perceive still another chapter at West Virginia University.

Source: "The Agricultural Colleges of the United States: Paradoxical Servants of Change." Paper presented at the National Association of Land-Grant Colleges and State Universities, Washington, DC, November 1961. Also published as *The Agricultural Colleges of the United States: Paradoxical Servants of Change*. Columbia, MO: University of Missouri Press. November, 1961.

How to plan and execute development is one of the world's leading questions. What development means in sharply differing histories and cultures weighs heavily upon those nations [that] seek it and are willing to pay the price of change, and also upon the great sovereign powers for which it has become a necessary element of diplomacy. The search for workable models of economic and social development grows more anxious and precarious by the moment. What is at stake is the discovery of that combination of population, resources, and old and new institutions [that] may set free the self-generative forces, latent though they now be, in given societies. Accordingly, any experience [that] suggests itself as a revelation for understanding development organizations is of great contemporary significance. It is in this special sense that the agricultural college is worthy of a centennial observance in the year 1961. And it is not unfair for the same reason to ask the leaders of agricultural colleges: what are the chief attributes of the colleges as development organizations in terms of their national design, their response to national purpose, proficiency in their organization, their special organizational linkages, and the nature of their access to other strategic groups?

A whirlwind of activity in the remaining weeks of 1961 brought the provost's duties to closure. We made occasional trips to Morgantown, West Virginia, for press conferences and to meet university, community, and state leaders. These contacts provided initial insights about how to begin the new work, even to make certain moves before arrival. The same may be said for an invitation to appear in January 1962 before the budget and other legislative committees in Charleston, an event necessitated by the illness of WVU's acting president.

My final professional duty at Michigan State University was to attend the January 1962 meeting of the board of trustees, give my analysis, and recommend that the College of Arts and Sciences be made into three distinct colleges. The board approved this last recommendation, and I quickly entered the automobile waiting at the door. I was joined there by Catherine, Paula, and Thomas, and we departed for Morgantown, West Virginia, to begin a new personal and professional chapter.

III

WEST VIRGINIA UNIVERSITY

REVISITING THE LAND-GRANT IDEA

A NEW BEGINNING

THE MOVE TO Morgantown in January 1962 took the family home, but with a lingering sadness for departing good years and memories in Michigan. Both Catherine and I relished the West Virginia people and their hills and landscapes. Paula was about to enter her third year of high school. Then seven years old, Thomas was awed by the large house of the WVU president in the middle of the downtown campus. And I felt that our future lay in serving the people of West Virginia, indeed for the remainder of my career! Board chairman Forrest Kirkpatrick and I informally agreed on a term of five years. The family and I would then join the board of governors to evaluate performance, take account of my quite special concerns for family health, and decide a future course.

When a new university president arrives, one may be sure that the new appointee will begin an immediate assessment of the present situation. Such was the case at West Virginia University (WVU) in early 1962. Having experienced a transition period for more than a year, Dr. Clyde Colson, beloved Dean of the College of Law, had served well as acting president. Colson appeared more than ready to depart the office. He was on his way out the door as I was on my way in, on the very day we arrived! I asked if he would remain to share his overview and the current agenda, but, no, he disappeared quickly through the doorway. He returned later to exclaim, "How two new problems will show up while you work on the present one!"

My predecessor had been Elvis J. Stahr, who, after a brief tenure, became secretary of the army in President Kennedy's cabinet. By his effective efforts, several key leaders were in place, all destined to join me as the institution's fifteenth president. John Golay, arriving from Chicago just as Stahr departed and still unsure of his assignments, continued as provost. Robert Munn, university librarian, brimming with insights about the state and the university, had an talent for planning. Ernest Nesius, dean of the College of Agriculture, was already a national leader in university outreach. Irvin Stewart, a former president and then professor of political science, who had wisely guided WVU into becoming a genuine university, gave me support without reservation. The director of a new community college in Parkersburg, a part of the WVU system, Todd Bullard prepared me in political science. He was soon appointed president of Potomac State College, also a constituent division of the university. A few years later, in an entirely different setting for both of us, Bullard would join me in a lengthy and productive colleagueship.

Carl Frasure, dean of the College of Arts and Sciences, shared his remarkable knowledge of state political organization. Joseph Gluck, long-time dean of Student Affairs, introduced and guided me within the student body. Kenneth Penrod and Clark Sleeth, respectively vice president and dean at the Medical Center, taught me the realities of that still new system. In the president's immediate office, the following toiled in a manner never to be forgotten: Harold Shamberger, a wise student of public and legislative affairs and never ceasing in getting his job done; Donald Bond, then effectively initiating the WVU Foundation; Mary McDaniel, who, as executive secretary, provided ceaseless assistance; and, soon to join as special assistant, David Nichols, a young and creative humanist.

A planning effort soon emerged from this company of colleagues. It focused on three challenges. The first aimed to strengthen the basic disciplines, better relate them to each other, and give special attention to those of clear relevance to the state (e.g., the biological and medical sciences, engineering, law, the creative and performing arts, and proper use and development of natural resources). The second provided for a review of the physical plant, then awaiting decisions about the respective functions of Morgantown's three campuses. The third challenge was to define the future role of a land-grant university in West Virginia.

To learn of what resulted from the plans to enhance interdisciplinary strength and improve the quality and organization of campus facilities, the reader should turn to other historical documents. Of special importance is the book written by William T. Doherty Jr. and Festus P. Summers, *West Virginia University: Symbol of Unity in a Sectionalized State*.[2] As of my entire account herein, so this part on WVU: these reflections are about how universities may engage with society. However, this emphasis depends greatly on a university's internal strength, an axiom to be emphasized by selected excerpts from my writings in that period. Clear from the outset of my thought about the roles of WVU, and public universities in general, were notions that they could not adequately serve the development needs of a state if only slight interaction and cooperation exists between the disciplines, departments, schools, and colleges. Given early opportunities

---

2   Doherty, Jr., William T., and Festus P. Summers. *West Virginia University: Symbol of Unity in a Sectionalized State* (Morgantown, WV: West Virginia University Press, 1982).

to reflect on this manner, it was possible to take up this challenge and explain its relevance at WVU.

Source: "On the Unity of Scientific Disciplines." Address presented to the West Virginia Academy of Science, West Virginia University, Morgantown, WV, April 27, 1962.

[Our plan at WVU] is to determine academic goals and coincide our educational hopes with economic, organizational, and public needs.... We propose to provide greater depth than we now enjoy in those areas [that] are relevant to West Virginia and capable of true eminence.... More and more of the real world concerns call for multidisciplinary approaches or mergers of technical and socioeconomic phenomena associated with the density and distribution of the people and the pressure of their tools upon resources. It is safe to say that we do not yet have an interdisciplinary theory of development [that] incorporates the area, resources, population, culture, institutions, science and technology, and a theory sufficient to predict the locus of self-generating mechanisms in a given society.... We ought to be troubled by the divergence between the nature of the world's interdependent problems and our ability to gain a conversation between the relevant disciplines.

By 1962, my career, which had begun in West Virginia in 1939, placed me in what might be entitled the anatomy of a peaceful revolution: a new age of science and its application through technology. The changes to agriculture and rural life had greatly quickened from my youthful 4-H days, from my stretch as a county agricultural agent, and then to sixteen years mainly serving the outreach of Michigan State University. The technological impact on American agriculture in that short period had alone produced remarkable successes as well as unintended and troubling consequences. Among these interests were the changes brought to land-grant universities, a concern expressed in the previous chapter. The needed accommodations of the land-grant university were of great interest throughout the 1950s. To direct attention to them, in light of overall development challenges facing West Virginia, and to strengthen the engagement of WVU with them, became the inner logic of my term as the WVU president.

The assignment went much beyond holding the job. It had become a calling. West Virginia is the only completely Appalachian state, an area of instant natural beauty, the homeland of a warmhearted and frank people, and a corner of the nation that inserts itself into the middle of an enormous eastern seaboard population. In 1962, West Virginia seemed ready to launch and continue its new practice of bold ideas, their imaginative combination, experimentation to strengthen old institutions and create new ones, and resolve to mobilize and focus the state's human and technical resources. Given such aims, what should be the role of WVU? The chief challenge seemed one of how best strengthen the public role of WVU by defining a mission based on an adequate theory and philosophy of development, one that both those within and without the university would find agreeable. I was determined to soon place such a mission before the public. An opportunity to do so arose in the early weeks of starting the new job, as evidenced in this address I prepared for a key group of faculty and Morgantown leaders:

Source: "Education and State Development." Presentation delivered to a forum of university faculty and community leaders, Morgantown, WV, March 15, 1962.

Among other distinctive features of our [Appalachian] region is an apparent difficulty with investing in such essential services as privately and publicly sponsored research, an overall sound system of elementary and secondary education, and adequate social, health, economic, and political institutions. Although the wider the adverse divergence between a region and the national norm the more it needs to invest in human ability, the hard fact of the matter in a technical society is that because of this distance, investment in ability is not easy to come by. Then the circle becomes truly vicious....

Another distinctive feature takes root in the cultural and residential stability of the southern Appalachians, the difficulty of rapidly changing farms and forests and water into new land uses of larger scale, and the problems of building a vital system of education from bottom to top. [Without such], youth are encouraged to seek their livelihood elsewhere, people of maturity to stick it out, and [leading to] the departure of excellent and devoted teachers, technicians, and managers. Unfortunately, they are a greater loss to the region they leave than they are a gain to where they go.

We should ask ourselves just what this combination of factors boils down to. I believe it is children. Neither families nor communities are able to invest enough in children for them to keep up their pride in the home area and at the same time provide them the necessary ability to meet these regional factors head-on. Soundly based resource development can't be any better than the willingness to invest in children!

Thinking through a theory of engaging a university with a state must begin with the agencies it possesses for doing so. For the land-grant institutions, this means such traditional entities as the Cooperative Extension Service and the more general adult education programs normally administered by General Extension divisions. What their future roles might be was a concern of high order at WVU in 1962. The Michigan years had also included this urgent concern, especially how to reorganize the major outreaching agencies within the land-grant university. My rationale and manner of organization for doing so was taken up in some detail during the 1950s. A summary of such interests was published in 1958.

Source: "Extension Education in the Land-Grant Universities." *Farm Policy Forum* 11, no. 4 (1958): 8–14.

> The field-level federation of the two services might entertain experimentation at the field center with administrative techniques of coordination, viewing the federated field center as representing the regional community in response to ecological, industrial, occupational and commodity specialization, and consideration of locating this center at a community or regional college.
>
> The second span of experimentation is at the organization and administrative level of the land-grant university itself. [This includes] the issues of how to administratively attach the state extension director; the extent to which each academic division should possess its own off-campus resources; and the proper organization of Extension work in home economics and boys and girls club work. Other functions also need to be examined: maintaining the forum and its dialogue that relates the

whole university to the whole community in which it rests; arranging the conditions by which interdisciplinary centers and institutes may emerge and be sustained; [creating] imaginative designs for continuing higher adult education; and discovering the criteria of relevance which govern the deployment of university resources in university-like ways.

The formal inauguration of new university presidents continues as a legendary ceremony. Such could not be escaped at WVU! With the date set by the Board of Governors for April 11, 1962, what might be properly said in an address remained much on my mind. With the planning venture, cited above and on its way, having the inaugural message summarize the highlights of a master plan grew in importance. My centennial address on "The Agricultural Colleges of the United States" (cited in Chapter II) had organized the themes of the years at Michigan State University, becoming the backdrop to the new chapter at WVU. The inaugural statement needed for the April assembly built upon that past in light of the new context provided by WVU and the state of West Virginia. The inaugural address aimed to underscore the tentative plans in mind for the university itself, for the developmental needs of the state, and how these two initiatives might be joined. Two major points about them are found in the excerpts that follow.

Source: "Inaugural Address, April 11, 1962." Published as *West Virginia University Bulletin* 63, no. 4–2 (October, 1962).

The second invention is a series of regional arrangements in West Virginia, located [adjunctively] with appropriate institutions wherever possible, so that the University and the state college and university system especially may combine their respective strengths for a more convenient and powerful assistance of our people. The state would, in breakthrough fashion, be served by the joint combination of such resources in convenient centers [that] offer broadened technical and educational information, sponsor the wise convergence of the undergraduate resources of the state colleges and graduate resources of the university, and coordinate stronger programs, in cooperation with state and federal agencies of regional development within the state. Such inter-college regional centers could also help higher education to better backstop, support and join with principals, superintendents, and teachers in making the public school system the powerful instrument of development it must be if the new urgency in West Virginia is to be answered. The alternative to unselfishly merging the best we have may be, as so many places risk today, the colonizing of our state into unilateral, unrelated, poorly supported, and wastefully overlapping educational domains.

INTERACTING WITH STATE INSTITUTIONS

WITH THE FORMAL installation completed, and the focus of a strategic plan taking form, comprehending the state grew as an earnest duty. At the same time, several projects had been launched on the campus, all outcomes of an emerging plan. Emphasis grew upon the campus physical structure by directing attention to a model that would turn the three campuses to maximum advantage. While the downtown campus would serve as rather the social center and the home mainly of the arts and sciences, the other two campuses would feature professional and outreach functions. New university construction went to the drawing boards: a new university student union, a creative arts center, publicly and privately built residence halls, a new forestry complex, and requisite parking facilities.

The plan also called for a core curriculum and the reform of academic governance. Disciplines and programs were reviewed in light of what might be unusually distinguished and relevant to the State and region. Special attention was paid the biological sciences, to be integrated at the research and graduate level in a Graduate Institute, as well as the medical and related programs. Similar reasoning was directed to forestry, certain areas of engineering and physical sciences, and the preparation of public school teachers and leaders.

Some new ancillary offices and key leaders came upon the scene. These added to the lasting pleasure of recruiting and aiding the development of younger colleagues. An Office of Student Services was established and Michigan State's David Hess invited to lead it. Also from MSU came Stanley Ikenberry to head a new Office of Institutional Research. He would later become dean of WVU's College of Education and Human Resources, an official of The Pennsylvania State University, president of the University of Illinois, and president of the American Council on Education. Of great importance to the university's future was the move of Harry Heflin from the presidency of Glenville State College to become vice president for Administration. This esteemed friend and mentor would remind me with one aphorism after another, saying, "Paul, you would do better to walk steadily rather than run headlong into the future." Heflin would contribute much to West Virginia, and later served as the WVU President.

Despite such internal steps, however, my chief resolve was to better comprehend the state before tackling how best to update WVU as a model of state and land-grant universities. This meant learning of the state's social, economic, and cultural institutions, both private and public. Also to receive close attention were the state's governmental agencies. This interest continued and even stimulated regional and national interest in WVU's proposals of service to the state. Rising as a crucial and perhaps most important principle was the attempt to build a genuine partnership of trust and cooperation among all the colleges and universities of the state, both private and public. No fostering of a state's social and economic development seemed possible without it. Accordingly, my first months on the new job went to a program of traveling, speaking, and consultation with state officials and academic leaders in the state. A later paper, and excerpts that follow, indicate the level of importance that I came to attach to the trustworthy relationships of state and land-grant universities with the technical, legislative and executive responsibilities of state agencies and the political bodies charged with overseeing them. One such presentation also carried such views to the national level.

Source: "The States and the Universities: Cooperative Managers of Knowledge." Address delivered at the Fifty-seventh Annual Governor's Conference, Minneapolis, MN, July 27, 1965.

That governors and university presidents should discuss public higher education together is both good and natural. All of us know the claims [that] state universities make upon resources. All of us remember that an initial act of each new state was the founding of a university. It is safe to say that the relations between state governments and state universities are among the most illustrious in American public life. Governors and university presidents also share a common uncertainty. They are not very sure that the efforts under their respective directions are equal to the need. On the one hand, academic leaders observe the gulf between the quality of life and the very knowledge [that] their institutions have produced to achieve it. On the other, state executives struggle under incredible demands for local services. Both of them must choose continuously from among many complex alternatives.

[A major concern today] refers to the need of careful university statements about what long-term assistance the academic institution may contribute to state planning and development. The ideas of public officials must be pooled as these statements are written. [These conversations will] include such points [as the] following: the preparation of able personnel to staff the public and private aspects of statewide development; the conduct of sound research [that] is relevant to the needs of the state; creative ventures in adult education for elected and appointed officials; the study of alternative patterns of institutional reform for local government, regional, and metropolitan centers, the states themselves, and, particularly, of the public school establishment; the stimulation of research in functional areas of state development, such as transportation, manpower utilization, environmental science, tourism, and recreation, housing, capital structure, diversification, public health, and human development and learning.

Invitations to meet West Virginia's people, and to address one audience after another, gave me further opportunity to interpret WVU's mission in a collaborative mode and in light of other colleges and agencies. I spent much of 1962 in this way, attending meeting after meeting to join in their deliberations. This experience enabled me to gain a more comprehensive understanding of the state itself, and add new knowledge about the state's cultural and political history and its socioeconomic structures. Of continuing pleasure also were the opportunities to become acquainted with other academic institutions and their efforts on behalf of their own communities and the state.

Source: "Education and Resource Development." Address delivered at Alderson-Broaddus College, Philippi, WV, May 4, 1963.

> Our various institutions of higher learning in West Virginia must be seen partly as an investment in development, which is to say an investment in people. To do otherwise means that we have either failed to understand that there are no magic wands or that we have backed into the trap of seeking simple overnight solutions to complex century-long problems. And we shall pay the price of good people who come to our colleges and universities, gain experience at West Virginia's expense, and pass on to another destination more competent than when they first came.

I was invited to participate in planning the state's centennial celebration, thus providing further experiences to ponder West Virginia's past and future. I gained insight after insight from many specialists in the private and public sectors. The experience also provided an acquaintance with many thoughtful people in the other colleges and universities. Viewing the context from which West Virginia had emerged and reflecting on what the future might hold raised my thinking to the macrocosmic level. Since I was recognized as one of those engaged in this manner, requests arrived, rather stimulated by centennial themes, to speak on related topics. For example, West Virginia's Centennial Celebration Committee asked me in early 1962 to write a closing chapter for its centennial brochure. Delivering one homily after another on social and economic development in that period stimulated brief essays on the state's future, from which the following excerpts are taken.

Source: "Tomorrow." In *West Virginia in Color: Official Volume of the West Virginia Centennial*, edited by Harry Schaefer. Parkersburg, WV: North American Color Press, 1963.

We will be required to take all aspects of our environment into consideration and unify them into one complete and complex program of development. This planning should provide for better intrastate highways that will be linked with the interstate highway system, so that driving time from New York or Philadelphia or Washington to any point in West Virginia will be much reduced. Planning must polish our natural beauty for recreation and other uses, cause streams to sparkle, and place community renewal programs on the drawing boards.

Tomorrow will not wait for West Virginia, and whether we like it or not, our progress as a state will be judged not only by our own measurements, but by the standards of the nation. There is little reason to expect that West Virginia's second century will be easier than the first. Economic and social development [is] a dynamic that permits no escape and one that sets ever higher goals that are constantly renewed and invigorated by those of vision.

Source: "Remarks." Address delivered to the West Virginia State Medical Association, Lewisburg, WV, August 22, 1963.

A broad partnership of the health services is needed. We must call out more strongly than we have about the importance of health problems and services to the social and economic development of the state. As West Virginia University seeks to find strategic courses of action for development, so must the Medical Center point and work upon such issues as our poor relative position in unmet medical needs, that we do not have enough physicians, dentists, and nurses, and that many smaller communities are unable to find even one physician to serve them.

The Medical Center is a new vehicle in our midst to help us join hands in that service. And might we do so with compassion: for those children of the highlands who have the look of half-health about them; for all our people who have been pushed aside from the main stream of American public life; for all those who will never know the delights of the Greenbrier [Hotel]. In these days when academics and other professionals may be tempted to selfish gain and vindictive jealousy of each other, such compassions will surely be to our everlasting credit.

Source: "Remarks." Address delivered at the West Virginia Bar Association, White Sulphur Springs, WV, September 1, 1962.

There is little doubt that a critical function of private and public institutions in society is to facilitate the transitions from one set of traditions to another. And it seems to me that both the law and the institutions of education are in the middle of these demands.

Law itself bears witness to the pressures of change as the new requirements of society are met. It can never be fully attuned to today's demands because the laws change a few paces behind them. Institutions of higher education and the law are among those [that] are the more thickly rooted in the past, and though both rightfully cherish the wisdom that the past has given, and use it to set up guidelines for all further activity, too often these rules destroy the most fruitful elements of change through unsatisfying compromises between the old and the new.

Public education in 1962, as in the previous years, could only be emphasized greatly in the state's development; indeed, it centered the process. No topic seemed more urgent to me as this statewide reconnaissance was made than to openly link campus resources to the development of public education. Accordingly, certain areas of importance to resource development were added to WVU's College of Education, leading to its being renamed the College of Education and Human Resources. Stanley Ikenberry became its first dean.

Source: "Remarks." Address delivered at two regional meetings of the West Virginia Education Association: Keyser, WV, October 10, 1963; and Parkersburg, WV, October 17, 1963.

At this very moment, as we labor over new goals and the methods to achieve them, new pressures and demands descend upon the public schools with relentless frequency, while more and more critics rise up to fix blame for the juvenile delinquent, the unemployed worker, the school dropout, and for virtually every fault of human character. The public keeps turning over to you the responsibility for developing morality, intellectual ability, ethical values and conduct, vocational skills, and almost every quality [that] used to be the joint property of the family, the community, and the individual. The teacher turns out to be a bulwark of universal knowledge, a spiritual guide, clergyman, psychologist, vocational expert, sometimes mother and father…all this commonly on the salary of a good baby-sitter….

[An] important form of articulation requiring a new and stronger fiber is that between your system and that of higher education. We talk much of these relationships, but you recognize that most of them are mediated by arbitrary decisions of college and university representatives, on the one hand, and by state authorities, on the other. We need more honest talk together about the whole educational process, from kindergarten through the college degree…. What I am trying to say is that the system of elementary and secondary schools can't come up with higher standards alone, and with resources [that] help attract and hold well-prepared and devoted teachers and leaders…. Education problems belong to the schools to be sure, but they also belong to every sector of community life…. [Today] the searchlight of public criticism is shifting from the public schools to the institutions of higher learning [and] out of it will come a greater understanding of the links in the circle of educating people; that after we suffer enough through this period of blinking into the glare under the lights, there will spring up a new comradeship between the levels of education and the agencies and services of the community.

A notable part of the centennial celebration in 1962 was the acceptance of President John F. Kennedy to provide the climax by speaking in

Charleston from the steps of the state capitol building. Immediately prior to that event, the president had invited the presidents of state and land-grant universities to the White House to discuss matters of national importance. At the reception following in the Rose Garden, and at my turn to be introduced to the president, he exclaimed to me, "I go tomorrow to speak at the West Virginia Centennial Celebration."

"Yes," I said. "I know. I will introduce you!"

Kennedy quickly responded. "Well, come ride with me and enjoy the flight over!"

Sadly, I had to decline, as my preliminary tasks at the celebration made such a "ride" impossible.

A steady rain fell on Charleston that next day. Throughout the ceremony and the address by the president, he refused the assist of an umbrella; at his side, I declined as well. Among my treasured photographs is one of President John F. Kennedy and me standing together at the podium with Governor Wallace Barron and other state personnel. It was taken and sent affectionately to me by an unknown lady in that quite dampened audience, and remains a proud possession to this day.

Striving to understand the cultural and institutional organization of West Virginia had as its aim the enhancement of cooperation within it. With development as the theme, the influence of business, industry, and labor was of great importance. However, coming to grips with the economic infrastructure (that is, beyond agriculture, in which the university had long been involved) seemed a paradox as my tenure began, and remained a paradox at its close. Not that interest and support failed to come from this sector, but industrial influence seemed often mitigated by the extensive resource ownership and management located outside the state. Surely was this a major challenge for WVU, and to prepare for it was in order. This meant strengthening the university's own resources and organization for partnerships with the economic sector. An early step was also to work more closely with the state's labor movement: its leader at that time, Miles Stanley, became a trusted friend of the university and of me. Also, one Emery Bacon, education director of the US Steel Workers Union (and "dean" of others so engaged in the labor movement) was attracted to WVU as special assistant to the president.

But a glance at West Virginia's economic structure in the 1960s revealed the continuing dominance of a natural resource–based industry. The coal-producing enterprises were reeling from sharp declines in customary need for unskilled laborers using hand tools in the mines, due to such new technologies as the mechanical coal digger. The issue of industries based upon extraction and little product refinement had clearly to be placed on the table.

Source: "Remarks." Address delivered to the Fiftieth Anniversary Conference of the West Virginia Oil and Gas Association, Jackson's Mill, WV, September 11, 1964.

For nearly a century, West Virginia has ranked near the top of the states in value of minerals produced. In each of the last five years, West Virginia has produced minerals valued at over $700 million. This mineral wealth, including coal, natural gas, oil, salt, clays, sand, limestone, and such other resources as forests are the basis upon which the economy of West Virginia largely rests. The fortunes of West Virginians are almost wholly reflected in the ups and downs of the mineral producing industry.

It is ironic that West Virginia has been called the Switzerland of America, for Switzerland is as poorly endowed in natural resources as West Virginia is rich. Among the forty states [that] our state outranks in the value of its minerals are New York, Connecticut,

Ohio, Michigan, Indiana, Wisconsin, New Jersey, and Massachusetts. An advantage of natural wealth gives no clear assurance of a state's high achievement, economically or culturally. If there is one lesson to be learned here, it is that a high level of economic and social growth comes from something else: an investment in people greater than the investment in natural resources. This investment is achieved through education and ever stronger institutions, and community services.... [In an economic sense], natural resources are unimportant in themselves unless people who develop them into more refined uses are capable of doing so with ever greater skill and intelligence. Our most precious resource is people.

Source: "Wood in West Virginia's Future." Address delivered at the West Virginia Wood Utilization Conference, Charleston, WV, November 1, 1962.

[Forestry and wood utilization] are among those areas [that] the university declares it will not give way on and, rather, for which it will strive for excellence. Such reasoning is behind placing improved forestry and wood utilization facilities at the very top of the university's capital improvement program. We are more than grateful that the distinguished governor of the state, members of the Board of Public Works, and members of the legislature...have all seen fit to honor and support this priority as their own.... We live and work in a state whose personality rings most vibrantly because of its forests. Two-thirds of its land area is commercial forests. Ninety percent strong in hardwoods, West Virginia's forests orient to the young saw timber side and account for almost six percent of the hardwood saw timber in the United States. [We also sense] the unusual symbiosis between trees and terrain, between wild life and pastoral beauty, between water and the natural formation of industrial-agricultural regions, and between mountain and valley vistas. However, the personality of this state is one thing; converting it to more productive and intelligent use is quite another.

Source: "The Role of Conservation Education in West Virginia's Future." Address delivered to the Governor's Centennial Conference on Conservation, Charleston, WV, April 3, 1963.

Nature forces man to think and act with a spirit of wholeness. He is in instant trouble if he acts unilaterally upon a resource without regard for other resources [that] are forever related to it. Since man is perhaps the only higher form that insists on using the same channel for the removal of his wastes and for the intake of necessities, his use of water is paradoxical. He slashes his forests, only to live uneasily in the midst of the storm. In draining his mine, he kills his fish. In tearing out minerals, he wounds the beauty of his community. And the price of forcing his soil is often that he must leave it. In short, without an eye toward wholeness, man frequently destroys a resource while he is developing and using another.

[We must discover a] philosophy and practice of resource planning. No more critical issue exists in the conservation education field than how to reconcile the principles and limits of planning with our determination to use private property as we see fit. Indeed the entire course of the conservation movement in this country has struggled through a rough terrain of planning the public welfare with controversy over individual rights. And only has the past quarter of a century seen the idea of planning increasingly freed from suspicion. In and out of the resource field, this issue forms the eternal struggle of how to achieve public planning which is responsive to individual welfare, and how to achieve individual action [that] contributes to total benefit. [In West Virginia] we have an unusual laboratory for testing the dilemma of modern technological man: As he refines his technical knowledge and skill, can he retain an intimacy with the reality of his fellow beings in nature and culture, and by so doing continuously renew his religious, aesthetic, ethical and artistic values?

"Circuit riding" throughout West Virginia in 1962 and 1963 was, of course, an extraordinary experience in personal learning. Looking at environment as the interdependence of multiple systems grew in interest, I sensed that the pyramiding of economic and technological changes demanded a complementary improvement in social organization and administration, a central theme in my previous training and experience. To effectively mediate these changes, more emphasis was needed in communication among the state's leaders and their organizations. Knowledge and information were to be more the instruments of such mediation. This change, if no other, asked of WVU and all educational institutions what they proposed as a response. Imagining and creating new forms of interdependence within education and between education and the state's infrastructure, were visions that should be a key part of the university's mission as well as that of the state's whole educational system.

As my spoken and written excerpts of "visiting" the reaches of West Virginia suggest, I had gained a new appreciation of the natural beauty of the state. The same may be said for my concern that the state faced threats to both the aesthetics and utilities embodied in its environment. The office of the WVU presidency offered itself as a bully pulpit on such issues. The Board of Governors decided that the president should deliver the WVU commencement addresses. An early one, and not without resulting arguments, gave focus to the environment.

Source: "The Untidy Society." Commencement address delivered to WVU graduating class, Morgantown, WV, May 31, 1965. Also published by Cornell University, 1965, and by the Division of Extension Research and Training, USDA, June 1965.

The people eat too much and exercise too little. Its amphitheaters outdo those of ancient Rome and Greece as tens of thousands of unfit oldsters sit down to watch increasingly soft youngsters win for them. It will park its automobiles in flowerbeds rather than walk a city block. To give "kicks" to an unloved boy, you can be silently stabbed—in a subway, on an open corner, in the heart of a university campus. The Untidy Society stages great spectacles about the corruption in public and private life, yet produces few great moral advances. It can turn dark-skinned people away at the church door, or use a courtroom to attack civility. It can make a ghetto out of the heart of the city and then desert it for suburbia.

The Untidy Society will make it difficult for you to be a participant. It will try to make you a spectator. It will have you parrot scraps of information without any grand

design. It can influence whole universities. How else
may one explain magnificent campuses surrounded by
the worst slums of the nation and haphazardly planned
communities? Perhaps you may better appreciate why
I am so determined to enlarge the public obligation of
this University. Whether as graduates, faculties, or whole
universities, we may learn from Alfred North Whitehead
when he said: "A merely informed man is the most useless bore on God's earth."

If WVU and other educational institutions were to demonstrate effective collaboration, they had to do more of it within their own organization.
This challenge described much of my service at Michigan State University,
though with less success than hoped for. With continuing need, both West
Virginia and WVU gave another chance to foster collaboration among
campus disciplines and demonstrate it further with linkages to external
agencies and institutions. What was coming to mind in this regard, however, carried with it a notable degree of risk! On one side stood traditional
campus needs—student learning and life, building new facilities and mod-
ernizing others, curriculum improvement and academic governance. All
these spoke of marked need and interest. On another side, the university
was viewed as a development organization. A danger loomed: was too
much being attempted?

Another tension emerged from how to balance the particular needs and
visions of WVU with those of other colleges and universities. The some
twenty-one private and public colleges and universities of West Virginia
could hardly escape competing for limited funds. Plans to rationally assign functions among several institutions were usually met with outright
skepticism by the respective constituencies. And in collaborative ventures,
could WVU, the state's most comprehensive center of higher education,
be trusted not to disproportionately enhance and protect its own situation?

Indeed, after an Association of College and University Presidents was organized, of which I was elected president, a puzzled member of the WVU Board of Governors asked, "Paul, just who are you working for?"

However, despite the risks and tensions, my firm goal grew to advance WVU as a leader as well as a trustworthy partner in devising a coordinated state system of higher education, rather than a strong-armed competitor giving little thought to the welfare of other institutions. I felt privately that to do otherwise would prompt state authorities to eventually establish a formal coordinating board.

Source: "Remarks." Address delivered to the West Virginia Association of College and University Presidents, Charleston, WV, November 15, 1962.

> [It] is imperative that our colleges and universities in West Virginia come to a better understanding of each other, of the strengths and weaknesses of each, and how each may better serve the state. Our institutions, both public and private, must move together for the benefit of all and for each. Otherwise, we shall be guilty of acceding to the temptation of every developing area: the bitter and petty limitations of sectional rivalry.

Source: "The Role of the Liberal Arts Colleges in Our Time." Address delivered at Morris Harvey College's Seventy-Fifth Anniversary Convocation, Charleston, WV, September 27, 1962.

> More and more of our institutions of higher learning should dare to be different but all cooperating to define and achieve a common destiny. Both the small college and the large university must find genuine causes upon

which to stand together. Common duties are immersed within the deepest layers of the American heritage. We must recognize that somehow, in the end, an educational opportunity must be extended to every individual, subject only to capacity and diligence. The political philosophy of the United States builds on the enrichment of democratic institutions by means of the continuous re-education of the people; our economic philosophy depends on a creative people who understand not only the application of technology for economic growth but also its unexpected consequences

THE WEST VIRGINIA CENTER FOR APPALACHIAN STUDIES AND DEVELOPMENT

THE PERIPATETIC MONTHS of 1962 gave me the chance to join with many others in learning of WVU's potentials. Such learning had filtered through a relevant background of more than twenty years—becoming an adult in West Virginia, a graduate of WVU, a county agricultural agent in two major agricultural counties in the state, and years of seasoning in the functions of university outreach at Michigan State University. Entering 1963 seemed, as it would for the remainder of my career, a key professional period of my life. The events, research, and writing of the previous years, the immersion in field duties through 1962, and the insights of colleagues at WVU and elsewhere, all moved inexorably to fashion an idea to transform how land-grant universities might best serve their states and regions. This idea was to establish the West Virginia Center for Appalachian Studies and Development.

Certain of the sinews of this idea had preceded my arrival. Former President Irvin Stewart had led WVU into becoming a genuine university and patiently built it into the life of West Virginia. My predecessor, Elvis Stahr, continued the theme by establishing a Center for Resource Development. He also helped inspire a center for graduate studies in Charleston. A cadre of experienced leaders at WVU was already influencing the land-grant system as a whole. Importantly among them were Ernest Nesius (Dean of Agriculture), Kenneth Penrod (Vice President for the Medical Center), Harold Shamberger (Public and Political Affairs Associate) and J. O. Knapp (long-time Extension Director). All became my mentors; they were also prepared to do more. The campus mood in 1962 also welcomed ideas promising to strengthen WVU in state planning and action.

No small bias resided in me! While tuned to academic ideals of teaching and scholarship, universities, in my view, should exhibit distinctive personalities shaped by their history and context. Too many of them, seduced into imitation of others, seemed intent to enter races that they could not hope to win. In 1962, and still the golden age of higher education, enrollment growth continued apace. The same could be said for support from private, state, and federal sources. Universities could afford to be themselves and strive for their own brands of distinction. Thus, at WVU, in the most Appalachian of all the States, it made sense to strengthen this identity by means of a West Virginia Center for Appalachian Studies and Development (soon to be informally called the "Appalachian Center"). It was not a ploy to garner financial support, as later pundits would imply. Nor was it to downgrade emphasis upon disciplinary and professional fields; rather, it would serve to link them to each other and to strategic goals.

This step seemed especially correct for land-grant universities. They had been the chief "development organizations" in bringing the age of science and technology to agriculture. They became major actors in the ongoing shift from rural to urban society. Out of this transformation sprang the need of new and different applications of science-based knowledge. Were these uniquely American universities ready to take them up? I felt not! Public service philosophies, methods, and mechanisms (e.g., the Cooperative Extension Service) had not been seriously and broadly adapted in and by the whole of land-grant universities. Nor had they become tuned to the very problems in urban industrial society that their previous service had helped create.

At bottom, the Appalachian Center was a device in university organization and administration. Three aims were foremost. One was to recreate the Cooperative Extension Service as the field arm of WVU as a whole. The second would define the General Extension Service as a campus-wide instrument for drawing upon campus-based resources for outreach efforts; this second aim would strengthen resources for outreach in most if not all the departments and divisions at the university, a movement to be coordinated at the university level. The third aim would devise a university mechanism to foster collaboration with private and public entities within the state and region, including other colleges and universities.

The Appalachian Center promised both a useful and distinctive approach of WVU in the state. But provincialism needed to be avoided. Ideas of public service and outreach functions by colleges and universities were springing up throughout academic life. WVU would gain and contribute in movements to advance broadly the quantity and quality of higher adult education. It seemed clear in the early 1960s that the appearance of a knowledge-centered society would bring both opportunities and pressures to colleges and universities. Enthusiasms and commitments among adult educators were gathering for such a leap forward. But such a spirit was less evident among the faculties generally. Reform seemed imperative, and my thought and writing continued to focus in that direction.

Source: "New Missions for Old Programs." *Journal of Higher Education* 25, no. 8 (1964): 450–458.

> Until recently, when people spoke of the land-grant college, it was not quite certain whether they meant the agricultural college or the institution as a whole. However, in the past twenty years the land-grant institutions have broadened and deepened their fields of study. In many

of them today, almost 50 percent of the undergraduate students are enrolled in the division of arts and sciences. New needs and priorities in American society have elevated basic science, corporate administration, international studies, and engineering. ... The recent penetration of one discipline by another has made old administrative charts obsolete...and more and more, the issues [that] count today call for interdisciplinary solutions rather than answers attempted by discrete segments of knowledge.

Enhancing the interests of WVU faculties in a new age where problems cross-cut the traditional disciplines demanded open and continuing discussion. Federal support of research had properly elevated attention to problems of this kind and asked what priorities might be established by both faculties and supporters. Such were the beginnings of what, thirty years later, would be launched as a major motive in American higher education and be termed "engagement" with society. But in the 1960s, the WVU reforms called for similar linkages between research capacity and the outreach functions. Relating disciplines on the campus, and sharing them through an improved delivery system, was of fundamental importance. Much time in 1963 to 1964 went to advancing these connections.

As might be expected, the people of the state and those of the legislature took evident interest in any step bearing upon social and economic development. However, the organizational subtleties were difficult to explain, although this was attempted on many fronts. Needless to say, such reflections needed to be shared and advanced with central planning and budgetary bodies of the state. As the following two excerpts suggest, the planning for assisting statewide development was being well received. However, many puzzles remained evident on how to include the inner regions of the whole of WVU.

Source: "Remarks." Address delivered to the Board of Public Works during the 1965–1966 budget request. Charleston, WV, December 7, 1964.

There are occasional moments when progress depends on how well a few leaders may sense the time for action and come up with a peak performance. If the opposite happens, a propitious moment is lost and a new wait begins for another one…. The ten-year accreditation team of the North Central Association of Colleges and Secondary schools wrote in its report on WVU in 1964, "The [West Virginia] University has moved ahead with an overall plan for future growth that is both imaginative and comprehensive. Few universities have taken such a long view and made such long-range decisions." Every member of the Board of Public Works has made himself felt in this planning. Every member of the faculty has had ample opportunity to be involved. No other board of trustees or state university president has spent more days and nights in the past three years to bring a university's objectives before the people.

A new computer center now functions for the good of the entire state. An educational television system is about ready to come off the drawing boards. The Medical Center is already unique about the country by reason of its low-cost teaching hospital…and the multiphased nursing curriculum is known broadly as the "West Virginia Plan." Never has the university been more determined to help the people of this state, as indicated in several cooperative ventures in statewide planning between our College of Engineering, the highway department, and the Appalachian Center; the technical backstopping by the university on behalf of the State's Economic Opportunity Program; the National Science Camp; the new Institute of Water Resources Research; the expanding efforts in air pollution work; and the services of the faculty for the Governor's Council of Economic Advisors.

Source: "Remarks." Address delivered at a retreat of the WVU Council of Administration, Blackwater Falls, WV, April 13, 1964.

I believe this council, in open and free discussion with our faculties, should unravel several themes [that] are at a level freeing them to review our [present] administrative structure: the environmental sciences (cutting through the physical, biological and social sciences) and argued on the premise that this is the future issue of American society: resources utilization (with recognition given to natural resources and materials utilization); the creative arts; and the nature of development (with reference to family, community, economic, and governmental institutions).

What do we mean by "center" and "institute"? What is the difference, if any, between a school and a college? Are there other flexible devices to encourage continuous and dynamic interaction between disciplines, between the disciplines and the professional areas? What can be centralized and what must be decentralized? What are the alternatives and what do they cost? Please be assured that I recognize how any major decision in a university is really one of compromise. Each forward step upsets many delicate balances [located] in the structure of any university. I join with you in realizing that a university cannot be governed by simple answers. Yet, without disciplined leadership a university on such points can find itself on the edge of triviality and undue waste. It is about this that the council must learn to speak more with one voice.

The Appalachian Center built upon the transfer of the Cooperative Extension Service from the College of Agriculture and Forestry to a university-wide status, enabling it to serve as the field arm of the entire university. This transfer had to be approved by the CES itself, college faculty and leaders, and interest groups throughout the state. Furthermore, since an early law had fixed the service in the College of Agriculture and Forestry, approval of the West Virginia Legislature, a risky venture at best, must be secured. Two giants for successfully achieving these approvals stood out.

The longtime and nationally esteemed director of the West Virginia Cooperative Extension Service, J. O. Knapp, went up and down the state to interpret and urge these endorsements. "J. O.," as he was widely and affectionately known, led in securing approval of the legislature without a single dissenting vote. This remarkable achievement endeared him all the more to me (and to others); indeed, it was a further act of mentoring me, as he had previously done when notably granting me a leave for graduate study in 1945.

The other major helpmate was Ernest Nesius, dean of the College of Agriculture and Forestry and the initial WVU vice president for the Appalachian Center. He had managed the College with distinction while leading a major international effort in East Africa, comprehending related reforms in Vietnam and otherwise throughout the United States and the world. (This significant global outreach would also enable my own return to Africa: among other notable experiences to confer professionally and personally with Julius Nyerere, the famed and first president of Tanzania.) Nesius toiled unceasingly to convene and interpret the Appalachian Center on the campus and throughout the state and beyond. He would go on to repeated honors for his unfailing service to WVU, Morgantown, the state, the nation, and the world. He and his wife, Margaret, continued as cherished friends and colleagues in the decades to follow and until their respective deaths some forty years later.

How the total resources of WVU might become involved was also in order, but was sure to form a challenge. Also, if the model of the Appalachian Center were to be honored, it would receive other units scattered elsewhere. These included the General Extension Division; the Mining and Industrial Extension Service; Continuing Legal Education; the Labor Extension Service; the Office of Communications and Visual Aids; and the East Africa Agricultural Program and its several contracts with the US Agency for International Development.

The Appalachian Center would anchor its mission in science-based knowledge. An initial step strengthened the Center for Resource Development and renamed it the Office of Research and Development. The aim was to employ the model of the Agricultural Experiment Station, then largely serving agriculture and rural development, and enable research and planning at the all-university level to be coordinated with that of other agencies. A new Water Research Institute soon followed and became part of that office.

Too little comparative understanding existed of how the state's sub-regions developed. New interests in "regional science" were expanding in some universities and suggested that this approach be adopted at WVU. To meet this need, the Claude Worthington Benedum Foundation helped create the Center for Social and Economic Research. William Miernik, a leading scholar in regional studies, was invited to occupy a distinguished chair and direct it.

The social and economic landscape of West Virginia had long felt the strength of the labor movement. Symbolized by the coal miners and John L. Lewis, and observant of the vast technological changes then taking place in resource extraction industries, stronger ties to organized labor seemed imperative. Two major steps were taken. An Institute of Labor Research, with Frederick Z. Zeller as director, was created; Emery Bacon also gave major attention to this interest.

This early focus on organization when creating the Appalachian Center aimed at galvanizing statewide development by better linking WVU to the state and the region. Three plans came into place. Following the philosophy explained in papers at MSU and WVU, six regional centers were formed. Believing that social and economic development would coalesce around regional employment and marketing areas, these centers would allow personnel to be recruited and grouped in specialties tailored to the needs of the region. Moreover, when imaginatively located, such regional centers would attract collaboration with other agencies and institutions. In these centers, the second aim proposed to consolidate and interpret official state reports and studies on development needs and strategies, and aid their public interpretation. The third and longer-term plan would give special attention to the Kanawha Valley. One of the six proposed regional centers, the already-present Kanawha Valley Graduate Center, was located amid a fourth of the state's population; in the principal seat of government, and within the expanding presence of research-based industry, Metropolitan Charleston was likely to grow as a major cultural and economic hub of statewide development. The Appalachian Center planners held these facts as the basis of a major challenge.

Creating the Appalachian Center carried with it the burden of balancing campus-bound resources with those engaged in public service off the campus. Perhaps to a fault, my concern for West Virginians influenced strongly what I thought best for the university. I seemed unable to modify this bias, and found it difficult to explain, despite the continuing attempts:

Was I but acting on one front and verbalizing on another? It seemed proper to share such doubts openly and strive to comprehend the responses. The following excerpt is one of such anxieties while serving WVU.

Source: "The University and the State." Address delivered to the Living Resources Forum, Morgantown, WV, January 28, 1964.

> [These plans] will not take place overnight; indeed many years will be required before the ideas of the Appalachian Center will be fully tested. It is also clear to me that we are committing ourselves to a larger task than our resources actually permit; we must find ways to improve our research strength in several fields and increase the number of personnel at both campus and field level who contribute to programs based on knowledge not heretofore provided. But the most important caution that needs re-statement is that the university will be just as strong out in the state as it is in its various departments, schools and colleges.... Everything that the university attempts will be influenced by what is happening at its heart, i.e., in the basic disciplines. A determined program of enrichments for these academic disciplines, which has already begun, must in no way be displaced by our plans and hopes for public service.

Helping create the Appalachian Center and trying to harmonize teaching and research capacities with the problems of West Virginians opened doors to wider personal national service. In the 1964 to 1965 period came elections and appointments to chair a national commission to explore the challenge in public affairs of public universities, and to chair the Council of Presidents of the National Association of State Universities and Land-Grant Colleges. Also included was service as board chair of the Center for the Study of Liberal Education for Adults at Boston University.

As the 1965–1966 academic year opened, a reasonable mobilization of interest in WVU's plan seemed apparent. Ernest Nesius had become WVU's vice president for the Appalachian Center. The program was under way along with plans for a suitable building to house its campus staff and host guests engaged in its activities. I had grown in my affection for the job and the breadth of its WVU duties. Whatever the assignment, I anticipated a life's career of relating education to the state's development. The close of the initial five years as WVU's president, a trial period as trustee Kirkpatrick and I had agreed upon in 1961, was nearing completion. I kept this informal agreement firmly in mind, given a continuing uncertainty of Catherine's health and the demands of the job upon the family.

Throughout the planning effort, interest continued on how best to arrange the university's presence in Charleston and the Kanawha Valley. In keeping with the outreach philosophy embodied in campus organization and the Appalachian Center, law and public affairs had persisted as disciplines to be strengthened both within the university and in statewide development. Partly stimulated by the need of new physical facilities for the College of Law, the planning proposals envisioned a law and public affairs center that would include that College as well as graduate programs in public administration, social work, community planning, and the Bureau of Government Research. Such fields held an essential relationship to each other in their professional contributions to governmental organization, regulation, and administration. Their common ground was the impact of practitioners upon government and of government upon the people.

However, more than any other of the reforms that sprang from a reconsideration of the mission of land-grant universities, the proposals in law and public affairs provoked the most controversial challenge during my tenure as WVU's fifteenth president. The controversy erupted and ended in the spring of 1966 with the premature release (and faulty communication on my part) of a planning report proposing a "West Virginia University Law and Public Affairs Center" to be located in the capital city of Charleston.

Source: "Progress Report on the Study of the Proposal for the Establishment of a Law and Public Affairs Center of West Virginia University." Statement to the press, May 9, 1996.

It is an objective of educational planning, as it has been at West Virginia University, that all activities of a given university be joined in close proximity on a single campus. Locating the Center on the main campus at Morgantown ensures close ties, and undoubtedly would lead to overall savings in administrative costs. Supporting physical facilities, including the main library and campus-sponsored cultural activities, would be more available to it. However, as the planning process continued, it became increasingly apparent that the great educational opportunity in law and public affairs is not in Morgantown but, rather, in the larger Kanawha Valley. Approximately eighteen thousand public servants are associated with state government, a large percentage of them in the Greater Kanawha Valley. The number of business managers in the region is increasing rapidly. It contains a substantial proportion of the state's population, improving transportation facilities, and a promising basis for one of the state's chief centers for industrial growth.

In making this report of progress, cooperation is sincerely sought in developing statewide concern for the excellence and effectiveness of efforts at West Virginia University to make such a center a most worthwhile venture. This report is made early in a program of discussion with interested groups with the public and private life of West Virginia. We enter into these discussions with the strongest possible belief that the area of law and public affairs is fundamental to the rapid development of the state. The Board of Governors and the administration of West Virginia University will give additional study to the proposed center and will base its final judgment upon more discussion and consultation.

The response of the important professional groups, whether on or off the campus, was generally negative. Clearly expressed was the concern with relocating important units off the main campus, an understandable one indeed. Perhaps in part due to the emphasis given the state's development and the rapidly emerging Appalachian Center, there was also fear that the proposed center would be defined as "service" rather than "academic." As the concern mounted, the planning report itself was completed and released on May 11, 1966. It stressed the importance of the College of Law and related programs to the public professions; the need of better relationships among these fields; and how their academic and public service missions would be strengthened in an area of concentrated population, need, and professional practice. The report also summarized the results of months of preparation and included detailed estimates of current and projected strengths of the respective fields as well as the longer-term steps to be taken. Following is the closing paragraph of the report and calling for open and utmost discussion.

Source: "Working Paper, with Reference to the Establishment of a Law and Public Affairs Center of West Virginia University." Paper prepared and distributed by the Office of the President, West Virginia University, Morgantown, WV, May 11, 1966.

> A university graduate center for the study of law and public affairs in the Kanawha Valley would appear to be a natural, logical, and appropriate extension of university programs. It would help fill needs crucial to the future of the state, yet not duplicate educational services already provided by other institutions while answering a great demand of education at the graduate level. Advantages of location in the Kanawha Valley have been outlined here, not merely to emphasize their importance over the advantages of remaining in Morgantown, but, rather, to submit them for analysis, study, and debate. We believe it essential, however, to force attention to the establishment of such a center, and also to the determination of its location.

While public leaders and newspaper editors were of many minds, it was soon apparent that the locational feature of the proposed center was unacceptable to major interests. Pursuing the matter further promised regional rivalries, a likely setback to collaboration with other institutions, and slow progress in outreach and the Appalachian Center itself. Concerned and informed citizens had spoken. Guided by the studied advice of the central administrative staff, especially such leaders as Harry Heflin and Harold Shamberger, I recommended to the Board of Governors that the planning proposal be withdrawn from further consideration. The episode added a powerful message to my thinking that had begun in the academic year of

1965–1966. Many new projects in academic, physical, and outreach functions had been launched in the previous years. Was it not time to slow down and consolidate those projects of highest priority?

Source: "Remarks." Address delivered at an Administrative Group Retreat, Jackson's Mill, WV, April 4, 1966.

For the past four years, one might term the present administration's effort as one devoted to program definition and outlining support for it. I am hopeful that the next chapter, which may be equally as long, will become known as one of program execution, with the major involvement of faculty, students, and other representatives of planning and action. In order to accomplish this, I recognize that certain alterations must come to my own style of administration. I have been giving substantial thought to this and to the following principles.... I am especially interested in discussions of the needed organizational model of the university; ...more of my time to a major responsibility of central administration, namely, coordination of the many elements generated by the planning process; looking forward to a year or two of much more interaction with representatives of the faculty, both in official governance as well as informally; ...planning to consolidate more of my time required for national and international projects in the Summer and off-season periods.... [T]he objective here will be that of strengthening the university as a functional system of relationships. We have a long way to go on this if our program plans are to be acted upon. As we move in this direction, I am quite confident that our self-consciousness as a university will be all the more apparent.

A SOMEWHAT ABRUPT END

THE CAPTION ABOVE is drawn from the aforementioned book, *West Virginia University*, by Doherty and Summers, a portion of their reflection on the end of my tenure as president in July, 1966. How such abruptness could happen to one whose intent, from 1961 onward, was to serve WVU and the state, in whatever WVU capacity for the remainder of his career, is properly to be explained.

To great degree, this whole account reflects the problem of achieving balance between family and career. There was my continuing interest to return to the scholarly life. Present were Catherine's bouts of uncertain health and vigor, occasional events through many years of her never-ceasing and courageous care of husband and children. These factors had long entered into our decisions about family, residence, and career. After initially declining for these reasons to be considered a candidate for the WVU presidency in 1961, they were later shared again with the chair of the Board of Governors before our arrival in early 1962.

Catherine's health declined again during 1964. As that year wore on, I came privately to the conclusion that I should not continue beyond the initial five years. Catherine's health plummeted late in that year. She had endured reasonably well the inescapable pressures of her duties, but they took great effect in that period. Indeed, during that fall, she felt it necessary for last-minute refrains from attending scheduled events. I had begun to formalize my decision to step down from the post. Then, driving home from a legislative committee meeting in mid-December 1964, the radio news reported to me that Catherine had been taken suddenly to University Hospital. Upon my arrival home, I was shocked to learn that she had taken an overdose of sleeping pills. Catherine remained under hospital care until she died several days later, with me at her side.

During her hospital stay, all my thoughts went to her expected recovery, the children, career, and the future. I privately resolved to take the next year and a half to bring the major projects of my term of five years to a close, thus be faithful to the informal understanding with the Board of Governors, and hopefully be permitted to serve the university and the state as a professor of sociology. Upon her death, however, this plan had to be set aside at least temporarily in the interests of fatherhood and WVU plans awaiting immediate action.

The focus of this chapter is largely on West Virginia's social and economic development as a special mission. In their account, Doherty and Summers take special note of campus physical planning in the 1964–1966 period when several campus projects were moved forward: completing the Creative Arts Center, readying the site for a new Student Union, the beginnings of a new athletic arena and physical education center (on land that had been saved after peacefully resolving the state's intention to build an armory on it!), a renaissance of the chemistry facilities, two new residence halls, repairs to Mountaineer Stadium, and the purchase of properties adjacent to the Evansdale campus, including a new home for the WVU president. Of unforgettable importance to me and my term as president was an agreement, after considerable negotiation, to purchase the lands of the Morgantown Golf and Country Club—lands capable of helping link the landscapes and programs of three campuses.

In that period of great personal loss and intensive work, I was also drawn into the rising interest of state officials to form a coordinated system for higher education. Governor Hulett Smith asked me to lead a state commission to explore the subject. Given my belief in the role of state universities in statewide development, and earlier exposure as a president of the West Virginia Association of College and University Presidents, this subject was of great interest. Given WVU's history and role, such a step was one of great importance. Indeed, in the previous years, envisioning all the colleges and universities cooperating voluntarily on behalf of state development had become my crucial aim. The underlying philosophy seemed correct, yet how best to achieve it remained elusive.

The excerpt following represents one among many references to some sort of collaborative system of higher education, one based on knowledge, trust and collaboration rather than simply installing an overall board with formal legal authority.

Source: "Education." Supplement on Education in the *Charleston Gazette*, Charleston, WV, October 1, 1965.

Evidence mounts to prove the causal relationship between education and economic growth.... We have come to agree that ignorance and poverty are one and the same, and that for a people to enjoy the benefits of the age, their abilities and understanding must expand given the newest knowledge being discovered and managed by the centers of research and scholarship. To put it another way, the knowledge "industry" is turning out to be the key enterprise of modern society.

We know that the future of West Virginia will be determined in large part by how well its organizations and institutions use knowledge in making decisions. We also know that this won't happen unless the institutions of higher learning are involved in the entire process as evaluators and advisors in policy planning. What we do not yet fully understand is how we can bring the best resources of knowledge into the service of public and private organizations responsible for executing policy.

To avoid wasteful duplication of effort, coordination of the institutions of higher learning has become essential. But an even more important reason for coordination is the increased strength that would be gained through the proper organization of resources. West Virginia has great potential for a unique and excellent educational system, but in order to achieve it, we must agree upon a long-range plan that would organize these resources for the sharpest impact upon the State's needs.

My service with the commission to explore the plans for coordinating higher education for additional collaborative efforts on behalf of West Virginia were cut short by my eventual departure. Yet the time was to begin more efforts to find the best solution. This puzzle would remain with me elsewhere in the years ahead. Models of coordinating colleges and universities seemed to fall into two categories. One features a coordinating body to facilitate budget, program planning, and voluntary coordination. This approach, avoiding the formal governance of the relevant institutions, risks wasteful rivalries among the participants. The other approach more strongly assumes both governance and administration of the member institutions, but reduces their independence and uniqueness.

My belief and efforts in institutional coordination would not diminish after departing WVU, which later accounts will share. The brief work in West Virginia revealed the puzzle that would go with me to similar ventures. Of one aspect I grew more certain: without sustained integrity and trust among its designers and leaders, no model of coordination is workable! Later experience taught me that cooperative effort among institutions cannot aspire to be healthy if planning on the home campus is sick. Planning of consequence within institutions may flounder first on the shoals of ivy-wrapped traditions, or, once getting past them, can hang up on those other reefs built to protect personal, professional, disciplinary or institutional interests. And when resources grow lean, alas, these reefs grow ever higher! The West Virginia experience stimulated a new interest in inter-institutional cooperation as but an expression of a shared ethic. Later would I learn that without such an ethic, cooperation is little more than the farce of a game, and coordination is overcome with disappointment.

As these professional considerations were examined and pursued, there were also new dimensions appearing in my personal life. Over and over would I reflect upon the informal discussions and agreements with the chair of the board and other trustees at the outset, mainly the informal agreement to a starting chapter of five years. Following and part of such thinking and its uncertainties, further reflections came following a surprise: my reacquaintance at a national conference with Dr. Francena L. Nolan. A noted rural sociologist with her doctorate from The Pennsylvania State University, upon my arrival at WVU she was serving as an assistant dean and director of WVU's program in Home Economics. Upon my arrival at WVU, she was also in process of reviewing and eventually taking the post of dean of Home Economics at the University of Connecticut. A few years later, after our reacquaintance at a 1965 national conference in Chicago, we were later married on the day before WVU's Commencement Service for 1966, This union of two personal and professional lives would happily endure until Francena's passing in July 2010. Further reflections on our lives and careers together will continue in the chapters to follow.

Immediately, however, the larger significance of our marriage in our respective professional lives provided issues for both Francena and me. She had earned a significant professional stature in her own life and career. Would she be able to continue to advance it at WVU? And in my case, whether as a professor or administrator, might it be more appropriate for me to remain with what had been started, such as the Appalachian Center and related duties? However, other campus issues needed to be addressed and provided unbroken attention. Moreover, campus responsibilities with the construction projects then under way deserved oversight reviews. So my thinking turned to an acceptance of these assignments and related issues and go forward. There was not the slightest hint in our minds of "pulling up roots and heading elsewhere."

But on the day before the WVU commencement exercises of 1966, with Francena having just arrived in Morgantown for a permanent stay, Secretary John W. Gardner of the US Department of Health, Education, and Welfare (HEW) called and invited me to an early visit. While president of the Carnegie Corporation of New York, Gardner had displayed a long interest in my work: the efforts in rural health at Michigan State University and later in the statewide development plans of WVU. For the latter he had invited me to New York City for a seminar with him and his staff to explain such planning. As was and still is recognized in today's intellectual worlds, John W. Gardner was one of the twentieth century's most brilliant and dedicated minds. He is still revered by all who knew him, not alone for his Washington leadership for some five years, but as the president of the still-famed Carnegie Corporation, and the founder and first president of Common Cause, to this day a positive civic organization working to enhance a balanced and creative social impact of our national political life. His small but famed book, *Self Renewal: The Individual and the Innovative Society*, needs to be read by every American generation, both those young and those not so young. [3]

We met in a few days. Gardner expressed his desire that I take the new post of Assistant Secretary for Education in the department of Health, Education, and Welfare (HEW). He explained that this position, along with similar posts in health and welfare, would have its incumbent lead a new Federal Interagency Committee on Education to secure more collaboration on education across the federal establishment. Of equal importance, he reported the White House, HEW, and the State Department to

---

3   Gardner, John W. *Self Renewal: The Individual and the Innovative Society* (New York: Perennial Books, 1964).

be working on legislation, rather a companion to the Higher Education Act of 1965, to launch a major landmark program of international education. The new assistant secretary would guide the legislation through congressional passage and funding, and then take up its implementation.

The month of June 1966, filled with project activities, writing, and a delayed honeymoon, also went to probing this option. Discussion centered on a mix of concerns: our children (Francena's just-married son, Michael; my daughter, Paula, a third-year student at WVU; and my son Thomas, then a ten-year-old); the evident risks then confronting Francena's promising career; my love of West Virginia and commitment to serving it; my quite special awareness of the pressures upon the spouses and families of university presidents; and the joys of professorial life to which I expected to return.

After an anguished period of confronting such issues, we decided that I should accept the post in Washington. Given the nature of that city, Francena would seek an appropriate assignment. Much activity followed to put matters in order for my successor. Routine FBI and other governmental checks on my suitability stalled an official announcement and complicated final duties. Throughout this transition, a sincere regret grew of departing unfinished tasks, but returning over and over to the decision, we concluded that it was the proper one. With deeply felt sadness, Francena and I bid adieu to an unforgettable array of friends and colleagues, and, for me, the hopes I held for WVU's part in the social and economic development of West Virginia.

A great sense of personal loss sprang from this decision due to my identity with the people of West Virginia. My past experiences—of boyhood, a student at WVU, as county agricultural agent, of outreach work at Michigan State University, and those expressed herein in the 1960s—all strengthened my fondness for Morgantown acquaintances and colleagues, and, always, concern for the people of the state. Such feelings never diminished as new people, jobs, and places came my way in a long life ahead.

West Virginians weave pride and independence into an individuality that includes a rare loyalty to each other and to home place. Their endeavors for a proper share of the fruits of modern society have made them hardier than most. They know how to stand up repeatedly once they are knocked down, and continue the most authentic neighborliness found in our nation. *These would remain my people!*

IV

WASHINGTON, DC

URBAN AND

INTERNATIONAL

DEVELOPMENT

A TRANSITION

WASHINGTON BROUGHT PROFESSIONAL contact again with the esteemed John W. Gardner, then secretary of the department of Health, Education, and Welfare (HEW). A notable American and former president of the Carnegie Corporation of New York, Gardner had greatly influenced higher education and many of its participants. I was among them. The contact renewed my long-tabled interest in international affairs. Francena's training and competencies would seek a new assignment. Meanwhile, our daughter, Paula, was completing her undergraduate work at West Virginia University, and our son, Tom, was entering a new school and beginning other experiences. Francena's son, Michael Nolan, newly married, would begin graduate study in rural sociology at The Pennsylvania State University.

New people came into our lives, including President Lyndon B. Johnson. I first met him at a preliminary interview in the Oval Office. After motioning me to a chair, he silently continued his attention to a stack of papers. Soon he looked up and asked, as I remember it, "Miller, do you have a PhD? When I replied in the affirmative, the president responded with a broad and mischievous smile: "See what I'm doing? As a former teacher, I find myself fixing up a lot of stuff written by people with all those degrees so it can be better understood. If you take on this new job, I want you to promise that you will help me clean up the language in this town!" Then, more soberly, he dropped his papers, spoke of his long interest in education, and asked me to sum up my own experiences and ideas.

West Virginia's US Senator Jennings Randolph assisted our move to Washington and introduced me to the appropriate Senate committee members for confirmation. Congressman Carl Perkins of Kentucky was present. An educational leader in the House of Representatives, and also a farmer, he listened with interest to a summary of my career read by the Senate clerk, especially the mention of the years in agricultural extension and my first job as a county agricultural agent. Then, with a sly grin, Perkins commented, "Dr. Miller, you seem to have gone downhill in your profession from the very beginning!"

Other acquaintances soon followed. One of a small staff already assembled in the office of assistant secretary for Education of HEW was Dr. Joseph G. Colmen, the deputy assistant secretary. Formerly director of research for the Peace Corps, Colmen quickly became an expert partner and lifelong friend. There was also Wilbur Cohen, longtime civil servant in Washington, key leader in fashioning the Social Security legislation, and then serving as deputy secretary of HEW. After Gardner, and then as the HEW secretary, Cohen became a trusted mentor. He also assisted Francena as she searched for a new job, which resulted in her early appointment as associate executive director of the American Association of University Women. After a brief period, she became the executive director.

The new work yielded many new associates: Harold Howe II, the commissioner of the US Office of Education; Charles Frankel, on leave as a philosophy professor at Columbia University to serve as the assistant secretary of state for educational and cultural affairs; Douglas Cater, special assistant to the president for education and related fields; and Joseph Califano, advisor to the president on domestic policies. These officials formed a core group that helped fashion my own efforts. They would join in support of what would follow.

In the year prior to my arrival at HEW, and unknown to me, several advisors to the White House had begun to fashion an International Education Act (IEA). Gardner, Frankel, Cater, and Califano were joined by James Perkins, president of Cornell University; Harry McPherson, an assistant to the president; Senator William Fulbright; Frances Keppel, then leading the Office of Education; and Dillon Ripley, secretary of the Smithsonian Institution. This planning led to an address by President Johnson on international education to some five hundred scholars and scientists at the Smithsonian on September 16, 1965. A similar message went to the Congress and was included in the State of the Union message on January 12, 1966. After the first address, the president appointed a task force to work on legislative drafts of the IEA, consisting of twenty representatives of government and higher education. This group, chaired by Secretary of State Dean Rusk, refined previous memoranda and other information as a background to the President's IEA proposal.

Also unknown to me, into this background went a report drawn under my own hand. This was part of a task I had accepted in early 1966 while at WVU when I agreed to join a task force on the role of professional schools in world affairs. As part of the task force chaired by Dr. William H. Marvel, another presidential advisor and president of the Foundation for Education in World Affairs, my job had been to produce a report on the international prospects of schools of agriculture and engineering. Such reports were among the materials that later went to the White House advisors, as above, charged with drafting the International Education Act for Congress. To be sure, my interest turned quickly to the agricultural sector, as the following excerpts from my written contributions in the report, published in the following year of 1967, and calling for more attention to the humanistic consequences of agricultural technology.

Source: Task Force on Agriculture and Engineering. *The Professional School and World Affairs: Agriculture and Engineering.* New York: Education and World Affairs, 1967.

> Agricultural colleges must confront the fact that technology has become a ruling theme of culture, and that it is a way of linking the heritage of the human struggle with the meaning of the human condition. Every student educated in the agricultural colleges should know something of these principles and how they apply to the agrarian revolutions around the world. Sir Eric Ashby, [a noted British leader in higher education], has suggested that every student studying applied science and technology, regardless of future assignments, should learn how to weave technology into the fabric of society, and thus take a place among the truly liberally educated.

Soon to be revealed were my major HEW responsibilities: coordinate the efforts to secure congressional passage and funding and then help initiate the International Education Act; establish and chair a new Federal Interagency Committee on Education; and lead the federal process to create a college for deaf students, to be named the National Technical Institute for the Deaf. The initial two of these projects had been made clear to me by Secretary Gardner; the third came as a surprise.

The Johnson administration gave special attention from the outset to the International Education Act. The president's major addresses at the Smithsonian and for the Congress built upon his early concern with the place of international education in foreign aid and development. His concern had a requisite history: the Fulbright Act of 1946 for the exchange of international scholars; the creation of the US Information Agency in 1948; President Truman's Point IV programs, which began with the 1950s; the Agency for International Development in 1961; and, by 1966, its contracts with seventy US universities to aid the development of some forty nations.

Such interests would spread: Title VI of the National Defense Education Act of 1958 strengthened university work in foreign languages and area studies; the Fulbright-Hays Act of 1961 helped prospective teachers learn foreign languages; and the National Science Foundation fostered international exchange of scientists and their scientific work. Similar interests and support also mounted in major foundations (e.g., Carnegie, Ford, Kellogg, and Rockefeller). The educational needs for international development would be analyzed in such publications as those by John W. Gardner and Charles Frankel.[4]

The second major assignment, to chair the Federal Interagency Committee on Education (FICE), struck a strong chord with my interests in social organization and administration. Secretary Gardner, believing that HEW might enhance cooperation among the departments and agencies of the federal establishment, saw FICE as a way to do it. To serve as chief of staff of FICE, I invited Emery Bacon, who had served WVU as presidential assistant for labor and industrial relations. A similar invitation was accepted by David Nichols, an associate at WVU, to also assist

---

4   Gardner, John W. *AID and the Universities: A Report to the Administrator of the Agency for International Development* (New York: Education and World Affairs, 1964). Charles Frankel. *The Neglected Aspect of Foreign Affairs* (Washington, DC: Brookings Institution Press, 1966).

in strengthening these efforts. Both remained in important Washington positions after my departure.

The third major assignment surprised me. Gardner asked, "Paul, what do you know of NTID?"

"I've never heard of it," I said truthfully.

"Well, you had better learn of it, for every time the President speaks to me, he wants to know where it stands!" exclaimed Gardner. I learned that NTID stood for the National Technical Institute for the Deaf, a new college proposed for deaf students, one of the many educational enactments under way by the president and the Congress. President Johnson never forgot the deafness of a parent or the memory of such close friends with similar interests as Judge Homer Thornberry, former Congressman from Texas, and his wife, Eloise. Thus, NTID entered and remained on my agenda, despite my being asked to leave the room when I appeared for a first meeting with the National Advisory Council on Education for the Deaf. This group had isolated itself from external influences to begin selection of a university to sponsor the new college.

INTERNATIONAL EDUCATION

THE BRIEF ACCOUNT herein of an extraordinary episode in federal legislation makes no attempt to tell the whole complicated story. For a more complete account, one good source is Theodore M. Vestal's book, *International Education: Its History and Promise for Today*, which analyzes the political evolution and ill-fated consequences of the International Education Act of 1966.[5] Vestal was an associate in HEW while serving as a youthful specialist in international education. Other important works on the episode are cited in Vestal's book.

---

5   Vestal, Theodore M. *International Education: Its History and Promise for Today* (Westport, CT: Praeger Publishers, 1994).

The International Education Act (IEA) was introduced soon after the president's State of the Union address on January 12, 1966. The House of Representatives secured passage on June 6, 1966, a result aided by such additional voices to those above. Clayton Powell (D-NY), chair of the House Labor and Education Committee, appointed John Brademas (D-IN) to chair a bipartisan task force to examine and hold hearings on the bill. Other supporters included Herman Wells, former president of Indiana University; David Bell, director of the Agency for International Development (USAID); Warren Wiggins, director of the Peace Corps; and Leonard Marks, director of the Information Agency. Brademas became the principal champion of the IEA in the Congress. Its passage raised hard questions: What would be the division between domestic and overseas emphases? Where and how would federal grants be distributed? Did not the IEA duplicate Title VI of the National Defense Education Act?

When I arrived at HEW in August 1966, the IEA had passed in the House of Representatives, but with reservations requiring further study. The bill went to the Senate on February 3, 1966, and to Senator Wayne Morse, chairman of the Subcommittee on Education in Senator Lister Hill's Committee on Labor and Public Welfare. The bill remained there until after passage in the House. Moreover, delayed by the alarm over racial riots in Chicago and other cities and national tensions over the growth in number of troops in Vietnam, the Senate hearings on the bill were delayed until shortly after my arrival in Washington. With a short lull expected in forward actions on the IEA, I entered a series of experiences of personal learning and action given to interpreting the IEA to members of Congress and the many constituencies within the educational community. Throughout the remainder of 1966, and for most of 1967, speaking and writing about the IEA with such audiences in mind grew into a major task. Such efforts, exemplified by the excerpt following, went into detailed explanations of both its aims and methods.

Source: "The Potential of the International Education Act." *The Phi Delta Kappan* 49, no. 4 (1967): 186–190.

President Johnson has introduced a new and vital role for international education [and opened] a new chapter in the history of international education in the United States. The International Education Act contains three titles. Title I provides grants to colleges and universities, nonprofit organizations, and scholarly associations for two purposes. One would authorize the establishment, strengthening, and operation of centers of advance international study. The second would aim to diffuse international studies to all possible segments of the undergraduate college enroll-ment in the country. Title II amends existing legislation, such as strengthening of Title VI of the National Defense Education Act (language and area centers), and of Title XI of the same legislation for a program of institutes in international affairs for secondary school teachers. Other amendments would encourage the exchange of students and scholars by facilitating exchange of currencies and extending loans to Americans studying abroad. Title III of IEA authorized funds to study the migration of the skilled and talented around the globe, especially in regard to the so-called "brain drain."

The first level of objective, to enlarge the international work of students and teachers, will call for reviews of current practice, experiments with new practices, sharing ideas among institutions, re-education of faculty, inspiring trustees, more study abroad, generalizing such experience at home, and improved participation of foreign students and faculty on home campuses. Another basic objective would insist that international competence flow steadily into the common culture. By means of more and better curriculum development, together with new visions of teacher education, building up higher education should also enrich the lower schools. Finally, another ultimate promise of the IEA...speaks to the future of cooperative technical cooperation. It is to be hoped that governments will nurture this activity without insisting that it be monitored for purposes of foreign diplomatic policy.

Senate hearings on the IEA moved slowly onward during the fall months of 1966, a period when the Eighty-Ninth Congress was coming to a close. Other domestic and military problems overloaded the Senate calendar in that period, casting doubts upon funding new legislation as the costs mounted for the Vietnam engagement. However, the bill was enacted by the Senate on October 21, 1966, only the day before Congress adjourned. President Johnson signed the IEA into law on October 29, 1966, while visiting Chulalongkorn University in Bangkok, Thailand. However, a serious snag was evident! The request of a budget to initiate the IEA (one million dollars to plan an initial effort requiring some $130 million) would have to await the review and action of the Ninetieth Congress. This division between the Eighty-Ninth and the Ninetieth Congresses of authorization and appropriation clearly highlighted a critical challenge to the future of the IEA.

In his State of the Union message on February 2, 1967, President Johnson included two other provisions of the IEA: one for a National Advisory Committee on International Studies, appointed by the president and located in HEW and chaired by the assistant secretary for education. The president also proposed to create in HEW the Center for Educational Cooperation (CEC), which would be "the focal point for federal leadership in international education." Originally proposed by the Rusk Task Force, and given independence on a par with that of the National Institutes of Health, the CEC would "channel communications between missions abroad and the US educational community; direct programs assigned to HEW; and assist private efforts in international education."

While awaiting the return of the Ninetieth Congress and the IEA funding challenge, attention turned in the recess to defining a national system of international education. To assist this effort, additional helpmates came aboard. One was Theodore Vestal, mentioned above. Others were Robert Leestma, a State Department specialist, and Ralph Flynt, a wise HEW observer of global affairs. Several consultants came into the picture, notably Glen Taggart. A former colleague, mentor, and friend from my MSU days, Taggart, with an extraordinary record of international service, and perhaps the first dean (at MSU) of International Affairs in an American university, seemed a promising candidate to be the initial director of the CEC. In early 1997, he gave special attention to defining CEC's mission and operation.

The lull between the Eighty-Ninth and the Ninetieth Congresses, together with such expert assistance, gave me more time to interpret the IEA at conferences of educators throughout the country. The chief aim was to strengthen and better organize the constituencies for securing IEA funding once the new Congress convened. Perhaps understandably, among the great number of interested constituencies throughout American education, and many as well in the international community, special interests were born and strengthened. My own efforts expanded not only in helping form the modes of operation for the IEA once it was funded, but perhaps more importantly in unifying common purposes among the many interested parties. The excerpts following are samples of that endeavor.

Source: "The Approaching Revolution in International Education." Address delivered as The Sixth Annual Grady Gammage Memorial Lecture, Arizona State University, Tempe, AZ,

February 6, 1967. Also published as a monograph, *The Approaching Revolution in International Education* (Tempe, AZ: College of Education, Arizona State University, 1967).

[The first important new element in international education is] the imperative need to establish a few university centers for graduate study and research, in order that the highest standards of excellence may characterize the capability of the country, and that a rapid multiplication of teachers and faculty may be forthcoming to accept the obligations advanced by both the private and public sectors. Such centers must respond to our relative needs for knowledge with reference to the major areas of the world, to disciplinary studies of the highest order, and to the several fundamental processes in international development, which are both disciplinary and professional in nature.

The second element refers to the need of improving the communication among our colleges and universities. The expense of mounting and maintaining international activity demands that resources be carefully shared. It also suggests that we recognize the difficulties inherent in attempting worldwide cooperation without living up to the same measure at home. If inter-institutional arrangements are to be among the prime innovations of higher education in the next few years...we may expect that international education will exact the greatest discipline of all for cooperative ventures.

As mankind gropes forward into larger and larger groups, education and compassion become linked together. This bond stretches across time, a paradoxical time, when we are capable of great brutality, on the one hand, and tenderhearted compassion, on the other, a time when millions have been killed by technological war, yet millions have been saved by technological medicine. Educators have much to bring to the outcome. They should know better than most that societies exist in a manner [that] is not true of the human beings who live in them. Men die; societies endure. No single bond surpasses education in uniting people across the boundaries of generations and nations, [and helping them] join in common activity and engage a common faith in the young.

Source: "Expanding Opportunities in International Education." Paper presented to the Twenty-Second National Conference on Higher Education, Chicago, IL, March 7, 1967.

The responsibility of the Center for Educational Cooperation (CEC) goes beyond the administration of the authority of the IEA. It is to become the focal point for leadership of the international education activities of the US Government.... Among its most immediate functions will be to assist a wider acceptance by American institutions of the concept that oversees experience of teachers and faculty members must not be considered a handicap in career development, in the computation of tenure and seniority, in the accounting of health and retirement benefits. This is a beginning, hopefully, of a close partnership of the Center for Educational Cooperation and the educational institutions of the nation.

The CEC is now formulating plans to set up under contract or to establish under its own auspices, if necessary, an American Placement Center to provide a central exchange for information on those who have internationally oriented specialties, experience and interest. Further, there is planned a central clearinghouse for operational data on training programs for international education.

[Moreover], there is also planned the positioning of senior educators as Education Officers at several of our embassies for coordinating all American governmental education programs in the country of their assignment. They will be education advisors to the ambassadors, and representatives of the CEC which will assist them at home and backstop their operation, a function that should be strictly and exclusively educational.

When the Ninetieth Congress convened in January 1977, a marked gain in Republican seats further reduced the chances for funding the IEA. Concern widened over the Vietnam War. Tensions continued to mount in American cities. But the DHEW budget request for IEA went forward: $350,000 as a fiscal 1967 supplemental appropriation; $200,000 to launch the CEC; $75,000 to fund and begin the work of the National Advisory Committee on International Studies; and $75,000 for a baseline study of international education in American colleges and universities. The request for fiscal 1968 increased to $36,525,000. From January through May, 1967, intense work resumed with Congressional committees and those national constituencies. The details of these negotiations may be found in Vestal's analysis. But the shock came on May 25, 1967, when the Congress failed to include IEA funding in its Conference Report on budget agreements. To many with sustained interests in international education, this event remains a mystery. While my role was pivotal, little can be added to Vestal's careful analysis, though I had to smile when Vestal wrote, "Miller had completed a conscientious and methodical plan for implementing the IEA. One wag commented that the IEA was the best-planned unfunded legislation in the history of the republic."[6]

The best one may say is that many problematic features of domestic and international events united at a critical moment in American political and international history. Champions in the House—for example, Brademas—had lost some allies in the election, especially with the death of John Fogarty (D-RI) and dissension over Vietnam and budget pressures. In the Senate, George Mahon of Texas, chair of the Appropriations Committee, clamped down on budget increases, and remained skeptical of both supplementary budgets and smaller requests capable of ballooning upward. Also, such international stalwarts as senators Fulbright and Morse refused to take up the cause. This they made clear at a breakfast with Frankel and me, at which they pointed out foreign policy disagreements with the White House, heightening Vietnam pressures upon the budget, and the impacts and costs of urban violence. Both men also exclaimed about the urgent problems of funding the great number of education bills previously advanced by the president.

Perhaps the implementation moved too swiftly in a short period to overcome issues on both the educational and political fronts! How would benefits be distributed among undergraduate colleges, the research universities, and the public schools? How "domestic" or "foreign" would the ultimate focus of the IEA become? How might the CEC conflict with AID and other Washington centers of international affairs? Such questions begged not only program answers, but also required translation into the political language of the Congress. Also, with IEA authorized by the Eighty-Ninth Congress and its funding delayed until the Ninetieth Congress, a breach was created in what had seemed a not unusual process of planning and action.

---

6   Vestal, *International Education*, 87.

Douglas Cater and others in the White House, and surely Secretary Gardner, never ceased their support. I suspect that the distractions of Vietnam and in American cities demoted the IEA in President Johnson's priorities, leaving him to believe that Cater, Gardner, Miller, Frankel, and others were getting the job done. Indeed, even with the defeat in funding in May 1967, the process carried on, pointing to Congressional action for fiscal 1968–1969. In the absence of a National Advisory Committee, an "interim secretariat" took the next step of drawing previous ideas and actions together in a report to the Congress: "International Education: Its Meaning and Possible Patterns of Development." And the interpretation and implementation of the IEA and the Center for Educational Cooperation continued. The grist herein was carried by steps of further interpretation and implementation. One stimulating and important step was mounted by asking key US scholars to submit carefully drawn papers that assessed major global sectors and made recommendations in thirty-two disciplinary areas in eight regions of the world. Similar explorations took place at ten regional meetings throughout the country, and there I met, spoke, or counseled with scholars and organizations alike. Samples of my activity in speaking are summarized in the excerpts that follow.

Source: "International Education: Prospects and Uncertainties for U.S. Universities." Paper presented to the joint Annual Meetings of the American Farm Economic Association and the Canadian Agricultural Association, Guelph, Ontario, Canada, August 15, 1967.

[As we strengthen international education in our universities] we must struggle with how to properly relate the disciplines to each other as they refer to problems and how to relate the disciplines on the whole to areas of the world.... It has not been easy to establish centers of energy for international research within the university and at the same time to keep them from drifting apart from the daily tasks of the faculty as a whole.…. The international theme suggests that universities are in a vital reconsideration of their roles in society. Nothing seems sure, little seems just right, and, at times, the university enterprise resembles a jumble of halfway purposes and discrete results. International education, if it is to perfuse the institution as a whole, rather than become a distinct field of study, will require better planning of institutional aims, strengthened ethical principles, revitalized loyalty within the university, additional devices of interplay among the disciplines, and fresh ways of reflection on the reality of problems.

Source: "International Understanding and Education." Presented at a regional meeting held at Yankton College, Yankton, SD, September 19, 1967.

Education can help by balancing between the history of human struggle, the present meaning of this struggle to society and forward explorations into matters of value. There is also the matter of feedback: how to share with our own people the international experience which our country gains. The everyday reporting of news is crisis-laden. But much more may be told, including the not so sensational but quietly evolutionary incidences of countless village councils in Asia, the patient building of schools in Africa, the difficult tasks of resettlement and housing in Latin America.

Source: "The International Education Act." Paper presented to the Modern Language Association Convention, Chicago, IL, December 28, 1967.

[In the post-war decades from 1945 to 1966], when the world was recuperating from the most devastating war in its history, when knowledge was exploding in new academic fields being created as fast as new nations, when the shape of the world was acknowledged by the introduction of language and area studies, our national record shows not one truly comprehensive attempt to examine the alternatives available to higher education, to propose choices, and to justify them in terms of experience and aims.... In what respects should the content of higher education be adjusted to become more relevant to the needs and desires of the individual in the world of 1990 and meaningful participation in the twenty-first century? What changes should be made in higher education to meet the needs of national existence in tomorrow's world of catastrophic threat and infinite promise? [In taking up these tasks], surely it is the search for a learning derived from or applicable to all cultures that is the most distinctively new and modern.

The rapid pace throughout 1967 to further implement and interpret the IEA never wavered. But the sense of doom grew when both Gardner and Frankel, my associates in the State Department, resigned their posts late in that year. As the costs of Vietnam in personnel and dollars mounted, so did the tensions involving the president and those who served to advance his program. One could sense this change in the diminishing discipline of program development that would flow from the White House. I shall always remember President Johnson, at a Cabinet Room meeting of several officials on human rights, as he tearfully described his visits with young soldiers embarked for battle sites in Vietnam: "In my day you had two weeks while on your way to get ready for the battlefield, but now these kids have only twenty-four hours!"

Inflation had risen to prompt "guns and butter" conflicts. Violence seemed ready to spin out of control, whether over civil rights, in cities, or on college campuses. The climax of the 1965–1967 interest in international education had passed by, and this at a time when competing interests among the educators were less than resolved. Then, when President Johnson announced his intention in March 1968 not to stand for reelection, seeking funding of the IEA was no longer practical. There was but one conclusion: In early 1968, the mission that had attracted me to Washington would likely fail. As an assistant secretary of HEW, it was time for me to emphasize other projects.

THE URBAN CRISIS AND EDUCATIONAL RESPONSES

THROUGHOUT THE TWO years in HEW, steady effort went to serving as the chair of the Federal Interagency Committee on Education (FICE). With Emery Bacon as the executive director, we strove to organize this body and inspire cooperation among the more than forty major federal entities (and many more minor ones) concerned in some way with education. However, and perhaps characteristic of such attempts in the Washington scene, how to enlist the interests of the principal officials, who insisted on sending representatives, remained a challenge and diluted FICE's potentials.

On October 16, 1964, President Johnson issued Executive Order 11185 to establish the Federal Interagency Committee on Education to (1) aid the secretary of HEW to "identify the education needs and goals of the nation," and (2) facilitate interagency coordination of existing education programs. The general approach became of interest in and out of the federal government. As the following excerpt indicates, the core of this effort involved agencies sponsoring large-scale education and training programs: the Office of Education, the National Science Foundation, the National

Aeronautics and Space Administration, the Department of Agriculture, the Atomic Energy Commission, the US Public Health Service, and the National Institutes of Health. Also, other major departments and agencies sponsored smaller but significant ventures in education and training—Treasury, Justice, Housing and Urban Development, and the Veterans Administration.

Source: "The Federal Interagency Committee on Education." Prepared for *Education Age* (St. Paul, MN: 3M Company, Spring 1967).

> The committee has established working relationships among the represented agencies and selected six issues for immediate study. One group is studying in depth the impact of federal programs on educational institutions, particularly on colleges and universities. A second group is studying the educational implications of manpower requirements created by recently enacted Great Society programs. A third group focuses on how education can be applied to the solution of urban problems, and especially the special needs of rural people who migrate to the cities. A fourth group works on the full ranges of federal student aid programs, and addresses the question of whether federally supported graduate students should teach in the classroom as part of their training experience. The fifth group is looking at a proposed government-wide storage and retrieval system of educational research information...and another group has taken up a related idea—a system of data collection to give an overview of the total federal education system.

While the IEA remained on the agenda, its drift into Congressional backwaters challenged the office and its staff to revise priorities and turn in other directions. Joseph Colmen, the deputy assistant secretary, and I devised a new work plan responding to a practical question: given the evident relaxation of the earlier discipline imposed by the White House, what can we usefully accomplish in the remaining period of the Johnson Administration? This turn began in late 1967 with the departure of Secretary Gardner and continued through most of 1968. There were urgencies with little time allowed them: helping complete plans for a community college on the Navajo reservation; support of educational programs for the handicapped; added emphasis on black colleges and universities under Title III of the Higher Education Act; and more interest in NTID, including a first trip to Rochester, New York, to help locate its campus site.

While giving new life to the program of the office, the tensions and tragedies of early 1968 were reckoned with urban riots, campus rebellions, and the tragic assassinations of Martin Luther King Jr. and Robert F. Kennedy. My office had provided minor assistance to the Office of Education on school desegregation; those early months of 1968 opened it wider. Suddenly, as a self-styled rural sociologist, I found myself more and more drawn into the urban and racial crises of the time. Such themes, and how education might address them, rose to displace those of international education.

I will never forget preparing two papers in the spring of 1968. They met different ends. One was not delivered at all, and the other, in one long night, was completely rewritten. The first, to have been delivered at the Founder's Day celebration of Tuskegee Institute, was preceded two days prior by the assassination of Dr. King. The second, delivered at the spring Commencement of the University of Florida, was immediately preceded by the assassination of Robert Kennedy.

With reference to the Tuskegee assignment, when we were not met by Tuskegee folk in Atlanta for the expected drive to the Institute, Francena and I proceeded on our own to that destination. Amid much obvious campus commotion, when we appeared at Dorothy Hall (the Institute's hostel), we were told by a student at the doorway that if we entered we would join the president and trustees held captive in the upstairs board-room by student action in the wake of Dr. King's death. We elected not to enter but to remain overnight with a faculty friend; we learned the next morning that Founder's Day had been cancelled. My paper, from which the excerpt below is drawn, was filed but not delivered.

Source: "Remarks." To have been delivered at the Founders Day Program, Tuskegee Institute, Tuskegee, AL, April 7, 1968.

In this period of national sorrow and mourning for the loss of a leader, a man of peace and nonviolence, a man of conviction and courage who understood people—black and white—and who appealed to reason, not emo-tion, we must praise those who, like Martin Luther King, have advanced reason in the struggle of human rights... As one also looks back on Booker T. Washington's life and achievement, [one observes] the extent to which he advanced the cause of reason, not in a time of peace and tranquility, but in a difficult time of tension and violence. As in our own times, Washington faced upheaval, high passions, and terrifying public disorder. In his situation, as in ours, there seemed to be no exact precedents to follow in solving the most urgent problems of a stricken society. In his own experience as a slave, he had seen how a system of servitude corrupted black and white alike in making work contemptible. Recognizing competence as the true freedom for any person regardless of time or place or prior condition, he set out to give his people a second liberation, from illiteracy and lack of skill.

Source: "Reflections in a Tragic Hour." Paper presented at the University of Florida Commencement. Gainesville, FL, June 8, 1968. Also published in the *Congressional Record* (with an introduction Senator Claude Pepper of Florida) 114, No. 102 (June 14, 1968): 5428.

My initial remarks, forwarded days ago to you, on the theme of "Not Education but Human Development," became useless in this tragic hour of sorrow. And they became useless in the early morning of Wednesday past when Senator Kennedy, in a center of luxury, giving of his vast vitality and brilliance in a stand against blood and violence, was struck down by them. Whatever else calls us aside and together, none takes precedence over weeping for his loss and the irretrievable death of still more of the national spirit.

The best of rhetoric, which I have never claimed, could neither depict nor remove the poignant visions of that tousle-headed leader, doing what he was destined to do, eyes shining, alternately grim and buoyant, necktie unstrung, caring deeply about what most of us, if caring, do too little. That Robert Kennedy, burdened with the violent loss of others he loved, could be consumed similarly, is so shattering to the commencement covenant that we can only pray together for the return to us of what it means to be an American.

Ours is a time of national sorrow, more so now by means of another shot, this time not on a motel balcony but in a kitchen corridor. How long must we endure it? We shall have to endure it for so long as we refuse to know ourselves. We shall have to endure until we heed those voices crying openly around us: "My relationship with you is ended." Our sorrow is the continuing process of isolation that deepens in our national life.... Robert Kennedy called out to us the urgency of shared purpose, not as a subversion of individuality, but rather to enhance us by helping us achieve a strength beyond ourselves. He has been taken from the quest, but, as we must pledge, not that message which he gave us.

A sudden action in the midst of the urban crisis of 1968, by President Johnson and the White House, shaped my remaining months as assistant secretary for Education in HEW. Among many responses at that time, the president appointed me to lead a White House Task Force on the missions of urban universities. Among its several members, combining such heads of major urban related departments as Robert Wood of Housing and Urban Development and selected representatives of major urban universities, was Cyril O. Houle of the University of Chicago. Houle had become a special mentor to me during the Michigan State University period, helping me to better understand adult education beyond its rural forms.

This group met in several lengthy and intensive meetings throughout the spring of 1968. Its major recommendation urged the White House and the Congress to revamp Title I of the Higher Education Act of 1965 (at that moment a modest support mechanism for continuing higher education). The revision spoke to decades of interest, by university, adult education, and labor union leaders, in creating "urban-grant universities," an appropriately modified application of the service tradition of the land-grant institutions. The recommendation called for a pilot effort that, if workable, would over time extend to universities in fifty major cities. But many proposals erected in Washington in that period were challenged by the political context that had stalled the international education effort, and this one fell victim to the same fate.

However, the activity added focus to what was already under way. The 1960s ushered in a new and enormous partnership of the federal government with universities, especially in support of research. Inevitably, interest arose in the public service role of these institutions. Old patterns and new reforms came under review and, as even introduced by the International Education Act, found their way onto the planning tables of academe. With an impetus provided by the White House Task Force on the urban missions of universities, my long interests in university organization and outreach were once more due to expand. Especially did the service in Washington stimulate ever greater concern for "compartmentalism" in the practice of education and learning, and how best to create more interdependence as problems more and more cross-cut the major disciplines, departments and colleges of the universities. Few of my papers and speeches failed to include this emphasis, to which the following three excerpts attest.

Source: "Impacts of Society on Higher Education." Paper presented to the Association for Institutional Research, San Francisco, CA, May 8, 1968.

[For today's university], the disorganization of the modern city is a challenge point...where the proper offices of government and higher education converge. Government, which is charged with doing for its citizens what they cannot do for themselves, confronts incontrovertible needs for action in the chaos of the urban ghetto. And the institution of higher learning, if we conceive of it as the vital center of discovering, organizing, and distributing knowledge, its obligation in the crisis of the cities is as compelling as that of government.... [This example demonstrates that] the interaction of society and higher education is a never-ending process. The problem for each is to contribute something relevant to the other, in order to receive its support in turn.... When society knows what it wants, it can ask for it with the hopes of satisfaction. When higher education comprehends its own assets and liabilities, problems and processes, it can cease to be the disorderly spectator it sometimes appears to be in the life of the national community and be instead the central clearinghouse for all that is best and most potent in the culture.

Source: "Reflections on the Federal Government and the University." Paper presented to the Sesquicentennial Celebration Conference of the University of Michigan, July 12–14, 1967. Also published in *The University and the Body Politic*, 133–141. Ann Arbor, MI: University of Michigan Press, 1968.

Suffice it to say that the usefulness of knowledge in modern society turns universities into centers of social action. In urban technical societies, economic growth depends upon human capital. Solving general problems with specific solutions demands that information is made accessible to people everywhere. As man [sic] turns from a creature living by manual labor to a being living by his intellect, the organizing centers of the society will turn to the universities for ideas and invention.... The university-government relationship is established as a predictable feature of the American system. The specific nature of the relationship is a puzzle; it has, nonetheless, become legitimate. Some of the fundamental principles over which there is little disagreement are as follows: that colleges and universities should serve the national and international communities in addition to the local community; that excellence in higher education is vital to the future of the nation; [and] that higher education must remain an assembly of free institutions, uncompromised by any sources of financial support.

Source: "Education for Community." Paper presented to the Southern California Industry-Education Council, Los Angeles, CA, January 18, 1967.

New institutions are being formed by public and private collaboration to eradicate slums, to reduce unemployment, and to attack the various afflictions of urban and rural poverty. As this assault moves forward, we can be sure that neither impassioned oratory nor massive transfusions of public funds are enough to sustain it. Without the collaboration of industry, education, and government, public policy fails to find the mix of resources that makes development at the local level an activity [that] is self-sustaining. This principle is the need for a sense of community by people where they live and work. They must see the essence and reality of the development process in their daily lives. People must see the need to care: about clean air and water, good schools and public services, about the cultural quality of the environment. Whether they live in city, suburb, or farm, people must care enough to want to participate in the tasks of development, whether as professional workers or citizen volunteers. And it is our job as laymen and citizens, businessmen and educators, public servants and industrialists, liberals and conservatives, to transcend the stereotypes and labels that divide us and

join together to make social and economic development a
sustaining feature in the life of the community. A "great
society" is one in which people care about community.

The White House Task Force on urban universities connected
to related projects. Clark Kerr, former president of the University of
California, had formed a commission to conduct an epochal study of
higher education in America. His notice would not escape application
of the land-grant idea in urban society. My long interest in this idea
was recognized and opportunities arose, in and out of Washington, to
comment on such applications. A paper requested and presented to the
HEW professional staff was adapted and given in several other forums.
An example follows:

Source: "Informal Education: The Rural Precedent and the Urban
Challenge." Paper presented to the American Dairy Science
Association, Ohio State University, Columbus, OH, June 16, 1968.

In the search for new approaches to the problems of cities, it is tempting to explore certain areas of past and
present success for useful analogies. One such is the
great saga, now more than a century old, of how universities helped turn American farms into the marvels
of productivity they are today.... Is the rural precedent,
perhaps the world's best example of informal education,
really pertinent to contemporary urban needs, or is it
only another panacea promising elsewhere more than it
can deliver? Aspiration, participation, mobility, communications, coordination, and time—these factors were
made to function creatively in rural society. Can they be
made to function as effectively in urban society?

Rural life built upon the family... The family was at once a social, economic, and occupational group.... [T]his kind of solidarity, grounded in interdependence and strengthened by the habit of cooperation, is seldom found in the deprived centers of American cities.

There was a symmetry in the organization of rural society. It featured rather formal authority, embodied in counties, states, universities, and federal agencies, each free to act on a part of the total effort. There is no such clear structure in urban society. Our cities have become jungles of competing interests, with power and responsibility divided and the citizen apathetic or cynical from too bitter an experience of social chaos.

The progress of rural society bypassed the really poor... there may be serious limits on what [the rural precedent] can teach us about helping the urban poor.

Whereas the land-grant college or university was the coordinator of rural development and a key element in the communications system of [rural] society, the university is not much more than a prestigious presence on the sidelines of urban life.

The rural and urban situations differ in the aspiration [that] people can bring to the development effort. The urban Negro, after long and social limitation, has less of the optimism, and, consequently, less of the drive that characterized both the rural pioneer and the city-dwelling immigrant of American success stories.

While analogies are helpful, they will not easily give us the methodology necessary for improving the quality of urban life. The rural precedent teaches us of the desperate need we have of a stable and coherent design. Without one, there cannot be the focusing of the public will so vital to success. [All in all] what has happened in rural America in the last hundred years may not show us exactly how to do it [in urban America]; what it does show us is that it can be done.

While at WVU an awakening to the underlying tensions in continuing adult education would influence my understanding of its application. Both curiosity and concern grew over the consequences of technology, then well on its way to join science as a major theme of American culture. How should education locate itself with reference to this theme and the likelihood that it would describe the twentieth century? This concern in one form or another colored the ideas and actions in Washington. Not unlike papers that served to unify thinking in the move from MSU to WVU, one paper perhaps best served this unification on the move to Washington. Basically to suggest the need of a Department of Education with full cabinet credentials, the paper addressed the proliferation of educational programs in the federal system—"more than four hundred separate educational programs scattered throughout the executive branch, and more than three hundred of them relating to the education of adults."

Source: "A National Policy for Adult Education." Conference keynote address delivered at the National Adult Education Conference, New York, NY, November 19, 1965. Also published as "A National Policy for Adult Education." *Adult Leadership* 14, no. 7 (1966).

[There is a confusion] surrounding what adult education means, and calls for a much clearer distinction between two broad areas. The first relates to the process of solving essential public problems by means of inserting knowledge and improved decision-making.... The classic example of this function is found in the ponderous application of knowledge to agriculture and rural life by the Cooperative Extension Service. The results...have transformed American agriculture, provided quality food and fiber at less cost to the consumer than in any other part of the world, released manpower resources to the nation at large, [and now] form the single most important technical export to the developing countries.... Yet this same example is also the classic documentation of the fact that inserting knowledge through individuals and groups for the solution of public problems may not, in the end, be education. For today, rural America stands with the poorest schools, the poorest community services, the poorest local government, the poorest educational and cultural attainment, and with a per-capita income of about half of that of its urban counterpart.

[But we also incorporate] a meaning of adult education that would define it as a uniquely personal experience with individual fulfillment and enrichment as the goal. The emphasis of the general extension movement within higher education has centered tenaciously upon individual learning throughout life as a principal objective....We have talked about the lifelong continuity of educational experiences in terms [that] we have not yet been able to match the means to achieve it; and on the other hand, unable to resist the pragmatic pressures of our institutions and the short-term interests of our clientele, we have not been openly courageous in proclaiming that individual learning is quite properly an end in itself....

[Are we not drifting] to a conception of adult education as a problem-solving technique for use against the public ills now everywhere about us? It is a concern that we risk making of adult education an even more diffuse activity—one [that] is splintered along the short-term needs and the agency motif. And it is a concern which ponders the distinction between culture and civilization: the former, that relatively small seminal social unit; the latter that larger organization which spreads and preserves culture but does not produce it. The grave risk of our new opportunities as adult educators is that we shall spend more time than we should in the preservation and spread of civilization rather than in the development of culture.

HEW's project to locate and establish the National Technical Institute of the Deaf (NTID), having been assigned to my office, was of steady interest. The object was to develop a college for deaf students with a career emphasis upon science and technology. Joined to this activity was my appointment to the Board of Trustees of Gallaudet University in Washington, the premier and oldest (private but federally supported) institution in the world for the education of deaf students. Legislation in 1965 provided for NTID to be part of a conventional university, with a selection to be made as noted above. More than one hundred institutions applied to be sponsors, with the Rochester Institute of Technology (RIT) in the final process of being selected upon my arrival at HEW. This institution, founded in 1829, was midway in building a new campus of substantial proportion.

Emphasizing applied science, embedded in career preparation, the school was located in a city with a large deaf population and the home of the renowned Rochester [public] School for the Deaf.

While NTID cannot be said to fit the emphasis of this account on adult education, its implication for worldwide influence brought genuine interest to me and my colleagues. Competent personnel, notably Phillip DeMarais and Ralph Hogue, gave this project much attention, moving it from the legislative enactment to its first Rochester activity in 1967. New colleagues appeared, among them Arthur Stern, chairman of the Board of Trustees, and Mark Ellingson, the RIT president. The duties with RIT were mainly to oversee its activation, especially the building program. While I was serving as a board member at Gallaudet University, an opportunity arose to help draft new by-laws that clarified its public/private status, settle its relationship to the federal government, and assist in selecting a new president. Following the service in Washington, I remained on Gallaudet's board for another decade, strengthening an already large interest in the education of deaf and hearing-impaired people.

WINDING DOWN

WITH PRESIDENT JOHNSON's decision not to stand for reelection, the future of my family took on priority again. Francena, while happily engaged at the American Association of University Women, joined in a common interest to return to campus life. Thomas's elementary schooling was ending, creating a convenient moment for a move. We had enjoyed some fifteen years of central administrative assignments, rather more than the five years once promised President Hannah at MSU. Should we not settle down with professorial appointments? We were tested immediately on this resolve: Arthur Stern, chair of the RIT Board, appeared in April 1968 to suggest my becoming a candidate to succeed Mark Ellingson, the Institute's esteemed president for more than three decades. But this and other similar queries were declined.

However, in spring of 1968, personal decisions were pushed aside by the not uncommon aim to tidy up a job before departing it. Two chores seemed urgent: first, despite the loss of the IEA, to establish a continuing presence for international education in HEW, and, next, to interpret that action to the educational community. To explain this strategy, several regional meetings of educational leaders in international education were conducted with the aid of Robert Leestma, an earlier advisor to Charles Frankel in the State Department; Wilbur Cohen, who had become secretary of HEW; Harold Howe II, US Commissioner of Education; and such stalwarts as Joseph Colmen, Theodore Vestal, and Ralph Flynt.

Mindful of the once-promised Center for Educational Cooperation (CEC), the outcome of this effort was to establish a new Institute of International Studies (IIS) in the US Office of Education. The IIS would improve and coordinate the programs already in operation, many already residing in that office, especially those of international personnel exchange, foreign language development, and area studies. A major survey by Flynt identified other programs in the federal system to which the IIS might be helpful. Robert Leestma was appointed director of the new institute in March 1968.

Located in HEW's US Office of Education rather than that of the secretary, the IIS could emphasize improvement of international education with reasonable insulation from the politics of congressional authorization and funding. In the new institute rested the hope that federal interest in international education would sustain until a better future arrived. This hope would be rewarded for the many years to follow with Leestma as the Institute's director. In his 1994 book, Vestal reviews this episode:

> Under Leestma's leadership, the IIS, with meager resources
> and little agency interest and support, carried on a remarkable

range of international education activities that helped maintain and even expand the field despite the budget constraints of the times. The IIS became the rallying point for fostering international education during the dark days of the 1970s, more so than is generally known. (Vestal 1994, 129)

The other part of the strategy for shoring up what had begun with the International Education Act, was a series of regional meetings at which the past, the situation in 1968, and possible futures might be candidly reconciled.

Grist for these gatherings came in part from the 1967 International Conference on the World Crisis in Education, for which my office provided staff assistance to the co-chairs, Secretary Gardner and James Perkins, president of Cornell University. After nearly a quarter of a century of American investment in internationalism—an investment of hope, skill, effort, and money—the experience in 1968 seemed to have fallen on hard times. The national mood, entangled in the Vietnam struggle, had markedly changed from the early days of the Marshall Plan and the technical assistance projects that followed. To talk over such changes and come to an understanding of them was the aim of the regional meetings for key educational leaders in international education. For with equal urgency of the Vietnam perceptions also came those of pressing domestic problems in American life. As it was commonly observed -- a priority list that includes the deprivation of our urban youth has little room for foreign aid!

Source: "Education and the Decline of Internationalism." Paper presented to the Southern Regional Education and World Affairs Conference, University of North Carolina at Charlotte, Charlotte, NC, February 29, 1968.

The task at home of infusing education with an awareness of the international setting in which American life goes forward has turned out to be more complicated than we thought. It was easy enough to persuade leaders in education that it would be a fine thing if every student could speak a foreign language and understand the relevance of other cultures to their own. It is something else to translate this into meaningful items of curriculum, to equip teachers to convey it, and to somehow make it part of the intellectual working capital of the community as a whole... Even where international emphasis seems strongest, as in the universities, it can fall short of what should be its true objectives. Specialization finds it easy to harden in some of the great international centers; the stronger they grow, the more separate they may become from the community at large and even from the parent university—frequently cultish, self-absorbed, and prey to a provincialism no less narrow for its exotic framework.

Despite the strength of these constraints, however, there is a new awareness that the effectiveness of working with either the international dimension or the crisis in social relations now so exacerbated in our cities lies in recognizing the extent to which the two are interrelated.... The same kind of sensitivity to people with different backgrounds that is called for in achieving international understanding is required for approaching the ghetto poor. Our problem in seeking world peace is interchangeable with our problem in seeking neighborhood peace. The dangers of failure are equally terrible in both—international wars abroad and social disintegration at home; they should yield to similar applications of imagination and good will. What we are able to achieve toward one will, in the end, be influenced by what we are able to achieve in the other.

With the Institute of International Studies invented and its director in place, my work at HEW seemed clearly over. My resignation was submitted and accepted, effective June 30, 1968. Work began on pulling ideas together on adult education, a request of a longstanding colleague, Russell G. Mawby of MSU days, who had become the principal program leader of the W. K. Kellogg Foundation. Meanwhile, Francena and I reflected further on the future. Our decision to return to professorial assignments enabled us not only to decline RIT's interest, but also other similar opportunities. My association with President Perkins of Cornell for the International Conference at Williamsburg, Virginia, in October 1967, had put me to thinking about a post in international affairs at Cornell University. A similar interest came from Chancellor Tolley of Syracuse University for both Francena and me, in adult education and the Maxwell School of Citizenship. Meanwhile, Chancellor Dean Colvard, leading in the creation of a new university in Charlotte, North Carolina, invited us to explore appointments there.

Also at this time, there were compelling events of family importance and interest, all of which related to how we might manage our own futures. Daughter Paula graduated from West Virginia University in 1967 and, supported by her election to Phi Beta Kappa, readied herself for graduate study in social studies and counseling. Not long thereafter, she marred Blair Thrush, who was soon to graduate from WVU's medical school. Michael Nolan, Francena's son, and his wife, Jeanne, would continue and each complete their studies for a PhD degree in rural sociology at The Pennsylvania State University. My son Tom was preparing to enter his final year in elementary school.

The upshot of these considerations and much discussion in mid-1968 was that we decided to go to Charlotte. A professorship in sociology and administrative duties in continuing adult education awaited Francena at Charlotte's Queens College, and I accepted a professorship in education at the new Charlotte campus of the University of North Carolina, as well as the post of first director of its office of university planning studies. I would also serve North Carolina State University at Raleigh as a professor of adult education. Thus were we destined finally for tenured and stable academic posts, to mingle our interests in the social sciences and adult education, and help create in Charlotte what in time would become a major metropolitan university.

So it was that the summer of 1968 found us packing up again. While we had doubted our fitness for Washington life and work, we had come to embrace the beauty, traditions, and intellectual stimulation of that city. Our awareness of national and international issues had been greatly elevated, in some respects rather more from defeat than success. Also, our personal growth accelerated with even brief exposure to the events and such persons as Lyndon Johnson, John Gardner, Wilbur Cohen, Douglas Cater, Charles Frankel, and Harold Howe II. I will never forget my days with my esteemed colleagues, notably among them Joseph Colmen and Robert Leestma. Moreover, mentors of an earlier time had rallied to the Washington projects and continued as my mentors, such as Glenn Taggart, Russell Mawby, Cyril Houle, and John Hannah.

Francena and I arrived in Charlotte in early September 1968 to begin what we expected to be a long chapter, likely one for the remainder of our professional careers.

V

CHARLOTTE AND UNCC

AN ADVENTURE IN UNIVERSITY PLANNING

CONSOLIDATING PROFESSIONAL INTERESTS

THREE FACTORS HELPED form our decision in favor of Charlotte. By moving there, both Francena and I could join in reactivating our professorial roles, hers at Queens College and mine at the new institution. The second factor would be the chance to join Chancellor Dean W. Colvard to devise the master plan for the new University of North Carolina at Charlotte (UNCC). The third factor promised a different experience, one of scholarship and teaching in adult education, urban civic issues, community development, and educational innovation.

Dr. Colvard was the deciding factor! We had collaborated on land-grant projects in the 1950s when he was the dean of Agriculture at

North Carolina State University at Raleigh, and my duties were expanding in Cooperative Extension work at Michigan State University. Our early lives and career interests were similar. His notions of how the land-grant idea might be adapted to urban society seemed profound, and on that subject, he had become a mentor. After his deanship at Raleigh, Colvard became president of Mississippi State University in 1960. He won national attention there for his efforts in relation to desegregation, especially in intercollegiate athletics and the 1965 peaceful admission of the institution's first African American student. His record as a humane and creative administrator, and one of impeccable integrity, gave strength to his selection as the first chancellor of the new university to be launched in Charlotte. Dean Colvard and his wife, Martha, exuded warm friendship and hospitality and inspired all who fell within their acquaintance.

Dr. Colvard's intentions were several. He believed that the effort of a university should begin at home—hence his concern for metropolitan Charlotte—and continuing adult education was slated as a major aim. Institutional governance should center in a democratic fellowship of constituencies both on and off the campus. He also possessed a keen sense of campus physical planning to enhance the disciplines and professions. He was determined to institutionalize innovation not only in planning but also in the conduct of the new university. Throughout the Washington experience, the upward surge of federal aid to colleges and universities implied forthcoming pressures upon them for more accountability and innovation. As my effort began in planning for a new university, I could do no less than grip "innovation" as a new "in" word in academe and surely to be given priority in Charlotte.

Source: "Clearing the Way for Innovation." *The Educational Record* 48 (Spring 1967): 138–143.

[Institutional insistence on autonomy] has stimulated the public in recent years to devise both formal and informal means of inter-institutional cooperation and exchange. Even today, however, it is safe to say that many, if not most, colleges and universities isolate themselves from each other and from other centers of intellectual activity.... The differences in quality among institutions of higher learning...far exceed our awareness of them [and] the motif of the curriculum remains enormously taxonomic. It is responsive to subject matter; it is not always responsive to human learning by different human beings.

Of course, the theme of adult education in Chancellor Colvard's own portfolio captured my enthusiasm and imagination. As in the other chapters of this account, this function received special emphasis. But what happened in Charlotte was much more extensive. The larger story of the new university may be found elsewhere, such as the books by Kenneth Sanford and Robert Rieke.[7] At the time of the move, new activities in adult education were involving me. They would mix with the new duties in Charlotte and add to this continuing interest. A major new assignment was to chair the Committee on Continuing Adult Education of the American Council on Education. I also began leading a graduate course in adult education at UNC-Raleigh in the fall of 1968. When I was invited to join the committee at the American Council on Education, one of America's foremost adult educators had just completed a major monograph under the council's auspices and asked me to prepare the preface.

---

7   Sanford, J. Kenneth. *Growing Up Together* (Charlotte, NC: University of North Carolina at Charlotte, 1996); Robert Rieke. *A Retrospective Vision: The University of North Carolina at Charlotte, 1965–1975* (Charlotte, NC: University of North Carolina at Charlotte, 1977).

Source: "Moving from the Wings." My preface to *Higher Adult Education in the United States: The Current Picture, Trends, and Issues,* by Malcolm S. Knowles (Washington, DC: American Council on Education, 1969).

[Today] the formal enterprise of education seems to be passing over some great divide of social experience.... Changing skills and attitudes equals the importance of acquiring them in the first place. Learning how to change because of change questions the monopoly of education by the young. The monopoly of educational institutions over the pursuit of learning is also weakening. In this sense, the links between society and education have become the frontiers of educational inquiry. Education itself is widening into a conception of human development. And it is moving from the classroom to the community.

It is surprising indeed how urban schools have been seen as centers of social services.... [And] no distinctive "Samaritan College" has been founded, a college that would reach out to the poor, teach the infirm, and encompass the needs of the wounded...the reduction of loneliness, the method of seeking, and...the joy of human fulfillment. New institutions are [also] possible that will define the learning space of the community no less great than the limits of electronic communications.

Source: "In Anticipation of the Learning Community." Paper presented to the Adult Education Association of America, Des Moines, IA, November, 1968. Also published in *Adult Leadership* 17, no. 7 (1969): 306–308.

If there is a crisis in education, it is a crisis of efficacy. It is not the condition of education alone. Social institutions of every kind seem slow to respond to those very needs which they help reveal. Great cathedrals sit bestride masses of people who live in abject poverty. A church stands on almost every hillside in the poorest sections of Appalachia. The clubs of the rich can adjoin the houses of the poor. Sickness can prosper in the backyard of the medical center. A child in the slum school can know more than his teacher than about the nature of the community. The greatest universities can turn their gates upon the ghetto, and, in the end, become one. These are the revelations [that] call out to us a new urgency that the master methodology must be the humanization of our institutions, a vast re-education of their self-centeredness. And it is this that we must solve if we are to anticipate the learning community.

Our limits to human encounter have been erased! Reading stands no longer as the only route to understanding the distant great. We can hear their music and see their works and hear about their backgrounds with a vividness and immediacy once unimaginable without first-hand contact. Even now, given the media of the electronic age, we cannot devise ways of understanding the prospects and problems of others not quite like ourselves. From our neighborhoods to the world community, mankind is in serious trouble indeed. Let us fervently hope, let us pray, that adult educators will be in the front lines of this process that will centralize and interconnect even as it decentralizes individual learning, that will enlarge the learning space to information points wherever they may be, that will recast the family as a revitalized instrument of culture growth, and that will swell the shared interest of every community, which is to say, by dialogue.

We are up against a rift as no other in the century...with the gulf between deed and creed.... It is not only true at home; it is also true abroad. One may see two master technologies in the world today: the technology of weaponry and the hostilities it can turn into an Apocalypse; and the technology of communications with its promise to bring people together—constructively, benevolently and humanely.

I carried with me to Charlotte a growing concern for the American family that sprang from my exposure to the deepening urban crisis experienced and felt in the Washington period. Francena's general work in family sociology helped me better understand the interplay between family, school, and community as crucial to the prospects of American life. Such a vision overlapped with and helped guide the early tenets of planning in Charlotte. Such references began to show up and expand in my papers for planning and probing the underlying tensions in American education.

Source: "Adult Education and the American Family." Paper presented to the American Family Life Association, Seattle, WA, November 9, 1968.

[We must] explore [these] discontinuities in family, community, and school, and how growth and experience in one of these sectors can provide growth and experience for the others. When the barriers between family, school, and community fall down, when each plans to enrich the others, when success as a father is valued equally with success at the office, when teachers, students and parents all join in learning by doing, then, and perhaps only then, will educational concerns for the family rise above the token gestures we make today.

Clearly my thinking about the planning tasks in Charlotte returned me to fundamental structures of community life, such as family, school, and neighborhood. Of similar importance was the cultural motif in America's southern culture. Two vectors were at work. The first was the challenge of our comprehension of our own family life, new marriage, and building relationships with our children and other kinfolk. The second vector would challenge us to upgrade our understanding of our first residence in America's southland. If UNCC would creatively become a distinctive and competent servant in the southern region, especially at that time in American history, my earlier training in applied anthropology would need revisiting for sound application. Francena joined in this same challenge, given her special interest in family sociology, as she took up her outreach duties at Queens College and joined me in relation to the new UNCC.

UNIVERSITY PLANNING

THIS CONSOLIDATION OF ideas around higher adult education and innovation carried into the planning process for the new university. To be sure, many other perspectives were necessarily included, on my part and by a great many other participants. How this wider planning for the new institution began and evolved will be found elsewhere, as indicated above. The following is skewed toward a focus on the promised outreach to the larger community and region.

The antecedent institutions of the University of North Carolina at Charlotte (UNCC) were three in number. Established for extension courses, the Charlotte Center of the University of North Carolina began in 1946; it became Charlotte College in 1949 as part of the public community college system. The College became a four-year and state-supported institution in 1963. Serving throughout this evolution was Bonnie Cone, the executive leader of both institutions. A former teacher in the Charlotte schools, her energy and imagination led to the action in 1965 of the North Carolina Legislature to rename the College and declare it the fourth campus of the University. While Dr. Colvard became the first chancellor and was charged with leading UNCC into becoming a full university, Bonnie Cone continued as a vice chancellor and took on a decisive part in the planning. She also became a ready mentor to me, as she had for many others.

Starting to plan brought two opportunities that the chancellor felt were of great importance. One was the chance for growth it gave to the Charlotte College faculty. Relatively young, most faculty and staff had come to the college prior to the decision to establish UNCC. Relatively inexperienced in the ways of a complex university, many felt uncertain about their own futures. Striving to involve and counsel them grew to be the most stimulating and perhaps helpful service I was able to give. To be remembered especially in this youthful cadre are Newton Barnette, Seth Ellis, John Chase, Barbara Goodnight, William Mathis, Douglas Orr, Larry Owen, Allan Palmer, Norman Schul, and Loy Witherspoon. Associated with this group and other helpmates was Dr. Hugh McEniry, who had come from Stetson University to serve as the new vice chancellor for academic affairs. He joined Colvard and Cone as a stellar mentor. Dorothy Lakin provided unusual technical and office support of my efforts.

The second opportunity grew from a key strategy in the proposed planning format—to invite external specialists in the respective planning categories to visit UNCC, and as leaders of campus symposia offer their own scenarios for a new university. The process promised an extraordinary learning experience for all. Throughout 1968–1969, some one or more of these specialists seemed present on the campus at any one time. One memorable example was a still relatively young professor, Henry Kissinger, arriving with his vision for international affairs in academe.

This exposure enlivened interest on the issues of higher education then current: how best to strengthen teaching; how to organize the disciplinary and professional curricula; how to incorporate mechanisms to insure continuing flexibility for institutional change and innovation; the public connections and commitments of the new institution, especially a focus on lifelong education in a dynamic metropolitan region; how to achieve participatory governance that would work; and to bring to the outcomes an understanding of an American society soon to be even more centered on how best to create, preserve, disseminate, and utilize knowledge.

Another early step was to create an Office of Institutional Research and set it to exploring concepts, options, and categories for the planning process. Some of these categories were traditional: the divisions to be established; a master campus physical plant plan capable of continuous adaptation; the extramural functions in and beyond the metropolitan community; institutional goals and the governance procedures for achieving and amending them; how planning, with both internal and external competencies, might be best sustained; and how to provide future development with research, testing and evaluation. Such preliminary framing of the planning process filled the agenda during the fall of 1968.

At the outset, a process went into motion that invited questions relevant to opening up a more formal planning process. The entire campus community was invited to formally and informally submit detailed questions and issues. These in turn were consolidated and shared with the campus community as rather the basis of the more formal planning process. From the overall summary of this introductory process, the sample below of such issues and questions are taken from a fuller statement that opened the door to the planning process.

Source: "Comments on Goals at UNCC." Statement presented to the faculty and staff of UNCC, February 17, 1969.

We must turn to the questions now ready to be studied, discussed, answered, converted to practice, assigned resources, evaluated, and developed into a series of steps for accomplishment.

What is the deeply felt yet feasible belief about the undergraduate student and the function of teaching? By what patterns will the intellectual resources of the university be arranged? Questions of research and graduate study, together with issues related to centers of critical mass capable of attracting faculty, spring from the capacity to form, sustain, and renew an intellectual community. How to create and share authority in the academic precinct is among the most complex of issues, and is of special importance to a new university still open and uncommitted. What is to be the nature of the linkages built and sustained with the larger community, a question of contemporary importance as the lines between universities and society may become less distinct, What systems and other instruments will be in order for decision-making in resource planning, allocation, management, and evaluation?

To take up such questions led to a study of how best to conduct the planning. The suggestions rejected were a single internal planning committee, the employment of a consulting firm, or the appointment of a larger commission to represent both internal and external constituencies. Instead, the idea that gained acceptance was evolving the form of a "study seminar" to include faculty, staff, administrators, students, patrons, and an external specialist noted for competence and interest in the chosen topic. A "seminar" would focus on a particular question, as those above, in depth. Moreover, throughout these focused discussions, a background question would be kept in mind: How might the land-grant university idea and history be adapted to become an urban metropolitan mission? This vision remained strong in the chancellor's interest. Such new inventions as "Urban Observatories" were also under consideration. Young specialists at UNCC were interested, notably Norman Schul, later dean of Social and Behavioral Sciences, and Larry Owen in institutional research. They became helpful colleagues in critically reviewing university planning models.

Importantly, leaders of Charlotte, a city exploding into a major banking and financial center, supported Chancellor Colvard in the adoption of such ideas. Soon to be established, for example, was a new industrial research park, an inventive partnership between UNCC and Greater Charlotte. Moreover, the urban tensions during the Washington stay had quickened my interest in adapting the land-grant university model to metropolitan regions. This brought to me some new professional opportunities, including membership in the Urban Affairs Committee of the National Association of State Universities and Land-Grant Colleges. Invitations came to speak of the challenges to urban life then mounting and what it might mean to the missions of both established and new universities. Such excerpts as follow suggest the influence of longstanding models in the land-grant institutions for rural development and how they might be modified and employed in urban contexts.

Source: "The Land-Grant Universities in an Urbanizing Society." Paper presented to program leaders and supervisors of the Cooperative Extension Service, Atlanta, GA, October 14–19, and Baton Rouge, LA, September 30–October 4, 1968.

The forces of the urban industrial society have had a cataclysmic impact upon the formidable system of the Cooperative Extension Service.... [There has been] a massive reorientation of the American scale of values from locality and parochialism to national and international purposes. Major planning and action events have come to be centered in metropolitan areas, the industrial establishment has joined with labor and government as visible centers of power, and legal pressure along with sweeping social change and movement have reduced the representation and influence of rural people in the legislative processes.... The old categories of rural and urban are no longer useful in planning the future by the land-grant colleges and universities, except as they continue to enrich our understanding of the distinguished heritage of agriculture, rural life, and the colleges themselves. The [land-grant] colleges, including extension work, must be willing to become more inventive with reference to their own reforms.

Given the size and complexity of Greater Charlotte, creating a new public university in its center would challenge the planners to find how best the institutions of the larger metropolitan region (the Piedmont) could themselves gravitate in closer relationship with each other and with the new university. Such a step would open wide the gates of creative public collaboration and administration, and strengthen the institutional framework for regional development.

Meanwhile, with widening social and legal reforms under way to address American challenges of race relations and human rights, the issue of building more comprehensive and community-wide collaboration was rising in the American scene. Questions became apparent on many fronts about how metropolitan-wide reforms in basic institutions might best be aided by public serving universities. Such influences added to my own growing assumption that universities must do more to assist such collaboration, and, especially, among the institutions bearing upon education

---

Source: "Adult Education and Community Conferences." Presented to the Pre-Galaxy Workshop, University of Maryland, College Park, MD, December 5, 1969. Also published in *Proceedings of the National University Extension Association*, Charlottesville, VA: University of Virginia, 1969.

> It is not unreasonable to ask if the university has not gone far enough, as a unilateral force, when intervening in community life. Rather, given the nature of urban society, should not the university devote more of its resources to strengthening the whole fabric of education in the community? Should it not help create new institutional forms, support them, prepare personnel for them, devise research and development plans, demonstrate and evaluate, all to enhance how every school and college might be better attuned to a more zestful and varied form of community learning?

When pondering the nature of an "urban-grant" university, attention had to be paid to how a new university might first demonstrate this meaning. While the wider concerns of the metropolitan community of Charlotte, Mecklenburg County, and the Piedmont Region of North Carolina could not be overlooked, one place to begin was with urban community education. A forceful and impressive renaissance had just begun in the city's urban schools and creative responses to challenges of race and equal opportunity were apparent. In the national picture, new concepts were circulating, including "learning societies" and their support with investments in "human capital." The UNCC aspirations embodied such ideas in concept if not in name: greater Charlotte viewed as a learning community to which the entire university would give leadership and inspiration.

Indeed, and not without elements of surprise and argument, rather than create a discrete division or "college of education," the new plan would call for an "Institute of Education," thus to engage the entire university with a concern for "education." And emerging from the urban tensions of the 1960s was greater interest in such notions as "community education" and "community schools." Voice after voice had begun to point out the need of the university system to offer more support of, and interest in, the elementary and secondary schools. This idea would become of ever greater importance in the years ahead, for rural and urban centers alike. Such an emphasis would also urge that community-wide learning be stimulated and supported in other community institutions and groups. The following excerpt was part of a call for new models capable of bringing community schools and universities into such cooperation.

Source: "Reflections on Urban Community Education." Paper presented to the Fourth Annual Convention of the National Community School Association, Detroit, MI, December 12, 1969.

> While countless other aspects of urban planning and development require the talent and knowledge possessed by colleges and universities, none of them has the priority that attaches to a new collaboration between higher education and urban schools.... While flexibility must obtain, and recognition be given to the importance of institutional integrity, educational institutions must be more willing to bend individual interests in the service of cooperative action. Herein rests the promise of sensible urban development.

[Another challenge would insist that] our imagination must soon catch up with the technology of telecommunications.... The meaning of "communicate" is to make common. Its purpose is the creation of community. In the same way, to publish is to make public. Both serve to create a public, meaning people with shared interests, the drive of our species to create and belong to communities. The creation of community, and to create a public of shared interest and purpose, must displace "rural," "urban," "agriculture," "commerce," and other limited nouns. [Our] society starves for renewed conceptions of education for such a public.

From the outset of our stay in Charlotte there grew a sincere appreciation of the pride expressed for the presence of a new and major university. Both the location and the creative process under way seemed right for demonstrating how such a relationship, and the actions sponsored therein, might well produce a model for uniting a metropolitan community and in which learning would expand into common practice. This also would mean advancing a citizenship for which continuous learning would be the hallmark. Both Charlotte and UNCC seemed ready to define and explore this, one with the other.

Source: "Metropolitan Approaches to Urban Education." Statement presented to the UNCC faculty, UNCC, Charlotte, NC, January 13, 1969

Of equal importance [is] how continuous education may enhance basic citizenship, those skills and values necessary to perform effectively in one's family, community, nation, and, increasingly, in a world community.... Given the facilities of most communities

and the degree of mass media proficiency, too little
has been done to combine formal and informal education for citizen learning.... The ultimate outcome of
the educational enterprise is whether or not it helps
everyone to live better as a good human being, in good
communities, striving for good local government, and
enjoying good art and music.... And educational problems themselves involve not only the functions of pedagogy but also serious humanistic, political, economic
and social choices.

A BASIC DECISION

By MARCH 1969, UNCC planning was well on its way. Both philosophy
and methodology were being accepted as appropriate. National authorities
steadily arrived to challenge campus-wide study groups. A preliminary
plan was promised by the fall. More time became available to consider
other duties as outlined in the agreement with Chancellor Colvard: teaching at UNCC (a graduate course in adult education at UNC-Raleigh was
already under way); and writing a book on university outreach, encouraged by the W. K. Kellogg Foundation and already in process. Meanwhile,
Charlotte grew as a splendid place to live, and new friends and colleagues
joined to help fashion the plan for the new university. Not surprisingly,
Dr. Colvard never faltered in support of the respective assignments,

But other reflections had drifted to the surface. The efforts in
Washington and Charlotte, compared with the "line" administration
at MSU and WVU, were "staff" assignments. The earlier "line" functions seemed more to my favor. Moreover, a return to teaching at UNCC
risked delay as my duties in the Office of University Planning Studies
were judged by significant others as more important than a return to the
classroom. Vice Chancellor McEniry, helping me ponder the options, expressed strongly that the need was greater in planning and administration.

During this time, Francena, doing more with projects in continuing higher education, was exhibiting more activist interests in human service fields.

In April 1969, our occasional reflections were suddenly made more formal. An executive of an academic personnel search firm called on behalf of the Rochester Institute of Technology (RIT). As described previously, a previous and major assignment in the Washington years was to help develop the roles and location for the National Technical Institute for the Deaf (NTID). I had earlier declined an invitation to be a candidate for the presidency of RIT. Having been briefed on my detailed awareness of that institution, the search firm asked me to suggest persons suitable to become the RIT's president. After assembling several names and calling back to report them, a new question sprang out: "Might we add your name to the list of candidates?" After lengthy discussions with Francena and Thomas, who was then ready for high school, we found such an addition to be agreeable.

No need to elaborate further. In quick order, Francena, Thomas, and I went to Rochester to confer with the appropriate parties. Invited to accept the RIT post, we did so. Once settled, Francena would serve in a professorship with scholarly and teaching duties in a proportion and kind of her choosing. Having been part of its conceptual and establishment phases in Washington, we felt the privilege of seeing NTID through to completion. Also of great importance was the special challenge at RIT, founded in 1824, of helping define its course following the 1968 completion of construction of a stunning new campus for its eight constituent colleges. RIT, with deep roots in Rochester's past, and not unlike the startup of UNCC, faced a new and expanding future.

However, the decision was not easily reconciled. Given our ages, we could expect but one more significant professional chapter. The long desire for a full return to teaching appeared less and less likely. Our happiness in Charlotte would have to be found and nurtured elsewhere. We would enter into private higher education with our backgrounds limited largely to public institutions. But there were apparent similarities. Rochester was the hub of a major metropolitan region, and an older city of medium size that supported an exceptional array of educational, business and cultural institutions. It had been challenged by some of the urban and cultural tensions holding sway at that time. In short, in a place not unlike Charlotte, one could continue to advance the ideas of an unusual urban university. In the years to come, and at this writing some forty years later, it is good to know how UNCC would grow imaginatively into a noted university of considerable size and distinction.

We moved to Rochester in two segments: Francena and Thomas went first in late August to so that Thomas could begin his freshman year of high school with the rest of his class. I followed in October after completing planning duties at UNCC. It was a sad time, for we were departing a place for which affection was certain, both given and received, to begin anew at still another place, one still unknown and of certain complexity. The poignancy of departing Charlotte would never diminish. Of great importance was the loss of a daily partnership with Chancellor Colvard, an experience that would remain a highlight of my professional life. Indeed, my last meaningful act at UNCC was to center my reluctance for departing the colleagueship with him, this in an address to a gathering of city leaders who supported and helped found UNCC. My statement attempted to thank them and define Dr. Colvard's extraordinary gifts, yet remind others that the best plans in university life do not assure their accomplishment.

Source: "Reflections on a Departure." Remarks delivered to the Charlotte Rotary Club, Charlotte, NC, September 16, 1969.

> Chancellor Colvard is in process of bringing about a new kind of academic administration; he is "plowing new ground." As a humane person, he is allowing his humanness to flow into the sinews of the institution. He has

followed with invitations for all to participate in planning the institution's future. With a quiet and sympathetic magic, he has helped find tasks of importance and
then guide people into teams qualified to tackle them.
And he has not blinked when ideas outlandishly breaking all precedent come suddenly upon the table. Few if
any occupations surpass that of the university president
on challenges to personal character, the need of selfless
statesmanship, and the isolation in which high office
may place one. Dr. Colvard has won over them all...and
UNCC is superbly on its way!

By this time, the reader will have gained awareness of the esteem in
which I held Chancellor Colvard. His ways of administration would go
with me to the challenges and duties at RIT. The histories of the two
institutions differed greatly in dates of origin: UNCC newly founded and
RIT established in 1824. The former emerged mostly by means of public
support, while the latter evolved under private auspice. Yet both institutions resided intimately within their respective metropolitan centers and
the surrounding regions. Under Colvard's leadership, UNCC would be
successfully launched and, of this writing, is a large institution with unique
capacities for serving a major metropolitan community and region. And
his example and counsel, long and steadily important and accessible to me,
would continue until his death in 2007.

VI

$\mathcal{R}$OCHESTER AND $\mathcal{RIT}$, $\mathcal{P}$ART 1

$\mathcal{A}$ $\mathcal{C}$ULMINATION IN "$\mathcal{U}$RBANLAND"

THE INSTITUTE

DANE R. GORDON's definitive history of RIT, published in 1982, describes how a technological university evolved in a major metropolitan region.[8] In those and other accounts, one may learn how this historical project was led. They depict RIT's emergence as an innovative technological university. Actions of the respective presidents to help achieve this evolution are cited therein, including some from mine, the sixth president.

Accordingly, I ask to be excused for taking up a different theme in this book: an emphasis on the outreach of universities as embodied in adult and continuing education that enables the serving of local communities, regions, states, and nations around the world. Except when they seem

---

8   Gordon, Dane R. *Rochester Institute of Technology: Industrial Development in an American City, 1829–2006*. 2nd ed. Rochester, NY: RIT Press, 2007.

essential, specific institutional activities receive less attention. In moving to Rochester, New York, Francena and I served in an urban center of considerable distinction. It is one possessed of a unique history of relating community and academe. Moreover, our recent sojourn in Charlotte, North Carolina, had given us and our teenage son Thomas an experience about the place of a university in urban community life.

For an introductory glimpse of the Rochester Institute of Technology (hereafter RIT), four features deserve attention. The first describes how antecedent institutions merged to form RIT between 1829 and the 1969 opening to students of the National Technical Institute for the Deaf (NTID). The second refers to the remarkable leadership of Dr. Mark Ellingson, my predecessor as RIT's president for thirty-three years. The third outlines the unique partnership of RIT with the city of Rochester. The fourth sums up the "state of RIT" at the time of our arrival for the fall term of 1969.

BEFORE NTID

MY STATEMENT AT the inauguration ceremonies for the new campus of NTID drew from Gordon's history. I also drew from my efforts to help create NTID while serving in Washington, and in that connection from an early visit to RIT and Rochester. Preparing for the inauguration of the new NTID campus on October 4, 1974, I urged that we look at the history of RIT and how it evolved to the point of celebrating a new addition to a new physical campus. The aim of such remarks was to recall the sequence of events in the history of Rochester, from village to town, to its growing industries, and finally, to the city and the metropolitan area. This history, and how it has evolved, provided the context NTID needed to be the special institution it was and remained, both within its own right and within its evolution as a unique part of RIT.

Source: "Where is Mechanics Institute?" Address celebrating the new NTID campus, Rochester Institute of Technology, Rochester, NY, October 4, 1974.

On another October day in 1885, Eugene C. Colby came to Rochester from Boston to look into a job at a new kind of school, Mechanics Institute, which had been organized a few days before. A teacher of mechanical drawing, Mr. Colby had come to an interview with the new board of directors about teaching drawing and serving as principal. The visit lasted two days. The meetings took place in the offices of the businessmen who made up the committee led by Henry Lomb, head of the Bausch and Lomb Company and first chairman of the board of Mechanics Institute. As the discussions closed, Mr. Colby, in bewildered tone, exclaimed, "But, gentlemen, where is Mechanics Institute?" Lomb waved his arm around the room and said, "My dear fellow, this is Mechanics Institute!" Colby took the job and held it for twenty years.

Colby's question and Lomb's answer about Mechanics Institute, in 1885, was not to begin the institution we know today. Emerging from the Rochester Literary Company, formed in 1822, the Rochester Institute of Technology began as the Rochester Athenaeum in 1829. The dream of another committee of businessmen, it was led by no other than Nathaniel Rochester, the founder of the city [that] bore his name. Soon to follow in rented quarters would be Rochester's first reading room, the first kindergarten, the first meeting room for civic planning and the center for speaking, debating, and community ceremonies.

Fifty years later Rochester was well on the way as an important technical and cultural center. So Henry Lomb, an immigrant himself, and an observer of technical education in Europe, would join with others, employ Colby, and set Mechanics Institute in motion. Its mission would be to teach drawing, then engineering, arts, domestic science, and how to work and how to live. And the Athenaeum would live on, too, for in 1891 it would join with Mechanics Institute, so that two traditions, one cultural and the other technical, joined to form the Rochester Athenaeum and Mechanics Institute, and, in 1944, be renamed the Rochester Institute of Technology.

Thus the National Technical Institute for the Deaf became the fourth institution to be established and be made part of RIT. The orientations of the three previous institutions would continue. The first places the student at the center of the learning process. The second engages the surrounding community as part of good teaching and learning. The third makes general or liberal education arts the partner rather than the competitor of career training. In this manner, RIT learned from the outset to go its own way while sinking its roots in the culture of Rochester. Yet RIT learned how best to change with the times. The advent of NTID would also make remarkable how a private university and the federal government might properly be woven together. Thus would the hopes and plans of deaf people call upon the understanding of hearing people. At the same time, this new institution, one born of public sponsorship, was sure to challenge yet strengthen the resilience of the Institute as a private center of higher education.

MARK ELLINGSON

DR. MARK ELLINGSON became RIT's president in 1936 and served without interruption until my arrival on October 1, 1969. The accomplishments of that long tenure, while applauded and revered in Greater Rochester, have not been recognized as they deserve to be in America's academic history. During my years in the post, Mark Ellingson and his wife, Marcia, were devoted advocates and friends of my family and me. Without fail, the telephone would ring with his words of support when critical issues arose. His leadership of RIT built steadily and creatively upon the chapters outlined above, thus providing the basis for a dynamic technological institution. Such a record is not likely to be repeated. Yet his humility and desire to give me full latitude were so great that, until I overcame his reluctance, he refused to appear on the campus without my invitation or approval!

President Ellingson had a vision for RIT, and he gave his entire career to reaching it. Understanding that the rise of public community colleges would undermine RIT as a private two-year institution for career education, he set a course to form a technological university. His insights were as accurate as his personal talents were numerous. He mobilized the industrial leaders and families of Rochester in support of his small institution and guided them into service as board members and donors. He found small but struggling educational enterprises, moved them to RIT, and nurtured them into full academic divisions. Prime examples were the Empire School of Printing from Ithaca, New York; the School for American Craftsmen from Alfred University from Alfred, New York; and a Rochester proprietary school of business. And he would seize upon the interests of trustees, notably Hettie Shumway, to enter the national competition of over one hundred major colleges and universities desirous of hosting the National Technical Institute for the Deaf.

RIT began to grant baccalaureate degrees in the mid-1950s. Dr. Ellingson saw that the growth in higher education, the motley assortment of structures serving as the RIT campus, and changing land uses in Rochester's downtown all demanded a new campus location. For more than a decade he mobilized the energies and resources of RIT, completed a major fundraising campaign, put a team of five nationally known architects to work on a distinctive architectural plan for a carefully acquired thirteen hundred acres, and bonded a large loan from the state of New York. Sheer hope and courage entered the construction of the new campus! This immense project would stimulate more than a little skepticism, as when a trusted and notable colleague of an earlier day, learning of my appointment, exclaimed, "Paul, you are taking on the biggest white elephant in New York's higher education!"

President Ellingson possessed still other talents that were integrated into a rare charisma. He mobilized a small army of committed people on the campus and in the community. His support of and kindnesses toward the faculty and staff made them want to follow him, however arduous the goal. The same may be said of the board of trustees, forty-three strong in 1969 when I arrived, and largely made up of business and civic leaders. Ellingson toiled on his projects with countless others, as well as helping on theirs. Many were his skills no successor would likely emulate. One civic leader would say jokingly to me, "Mark knows exactly how all those in the community who like a martini want it mixed!" So, from a long familiarity with campus and community (he had been both professor and wrestling coach before the presidency), Mark and Marcia Ellingson developed and inspired a company of stalwart colleagues. They became my helpmates, and I often refer to their fellowship in the following account.

Dr. Ellingson also gave me a special gift beyond his continuous support and affection—the extraordinary linkage of the institution with

Greater Rochester. His entire career, and surely every waking hour, went to crafting such a partnership. His achievement enabled me to newly explore the notion of an "urban grant" institution, an updating of my service with "land grant" institutions. I also expressed to him an uncertainty and tension over my personal qualifications and interests for fostering career training in a technological mode. He assured me that the creation of a technological university was in process: what that vision would yield for the future was still open. In short, a new president, beginning in 1969 with a new campus, would have wide latitude in helping shape the outcome.

GREATER ROCHESTER AND RIT

THE FALL MONTHS of 1969 were given largely to getting acquainted with RIT and the community. I visited each of the forty-three members of the board of trustees, mostly at their workplaces. Many of the trustees were leaders of Rochester industries and agencies: visiting them on site gave me personal acquaintance with Rochester's business and industrial structures, especially when walking the factory and laboratory floors. So, I gained an overview of a city centered on science, technology, and the arts.

At the same time, these experiences gave opportunity to share my personal interests. I would have to examine them in light of new responsibilities. This meant organizing my beliefs again about how academic institutions help communities become better places in which to live and work. By this early sharing of experience and viewpoint, I could point out my early reactions to the new setting, an important urban community famed everywhere for its scientific and managerial strength. One need but mention its support of the University of Rochester, an eminent academic center with worldwide programs of music and art and an equally distinguished system of medical science and education. Other local colleges, museums, and cultural institutions also deepened my comprehension of a city where great corporate enterprises collaborate in support of science, technology, music, art, and medicine.

These tours of city enterprises helped me better understand the part I might play in a community willing to support other several smaller private colleges, each free to add a special flavor to dedicated teaching. There was also the willingness to create and add a public/community college, which, as an education phenomenon of the twentieth century, was a form of higher education established to enlarge opportunity for young people, no matter their station in life. There was also a special connective tissue in Greater Rochester that overcame the risk of such institutions being isolated activities. Taking account of the schools, libraries, science centers, art galleries, television studios, and newspapers, one could sense Greater Rochester as a kind of university itself. Such a notion, a city itself becoming a university in general form, sparked my first major Rochester address at the annual conference in 1970 of the Rochester Chamber of Commerce. Key points follow.

Source: "College and Community." Address delivered to the Rochester Chamber of Commerce, Rochester, NY, February 9, 1970.

> Over time, here and elsewhere, I have come to believe in the idea of preparing young people for needed vocations and professions; in the idea that learning by doing, by combining study with experience, is an important way to become a responsible man and woman; in the idea that a mechanic, a waitress, or a barber can go to school, one ice-slick night after another for a decade, rise in the order of things, or simply do better that which they are already doing; in the idea that taking an interest in one's own community, and doing it with imagination and enlargement, is one good route to prestige for a college; in the

idea that technology and art, culture and industry, can be wedded for the improvement of all; in the idea of a college which has embraced a city from a small and not very attractive island at its heart, and then fought its way to a fresher place; and in the idea of people of industrial purpose (like, among many others, the Rochesters, Lombs, Eastmans, Eisenharts, Gleasons, Gosnells, Gannetts, Shumways, Damons, and Clarks) linking arms with those of educational vision (like the Ellingsons) and all becoming more humane and productive by reason of it.

STATE OF THE INSTITUTE

MEETINGS WITH RIT's faculty and staff, by major divisions and, insofar as possible with departments, became a priority throughout 1969–1970. Since these units had completed the move from an old downtown campus to an entirely new one in the summer of 1968, a plan to achieve short-term adjustments in the conduct of RIT was clearly urgent.

By January 1970, I was ready to frame certain issues, tentative policies and next steps, especially those of concern to both the trustees and faculty. As to the former, it seemed proper to look carefully at RIT's mission in relationship to the enormous changes of technology leaping forward as a fundamental theme of human culture. An early introduction to these matters was shared as special papers for the board of trustees and the RIT faculty.

They attempted to characterize the central vision characterizing RIT. The statements included short-term policies and actions, especially those dealing with curriculum, student life, and budget needs. Of special interest loomed the challenges to the whole of education being brought by the growing strength of electronic innovation and application. Such trends would be of continuing importance to RIT and shape its future. With this in mind, my first significant remarks to the RIT trustees and the faculty emphasized that (1) student education and preparation for work must not only emphasize productivity but also adaptability for continual change and innovation; (2) all colleges and universities would be called upon to achieve better cooperation between public and private education and between secondary and higher education; and (3) RIT must be among the leaders determined to increase the efficiency of American education and reduce its excessive fragmentation.

Source: "An Uncommon University an Overview." Remarks delivered at a meeting of the board of trustees, Rochester, NY, January 20, 1970.

The devastation [that] technological change can bring to human competence and enterprise is altering the historic view of the school and college as mainly for the young. People, regardless of their formal schooling, are now forced continually to refresh thinking and experiences, whether for "making a living or living a life." Academe has been generally slow to blend learning technologies with effective utilization of teaching talent, the result of rigid curriculum and admission requirements, faculty recruitment and rewards too narrowly based on research training and competence, and failing to understand the changes in need, attitude, motivations, and interests of our students. We must resolve to examine every aspect of the student experience—grading practices, the contribution of residence halls, the difficulties of renewing faculty competence, the length of time spent in college, and the balance of class work and independent study.

Source: "A Statement of Beliefs." Remarks delivered to a faculty assembly, Rochester Institute of Technology, Rochester, NY, March 3, 1970.

The Institute should:

remain steadfast in preparing people for needed vocations and professions in urban technological society by means of inventive curriculum design, extensions in cooperative education, and the fusion of technological and general studies.

continue as a community-centered institution of higher learning, and doing so with expanding intellectual horizons. No city is any longer a unitary phenomenon, but, rather, a contributor to the national and international system. Technology has become the ruling theme of national and international systems.

bring into concert its various learning resources and technologies, including those of its National Technical Institute for the Deaf (NTID), in order to influence the efficiency of learning, without doubt a frontier of American education as whole.

sustain itself as a private institution, with an inventive core of studies attuned to the linkage of science, technology and culture, and all embodied in research, graduate studies, and service components designed to help meet public educational needs.

NAVIGATING 1969–1970

MY INITIAL ACADEMIC year of 1969–1970 was both memorable and strenuous! A redesign of the central administrative structure was begun and completed. This process fostered a fellowship with leaders of extraordinary achievements. Important among them was Alfred Davis, vice president for communications and development. He had compiled decades of an unparalleled record of fundraising and public service, serving also as general advisor to President Ellingson. In my term, Davis also took up the duties of administrative secretary to the board, and continued with extraordinary distinction (even during his retirement) until his death in 2008.

Edward Curtis Jr., an executive of the Eastman Kodak Company, briefly assumed the post in communications and development before turning to important public assignments in Greater Rochester. Another advisor to Dr. Ellingson was Dr. Leo Smith, vice president for academic affairs. Approaching retirement, and holding a vast knowledge of RIT, Smith became special assistant to the president for general administrative affairs. He was joined in the president's office by Loma Allen, with an equally vast civic knowledge and leadership in Greater Rochester, as special assistant for community relations. As administrative assistant to the presidential office, Josephine Dudley gave my efforts uncommon and loyal support throughout my full term and beyond.

During the initial year, the vice presidents for finance and student affairs, after years of hard and effective work on the new campus development, accepted posts elsewhere. To the first came James Buchholz, chief financial officer of the American Council on Education, who served with distinction for most of my term. Dr. Fred Smith came from a deanship at Oakland University to take the post in student affairs as well as a new deanship of complementary education, a post charged to animate the residence halls and other resources of the entire campus for the advance of campus-wide learning.

For the second year, perhaps the chief new appointment was that of Dr. Todd Bullard, then president of Potomac State College, as provost and vice president for academic affairs. He is cited earlier as a key colleague at West Virginia University. Ostensibly as chief operating officer, Dr. Bullard would serve with great effect throughout my term before departing to the presidency of Bethany College in West Virginia. A new and related post was also created during the year, that of vice president for instructional development and planning, and filled briefly by Dr. Edward Todd before he departed to a similar post elsewhere.

In this creation of a new administrative team, of great importance and pleasure was to include Dr. Robert Frisina and Dr. William Castle, director and dean respectively of NTID. Both men, with distinguished careers of national and international importance in the education of hearing-impaired people, had preceded me by a year or more as the first leaders on the campus to initiate NTID. A major activity in 1969–1970 was to secure final approval of the US Congress for the construction of NTID facilities on the RIT campus. Of course, the always-present challenge of NTID had grown ever more visible: how to devise and operate a model that would enable the integrated resources of both RIT and NTID to serve effectively as many as fifteen hundred students with serious hearing impairments.

A serious issue challenged that initial year, and became apparent upon my arrival: an alarming budget deficit in an institution of some four thousand full-time students and a similar number of part-time evening students. In my first year, the recorded expenditure budget ran to $23 million with a deficit of $2.7 million. Given the details of moving to the new campus, this deficit of 10 percent was not fully understood until late in 1969. In the background was a permanent endowment of $40 million that could give minimum help, but obviously needed much enlargement in the years to come.

These circumstances produced a wave of collaborative activity and planning on the part of the institution's faculties and leaders. A rare willingness arose among them to correct the imbalance. Immediate plans surfaced to enlarge enrollment growth by such newly attractive programs as a School of Applied Science and a resolve (and a new deanship) to link more effectively with community colleges in the northeastern region of the United States. The gap had to be closed quickly and new financial plans and procedures established.

At the same time, new experiences brought about a different kind of campus than had existed for the many years in Rochester's downtown. A new and small city had formed, with distinctive academic halls, large residence centers, food services, libraries, and support structures such as parking facilities. For an early period, the campus was bleak and awaited landscaping and new architectural features.

A second crisis in that initial year took root in the student protest movements throughout 1969–1970 in the nation as a whole. RIT was not excused from them! Many hours and snow-filled nights found Francena and me tramping "the quarter mile" to the residence halls to visit with students, learn their views, and come to know them as individuals. Characteristic of acutely felt events on an academic campus, leaders surface, as some did on this occasion. One such memorable faculty leader was Stanley McKenzie. A young scholar in studies of Shakespeare, Dr. McKenzie, viewed as a rising star in the faculty, was elected president of the faculty body on the same evening that the board of trustees approved critical actions explained below. His career continued to blossom, carrying him over time to become an esteemed teacher and scholar, dean of the College of Liberal Arts, provost and vice president of RIT...and also as an older and brotherly friend of Thomas, our son.

One might say, then, that in academic 1969–1970, two history-making challenges topped the agenda: the first was the continuing adjustment to a new campus, and the other the national events mounting through the year to climax in May 1970 with the tragedy of students killed at Kent State University, and subsequent student rebellions and conflicts throughout the nation. As did other colleges and universities, RIT found itself in round after round of discussions and issue resolution. It is a matter of pride and good memories that the official leaders of students, faculty, and at special meetings of the board of trustees and administrators all joined to meet and learn from each other rather than damage RIT by hostility.

Source: "On Crossing to the Seventies." State of the Institute address delivered to the faculty and staff, Rochester Institute of Technology, Rochester, NY, September 9, 1970.

[In May of academic 1969–1970], the events stimulated by the tragic affair at Kent State University were highlighted by two unforgettable experiences at RIT. The first, which will be remembered in all the years to come, concerns the unanimous action of the faculty Policy Committee to suspend classes for two days, May 7 and 8, in order that all members of the Institute could join in what came to known as the "alternate university"— that is, discussion of issues [that] the times had brought to the fore. The premise of the Policy Committee for such action was that this unexpected moment should be used to foster campus trust and confidence. Another event, on the evening of May 14, found some twenty-five hundred students, faculty, and staff gathered in the Union after a campus march for a candid and responsible discussion, thus marking a milestone in the movement forward as a truly authentic university. The Institute developed greater understanding and tolerance in May 1970. All learned in some measure that the doctrine of a true university is found in its insistence that all views are heard and that respect be accorded the holders of each.

After my initial academic year, the critical events in May 1970 joined to welcome, with some relief, the opening of the second year. The past year had been one of learning, review, and building an acquaintance with an institution and its people. Throughout that period, I had come to think of RIT as an uncommon institution indicated by the nature of its evolution since 1829. I found RIT to be unmistakably authentic, with a disposition to distinctiveness, innovation, and renewal. I also came to employ an "urban" prefix as a direct logistical reference. RIT bore the print of locating and being financed considerably by a major metropolitan area, itself an interesting example of an urban aggregation of people in contemporary society. Accordingly, the principles underlying such an institution became the core of my first annual welcoming paper for the faculty as the 1970–1971 academic year opened. Moreover, this paper outlined a strategic planning program, one with goals and steps for both short and longer periods of time.

Source: "Additional Remarks on Goals." Faculty seminar on the future, Rochester Institute of Technology, Rochester, NY, September 15, 1970.

[I would propose] that we think of the Institute as an "uncommon urban peoples' university." [Thus we would] explore and practice how best to sustain such a university as an advanced form of sensitive and humane community in which people live and work together cooperatively, democratically, and affectionately.

A "peoples" university would practice a special flexibility, formal and informal methods of instruction, full or part-time, in day or evening, in class, by television and other media, on one's job, all with the view of enabling the learner to proceed at his or her own pace. [Such a university] would also serve as a dynamic non-partisan center of intellectual and cultural influence in the immediate community, the region, and in society at large.

[We would have] the Institute as expert on the usefulness, implications, and meaning of technology in contemporary society. [Also to be stressed] are such themes
as viewing technology professionally as the training
ground for technical manpower, technology viewed lib-
erally as a ruling theme of culture for the solution of
human problems, and in relation to the humanities, art
and communication.

We would explore and advance the Institute's form as a
sensitive and humane community in which people live
and work together cooperatively, democratically, and
affectionately. Among the most imperative and urgent
challenges of our time is how a university may demonstrate this collaborative wisdom. If not in a university,
where else may such values be better practiced?

RESHAPING OUTLOOKS ON ADULT EDUCATION

IMPORTANT AMONG SUCH ventures was my continuing membership on the
board of trustees for Gallaudet University in Washington, DC. This first
college or university to serve deaf students was established in 1864 and
signed into law by President Abraham Lincoln. In addition, the opportunity arose for me to chair the Committee on Higher Adult Education of
the American Council on Education. This joined a related post of serving as the North American vice president of the International Council
for Adult Education. I was grateful to RIT authorities for supporting
such endeavors beyond the RIT campus; they also advanced my imagining RIT's future in global scale. And these broader challenges stimulated reflection and writing on serving the public viewed as a learning
community.

Source: "A Glance at the Future." In *Handbook of Adult Education*, edited by Robert M. Smith, George F. Aker, and J. R. Kidd, 151–165. New York: The Macmillan Company, 1970.

The gales of change are sweeping across the entire world. New forces—in Europe, in Asia, in Africa—are shifting the balance of power within their societies. New populations are demanding more voice in the management of society, as students are demanding more voice in the conduct of their own education. The United States among other countries is moving toward an entirely new life style, toward a more open society, and temporarily a more explosive one.

RIT and its diverse urban setting, together with the growth and widening demands of education, required more study of what meaning should be given to my interest in continuing adult education. How the field had developed and what forces had stimulated that development needed to be clarified. These subjects grew rapidly, not alone for more understanding of them, but also serving to underscore creative steps that might be taken at the Institute. My writing continued this emphasis.

Source: "The History and Philosophy of Adult Education." Lecture delivered at North Carolina State University at Raleigh, Raleigh, NC, September, 1970.

Five creative traditions of adult education fall within its compass. The first is found in the borrowings from Great Britain, especially as they stimulated the "Evening Schools and Colleges." The second uniquely American tradition is found in the extensive, far-flung system of county agricultural agents, the Cooperative Agricultural Extension Service, and how both are rooted in the federal government through the US Department of Agriculture and the land-grant universities, local county governments, and in a multitude of voluntary organizations. The third uniquely American tradition has been the more recent idea of the community college. We have yet to see in full the outcomes of its place in continuing adult education. The fourth and now exploding type of institution is that of the "conference center," a specific physical structure at universities, hotels, and also as private hostels [that] function between campus and community. The fifth innovation now looming in the whole educational enterprise is that of electronic technology and its role rapidly unfolding to revolutionize the 'learning' society."

The rapid rise of interest in continuing adult education and its new instruments at the turn into the 1970s drew its leaders into strategic planning. Notable among these endeavors was the continuing commitment to this field of the W. K. Kellogg Foundation, including a major commission and study of how it might best be strengthened. The aim was to conduct a baseline study of where the field stood and what steps should be taken to strengthen it. The commission appointed to conduct such an overview was led by the Reverend Theodore Hesburgh, president of Notre Dame University. A national conference to introduce its efforts was conducted at that university. The privilege was mine of delivering the keynote address and later adapting it to local and other audiences.

Source: "Continuing Education and the Academics." Keynote address delivered at the University of Notre Dame, Notre Dame, IN, January 7, 1971.

For a long time, many conferences have been called in order that their participants could worry on a group basis about [the following]: why people learning off the campus seemed less important and legitimate than [those] learning on the campus; why professors dismissed the effort as the nocturnal routine of tired men with tired books; why scholars failed to include adult learning in their best works; and why so many academic leaders ignored the lore of continuing education as helpful to linking college and community…. However, the doors have opened to continuing education and to the people who promote it, in and out of the universities…. Thus Peter Drucker can say that adult education is central [because] "We have to restructure our whole educational system under the aspect of continuing education." [Similarly], John Gardner can also comment, "The continuing education movement does not need special encouragement. It will develop at a rapid pace regardless of what the colleges do."

As the need for competent American workers became more imperative in the advancing technological age, industry itself grew increasingly as a provider of training and education for its workers. Both in amount and investment, industrial education loomed as a partner alongside the colleges and universities. Indeed, Rochester could feature itself in this regard, by the long development of a partnership with RIT with the provision of worker education and development.

Source: "The New Learning System in America." Address delivered to the American Society of Training and Development, Rochester, NY, October 14, 1971.

Educators are beginning to realize that the dividing line [between campus and community] must be erased if the needs of higher education's popular constituencies are to be met. Adult educators can serve as an important bridge between these constituencies and the academy. Adult educators understand that today's young people want new emphases in education to help them relate formal course work to the needs of society, and to search for solutions to social and political problems. They understand that middle-aged and older citizens desire new arrangements in education to help them adapt to social and technological changes, and to gain the means of influencing future changes. They also understand that disadvantaged persons long for equal opportunities in education to help them improve their knowledge and skills, and to enter the mainstream of society.

The presence of a hostel devoted to continuing education had once been among my responsibilities at Michigan State University—that is, the W. K. Kellogg Center for Continuing Education, the second among such centers under the Kellogg Foundation rubric. Furthermore, thanks to the acquisition of a hotel on West Virginia's Cheat Lake, close by Morgantown, more experience with such hostels for continuing learning came my way. Soon I observed with interest at RIT the presence of its downtown "main street" building, affectionately termed "50 West Main." The spread of adult learning hostels for "nonformal" education, if understood broadly and flexibly, promised a new centerpiece of the learning society. Called upon to keynote the dedication exercises for the new International Center for Continuing Education at Columbia University, my experience would continue with such centers and their national and international purposes.

Source: "Continuing Education Centers and University Communications."
Keynote address delivered at Columbia University, New York,
NY, March 28, 1972.

The idea began on a run-down farm in Ryslings,
Denmark, where Christen Kold, impressed with the
ideas of a Danish theologian named Grundtvig, proceeded to build a meeting room for fifteen adult students
along with a living room, a kitchen, and a sleeping loft
for teachers and students. By the time of Kold's death in
1870, his own school had been enlarged to accommodate
one hundred students, and, more importantly, fifty other
residential folk high schools had sprung up throughout
Denmark. The idea was welcomed in the United States,
notably the Lyceums and Chautauqua series, the efforts
of local and regional agricultural societies, and, later, the
translation of the English worker schools into an extension credit course system. Eventually, Grundtvig's own
son, F. L. Grundtvig, would establish a folk high school,
"Danebod," on the shores of Lake Benton, Minnesota.
Harold Benjamin, a trainee there, would go to the
University of Minnesota in 1936 to direct perhaps the
first especially designed Continuing Education Center in
an American university.

My attention to continuing adult education widened in the opening
of the new personal and family chapter in Rochester. Alas, however, the
dynamics at RIT in the 1969–1972 period would shelve earlier commitments. I greatly regretted having to set aside my book on the public service functions of universities, which had been prompted by the support
of the W. K. Kellogg Foundation. But meanwhile, when the Notre Dame

University project on the future of adult education drew to a close, the Foundation suggested that a book might present the perspectives of the three university presidents most closely related to that effort. Thus, the opportunity arose to share some of the major themes of my own unfinished manuscript.

In Part I, the president of Notre Dame, the Reverend Theodore M. Hesburgh, described the Commission's work in terms of the growth in America of a learning society, future curricula, public policy, and needed institutional initiatives. In Part III, the president of Michigan State University, Clifton R. Wharton, summarized the extensive efforts of a special committee on lifelong learning at MSU. Part II contained my contribution, which took up relevant and needed reforms in universities, with special reference to civic policies and other related challenges in American society.

Source: "Universities and the Learning Society." In *Patterns of Lifelong Learning. A Report of Exploration Supported by the W. K. Kellogg Foundation,* by Theodore M. Hesburgh, Paul A. Miller, and Clifton R. Wharton Jr., 33. New York: Jossey-Bass, 1973.

> Replacing the institution-centered "system" of learning with a person-centered "non-system" is tantamount to revising the Ten Commandments. But in the decade of the seventies institutions and policies have been adopted that defy the time-honored procedures governing education and training during our lifetimes. These institutions and policies are already testaments to the awakening of institutions to the space-free, time-free realities of the new educational lifestyle. The new concept...did not come about through the initiative of educators alone. Instead, it reflects new realities and is a response to

turbulence in society—the shift from rural to urban patterns of living, the imbalances between social and technological innovation, the growth of new knowledge and the obsolescence of the old, and the mobility of the student.

THE MISSION PARADOX

GOING TO ROCHESTER and the Institute placed me in a learning system that stressed the preparation for jobs. RIT adhered to a long-standing mission of "making a living and living a life." The RIT liberal arts college was secure in its contribution to every student, yet surrounded by eight other colleges mainly organized for career preparation. Moreover, the historic support of RIT by Greater Rochester and beyond gave major interest to career paths, especially in applied science and technology. Members of the board of trustees were, to great extent, from the industrial community. Their view of the Institute as a dependable source of trained workers for their enterprises was a chief reason for financial support. Indeed, in my initial visits, some such leaders, even trustees, clearly defined the Institute as a training center for needed technical workers: a few expressed the fear that "turning RIT into a university" might undermine this useful business and industrial mission.

My education as a college undergraduate focused on the technologies of agriculture. But my first jobs and experience and my study while in military service stimulated wider intellectual interests and directed me to subsequent graduate study. Such gave me pause during the RIT presidential selection process, an uncertainty discussed openly with President Ellingson. Two sides to this tension were apparent to me. First, there was a distinctive wholesomeness in observing students intent on a vocation of their choice. This intention was also enriched by the impact and promise of RIT's College of Liberal Arts. Moreover, also present was the longstanding and distinguished Institute-wide program of Cooperative Education and its related practice of alternate terms given to carefully planned work experience in a student's major field. But there was also a risk that students would regard their college years as something to be endured for utilitarian ends rather than as a stimulation and enjoyment in a companionship of learning.

Throughout my term as the sixth president of the Institute, it seemed clear that RIT was set on a course to become an innovative technological university. Whatever the nature of its long-term outcome, the 1970s would establish certain definitive guidelines for the future. This would be influenced by RIT's uniquely inherent strengths and those of the larger community and society in which such qualities would be anchored. All would surely influence and guide me in making and acting upon assessments of the future, both of RIT and the greater community in which it rested.

Historic experiences and analysis of them spoke importantly of the productive role of RIT in the life of the Greater Rochester community. Each gave steadfast support of this essential partnership. Serving industrial and other forms of development proved basic to the Institute's outlook. Gordon's subtitle to his history of the Institute—"Industrial Development and Educational Innovation in an American City"—captures this historic partnership of campus and community. An unusual example of this union is one novel idea of the earlier Ellingson years: "contracts" being drawn with business corporations to exchange community financial support for the Institute's provision to them of purposefully prepared people.

There were other noteworthy programs at RIT; they evolved from industrial highlights of Rochester's development. Key examples were those featuring the graphic arts, an industrial core of Rochester, such as Eastman Kodak, Xerox, and the Gannett Newspaper Corporation. By reason of their presence and support, the Institute elevated printing, photography, and other graphic arts to levels of world-class eminence. The NTID, given to the arts and sciences of communication, was added. In many respects, these emphases, and others of the graphic arts, seemed a ready example for helping set RIT's future course. A significant intellectual challenge was to comprehend how RIT's College of Graphic Arts might best be developed. Such an eminent role could establish a major plank for an emergent technological university in partnership with acclaimed industries that had nurtured it through decades of development.

Source: "The Role of Higher Education in the Changing Industry of Graphic Communication." Lecture given at the Graphic Arts Technical Foundation, Pittsburgh, PA, March 23, 1971.

The first redefinition is to view industry, business, and government and other sectors of society as centers of learning in their own right. The challenge in this is how to put it together with higher education. This means that compositors, bi-metal photographers, and printing production managers are no longer to be produced in one-third of the life cycle, but are produced and reproduced across the length of a lifetime.

The second redefinition is of information and communication theory. I mean that somehow we must induce in people an ability to receive information, to retrieve it for their own use, and to develop and assess its relevance to other information. Education is being changed by a revolution in information theory and technology, and it is likely a basic concept [to fall upon] those industries that focus on the graphic arts and communication technologies.

The third redefinition will find us forging anew what the industry truly needs and what is possible for the academic institution to provide.... Education must have access to the industrial laboratories to make learning real for their students. Industries must have access to universities to stay in business. And while each will overlap properly with the other in certain educational and training functions, one point is clear: neither can do the task of the other.

After almost two years of administrative duty, reading, observation, and reflection, the inner logic of the Institute seemed clearly to have it foster the applied arts and sciences. Moreover, given the composition of its schools and colleges, this focus seemed clearly on the educational needs of business and industry. While such new programs as social work and criminal justice were added, the future would likely carry forward this fundamental orientation during my term and beyond. My aptitudes for understanding industry in a metropolitan community were rather undeveloped. But RIT confirmed an earlier view that universities thrive best when they build flexibly upon core orientations long in the making rather than by too sudden choices of new values and perspectives, whether of faculty, trustees, or administrators.

Along with such study of RIT's historical links to the larger community came a flood of opportunities for both Francena and me to participate in the educational and business functions of Greater Rochester. Francena, serving as a professor in the College of the Liberal Arts, gave attention to family-related courses and studies. She also worked with other groups to form a new child development center on the campus. The same interest carried her into community functions, especially leadership positions in the volunteer sector. Community-serving assignments grew also ever larger in my own portfolio. In both cases, they provided us significant experiences with essential realities of RIT in its home community.

Of special and early importance to both of us was the request of civic leaders to lead a commission to review, overhaul, and reorganize the United Community Chest (UCC) of Greater Rochester. This project gave us better understanding of the larger community and augmented my own sparse urban experience. Rochester had been among the first cities to suffer race riots in the 1960s. These threw light on United Way's shortcomings in meeting underserved needs; the new project, the Committee on United Community Chest Structure, aimed at correction. The task carried on for almost two years, resulting in a new and integrated membership body of three hundred members, a board of directors, a carefully organized nominating committee, a council of [agency] executives, a planning, evaluation, and allocation committee, and a committee on social goals and policies. The privilege fell to me of keynoting the metropolitan-wide conference to accept the report.

Source: "An Essay on Relationships." Keynote address delivered to the Conference of United Community Chest Presidents, Rochester, NY, August 4, 1974.

[When it comes to the impact of change we must all] understand and appreciate that people invest time and energy to become competent in their tasks and that change normally threatens stability by suggesting that still more time and energy must go to gaining new competence. People do not wish to risk losing what they have already achieved, especially personal competence and stability. However, they will respond to those who produce the change when the need for it is explained, when they are involved in understanding the problem, when they are warned that change is coming, and when they are helped to acquire the new competencies ahead of the change. Also, people who stimulate change often try to do too much too quickly, and explosive stress may be expected when change is urged, all at once, in work skills, in how people officially report to each other, and in social relationships.

Another and not unrelated assignment was embodied by election to the board of directors of the Rochester Gas and Electric Corporation. The years of service to follow brought a useful introduction to both the field of energy and official business practice. This door also opened to other appointments in the business field, especially to the board of directors of Rochester's Monroe Savings Bank (and of interest here the simultaneous service of Francena on the board of the Community Savings Bank). Another example was an appointment to the board of directors (and as chairperson for a period) of the Buffalo branch of the New York Federal Reserve Bank. All such experiences in the business sphere brought not only new experiences but also friends and teachers in the years to come. One deserves special mention: Professor Eugene Fram of RIT's College of Business, who loyally served me as an advisor in such roles as above. Remarkably, he served RIT fifty years before retirement in 2007! He and his late wife, Elinore, became close friends and colleagues.

Balancing off these new experiences in a different but suitable direction was serving on the board of trustees of Nazareth College of Rochester. The years to come in that connection brought lasting friendships and further contrasts of educational missions in higher education. Trusteeship of a private liberal arts college provided another prism to view what was under way across town at RIT; the mix also provided an evaluation of higher education in its possible future forms.

Along with balancing such experiences, both on and off campus, one that came to encompass both sites seems worthy of more detailed reference. Its initiation began in my initial year at RIT, when the latter joined other sponsors to invite and help conduct a yearlong Urban Seminar in Rochester under the leadership of the Brookings Institution in Washington, DC. The seminar attracted one hundred Rochester leaders, especially younger men and women committed to active and continuing volunteerism. This continuing seminar was led by appropriate leaders, both in and out of the local area. Having experienced new career experiences in Washington and Charlotte, NC, that dealt with urban affairs, joining in the Brookings Seminar became a worthwhile experience for consolidating urban insights to help support the new job at RIT. Several papers had also been written in the transitional period, especially on the special challenges of developing the outreach of urban universities.

Given RIT's historic immersion in Greater Rochester, the seminar seemed apt for facilitating the development of RIT as a model for an ever more urban America. During the 1960s and beyond, the turbulence in American cities wrote a unique chapter in American history. This was a time when legislative and judicial reform was prompted with reference to minorities. This advance moved more quickly than innovations in metropolitan planning, despite valiant supports of such private sponsors as the Ford Foundation and such acclaimed models as the University of Wisconsin at Milwaukee. It was also a time for challenging universities to better cope with the growth of such tensions in American life, which grew ever larger in my own perspective.

Source: "Societal Impacts of Higher Education." Lecture delivered at the 1968 Forum for Institutional Research, San Francisco, CA, May 8, 1968.

The function of higher education is not to build subways or run the police department but to help people understand the possibilities and limitations of civic life expressed through social, political, and economic institutions. Educational "service" in the modern community involves trying less to alleviate felt needs than defining and analyzing public needs; and, moreover, teaching the dialogic disciplines of civic decision-making.... There is too little linkage in trying to tackle essentially metropolitan problems with revenues drawn from and shared with many competing jurisdictions. Moreover, there is the rise of cities to strain the concept of federalism.... The disorganization of the modern city is the contemporary challenge point [and] this means examining the gulfs... between economic levels, race and other cultural groups.

The period between serving West Virginia University and coming to RIT challenged me as a rural sociologist to widen my interest in urban affairs: chairing a White House Committee on urban problems and development; helping create a master plan for a new urban university in Charlotte, North Carolina; serving on urban affairs committees in national groups, such as the National Association of State Universities and Land-Grant Colleges; and experiencing the issues in public schools of American cities.

During the course of the Brookings Urban Seminar, the Rochester Museum and Science Center, one of Rochester's illustrious institutions, decided to close one of its programs. Called the Urbanarium, this center was designed to employ museum resources for enhancing public understanding of Rochester's urban challenges. Directed by Gene DePrez, a young and talented urban specialist, the Urbanarium seemed well fitted for an academic sponsor. After extensive consultation and discussion, both the program and director DePrez were invited to move to the RIT campus in late 1970. The W. K. Kellogg Foundation, with grants adding up to $500,000, plus support of the larger community, assisted the transition. Backed by the Brookings Seminar and the addition of the Urbanarium, RIT might thus broaden out from its long and concentrated support of the business and industrial growth of Greater Rochester. The opportunity of the joint happenings was to create at RIT a center for effective application of educative, innovative, catalytic, and coordinative skills. This center would come to assist and serve noncompetitively the great number of organizations and institutions intent on urban development in Greater Rochester. And of perhaps greater importance, it might lead in identifying and helping develop an added group of younger talented leaders of the community.

As the summing up of a professional challenge to link the past, present and future in clarifying a mission for RIT, several orientations would have to be integrated: the simplified and historic mission of helping students "make a living and live a life"; an urban metropolitan community in which RIT's roots were anchored; achieving a technological university of unfolding eminence in regional, national and international contexts; and building up ever stronger private and public auspices. Surely such demands would also have to take into account certain transitions in the external world that would affect the whole of academic life. In a more traditional sense, there also loomed in RIT's near future the need of policies and directions for teaching, scholarship, and outreach capacities sufficient to support appropriate doctoral degrees.

A TECHNOLOGICAL UNIVERSITY IN THE MAKING: REFLECTIONS

IT WAS MY custom, not unlike that found in other institutions, to sum up the "State of the Institute" at the opening of a new academic year. While this action normally focused on institutional development, options, and plans, it reflected on such themes as noted above and the main "outreach" emphases of linking campus and community. Following are brief excerpts relevant to RIT's efforts in this regard. These are taken from annual messages of institutional assessment to the faculty and staff. Each excerpt is geared to a pertinent issue or question as the 1970s unfolded at RIT, and for which the language then employed is relevant to the evolution then under way. The full texts of these messages may be found in a monograph organized by the two trustee chairs who served during my term, Arthur R. Stern and Richard H. Eisenhart.[9]

My initial address to the RIT community, when opening a new academic year, strove to define a model and a mission capable of honoring both RIT's long history and my dream of how it might distinguish itself as an emergent yet distinctive technological university. Perhaps needless to say again, this form was rather a dream springing from the past thirty years of my experience, with the flavor of pondering how the magnificence of the land-grant university might best be emulated and given direction in urban America.

Source: "On Crossing to the Seventies." State of the Institute address delivered to faculty and staff at Rochester Institute of Technology, Rochester, NY, September 9, 1970.

The Urban Peoples University would concern itself with both the young and those no longer young. It would interest people in further learning, whether at home, in the classroom, by means of the media, or on the job. Such a university would function fifteen hours a day, six days a week, for the full course of the year. While most institutions are not of this model and will not be in position to adopt it, few are closer to the vision than RIT. A question that must be basic to the planning and development of the Institute in the decade of the seventies is this: how shall we modernize and project the distinctive elements of the Institute, and examine them in light of educational needs in urban society?

---

9   Stern, Arthur R., and Richard H. Eisenhart, eds. *Paul A. Miller, Speeches and Papers, 1969–1978*. Rochester, NY: RIT Library, December, 1979.

Whatever the planning and outcomes of such anchoring definitions for RIT's future, the initial period at RIT would also have the imperative need to consider the future of the National Institute for the Deaf. Of course, this sentiment was strengthened by the experiences and memories therein of my 1966–1968 stay in Washington, DC, and serving among other original helpmates that brought this new institution into being. Not only did it join Gallaudet University as one of the two most significant academic institutions for hearing-impaired and deaf young people, but NTID was one of a kind, unique in the whole of education, in that it would, albeit with public auspice, be also part of a private academic institution. A crucial approach would be required, on the one hand, to provide RIT support to NTID and for the latter to share with RIT an evolution of fresh insights about human learning.

Source: "Perspectives on the Seventies." State of the Institute address delivered to faculty and staff at Rochester Institute of Technology, Rochester, NY, September 13, 1971.

[We must] help the National Technical Institute for the Deaf to become the great national center for deaf education that it is destined to be, and, in time, the great international center it is possible to be for research and development on human learning. And, moreover, NTID must function as part of a larger learning community, and help RIT remain alert to fresh ways of disseminating its strengths.

In detailed histories, each chapter of RIT's evolution had grappled with the specifics of providing job training experiences to Rochester citizens of differing ages and backgrounds, as from its mission statement the phrase of "making a living." With the success of achieving a stunning new campus and related program visions, the other phrase in the mission—"living a life"—had taken on greater strength. Of course, this was intended to rethink the various meanings of how one thousand one hundred years of institutions called universities had been widened and deepened. Moreover, in the latter half of the twentieth century, social, economic, global and technologic trends were combining to elevate and challenge the principles of academic life.

Source: "The Locus of the Educational Adventure." State of the Institute address delivered to faculty and staff at Rochester Institute of Technology, Rochester, NY, September 18, 1972.

> The academic institution enjoys an ancient mystique [that] finds citizens thinking of it as an advanced form of human enterprise. People the world over, most of them not having entered a college door, admire the idea of the college and want it to succeed.

> Why people are wounded and enraged when this admiration is betrayed springs up in part when teachers and students fail to think about and create what is presumed to be true and what is thought to be beautiful. This intrinsic value attributed to a college obligates every teacher and student to reflect upon the demonstration of the college itself; in short, is what it practices worthy of emulation.

While the overall missions of universities were in need of examination in the 1970s, another dimension was also emerging. This trend dealt with the upswing of students of all ages and backgrounds desirous of participation in both on and off campus programs. On this front, it seemed clear that RIT, throughout its long history, had made itself into a servant of students of all ages and backgrounds. Accordingly, the whole panoply of university life in teaching, research and service, and this in relation to a globalization of human activity, was demanding new forms of support and interpretation. And RIT had brought forth a unique model that had been developed and deeply rooted in the life and industry of Greater Rochester.

Source: "Reflections on a New Chapter." State of the Institute address delivered to faculty and staff at Rochester Institute of Technology, Rochester, NY, September 17, 1973.

It is safe to say that RIT would not be here today, nor Rochester the technically competent city it is, without the unswerving attention paid by this institution to sharing its teaching with part-time adult students. [But] at most colleges, continuing education has remained an orphan restrained in the back room, which is remarkable when we know that the best result of going to school is to learn how to learn, continuously and eagerly, as living a life reveals new puzzles. RIT, however, saw in continuing education a basic way to extend the teaching function and to elevate the competence of a whole community.

Sizing up RIT in the early 1970s in response to the widening and deepening of university functions would recognize the strengths of history. Of special importance were the long relationships with community and industrial leaders of Rochester itself. Despite the fact that RIT's long development was less known in the academic world than it properly should be, many decades of this evolution wrote the unique story of an especially vibrant relationship given by the local community to institutional creation and operation.

Source: "Finding the Way." State of the Institute address delivered to faculty and staff at Rochester Institute of Technology, Rochester, NY, September 16, 1974.

Deserving of special attention is the special tie between industry and RIT, in Rochester to be sure, but increasingly beyond. RIT and Rochester demonstrate how the tie surmounts the not infrequent unease between the academic and corporate worlds, and accept both the differences and similarities inherent in the work of the business firm and the college. This is an unusual inheritance.... Corporate leaders, the trustees and others, even as they guide their own firms across troubled financial waters, continue to depart their desks when asked, plunge into the fundraising fray, go to meetings by day and by night, and perform for RIT overall with the precision gained from evident homework.

The energies and resources of RIT, accumulated since the founding in the early nineteenth century, had been mostly accumulated from the business and industrial communities. However, in the post-World War II period, the changes in business and industry as well as those in the academic world all mounted in volume and intensity. As the new campus opened in 1968, technological revolutions affecting both industry and universities were under way and being felt. To meet the stated goal of becoming a uniquely organized technological university, RIT's visions, anchored deeply in Rochester and upstate New York, would require new visions fresh responses, and creative explorations.

Source: "To Make a Living and to Live a Life." State of the Institute address delivered to faculty and staff at Rochester Institute of Technology, Rochester, NY, September 16, 1975.

The meaning of work keeps growing as one of the most volatile parts of life. We once worked in America to save.

We worked next to consume. We seem now to work for enjoyment. In the bargain, even the idea of capitalism has changed. Every challenge of American values begins normally by the desire to change the meaning of work.... Sir Eric Ashby, in his *Technology and the Academics*, [exclaimed] that one cannot be a good technologist without the capacity to weave technology into the fabric of society, and, since technology is inseparable from people and their institutions, it is therefore inseparable from humanism.

Given such issues as introduced in annual presidential papers, it grew ever more clear in the early half of the 1970s that RIT must be responsive to several important issues. The accommodation to a new campus, the acquisition of NTID, the balancing of income and expenditure, and a sense of how to debate mission issues, had all appeared. However, the nature of RIT as an emergent university of importance had still to be organized for debate over mission accommodation to the obvious and soon to be evident impact of a communications revolution. Although a single address could not encompass all such factors, in 1976 three pressing questions seemed in order.

Source: "Inconvenient Questions for an Emerging Institution." State of the Institute address delivered to faculty and staff at Rochester Institute of Technology, Rochester, NY, September 7, 1976.

[The first inconvenient question] is that we know too little about RIT's client system, [meaning] three decision-making processes. One refers to the decisions [that] bring students to a campus in the first place. The second relates to conclusions drawn by the students about the value of their college years. The third is the sum of decisions made by graduates, employers, associates, and friends who accept and evaluate those who graduate.

[The second inconvenient question] is: Are we still ready and fearless to acquire unusual programs and make them succeed? When we gave a home to the National Technical Institute for the Deaf (NTID), RIT assumed the risk, as it never did in printing or the crafts, of relinquishing the traditional status that came from teaching those who are the most gifted in society.... Is it possible that we tire from the daily challenge of the most audacious acquisition in RIT history? Are we still willing to risk institutional status and our own as well? Now that the first hurrahs are over, will we be apt at seizing upon the NTID presence?

[The third inconvenient question] is the offspring of the other two: How unconventional do we want RIT to remain? How willing are we as individuals to consign our careers to an unconventional college? RIT is curiously part academic and part community, which explains its rare strength, a form of hybrid vigor. Will we continue as leaders of community and continuing education? Will we blend study and experience into new forms of career education and planning? Are we ready to enhance cooperative education and take it beyond the method of financial aid it tends to become?

RIT's long association with business and industry, and its programs of cooperative education for students, had resulted in a pragmatic institutional culture of students and faculty. The challenge to administration to promote and execute appropriate planning could be viewed as the expected whim of the administrator, and then ignored. Accordingly, and given the challenge of the institution to broaden and deepen itself as a genuine university, planning had to be perceived as the pursuit of learning by not only trustees and administrators, but by all the constituencies on and off the campus.

Source: "Confidence or Fear in a Convulsive Time." State of the Institute address delivered to faculty and staff at Rochester Institute of Technology, Rochester, NY, September 6, 1977.

> Planning is a way of learning together. I believe this definition will help all of us to become more ready for a new and more turbulent future. Conscientiously done, such planning promotes our trust of each other, a form of human capital [that] RIT cannot, nor can any institution, do without. [I suggest] some questions for such planning that I hope will stimulate us to a common response: How shall we make use of our independence; what should we expect each student to learn…and how will we know that we and they are succeeding?

My final overview address would point to termination as RIT's president in the 1978–1979 period, although the likelihood was not yet fully decided. But it was a time to summarize some major strengths that would be called upon to determine RIT's future. RIT had overcome the strains and costs of joining the building of a new campus to the needs and challenges of how best to become a genuine university. Moreover, its long history had been anchored and shaped in ways that would not only see it become a genuine university but one also possessed of groundbreaking emphases in the years ahead

Source: "RIT: Living at the Level of its Time." State of the Institute
address delivered to faculty and staff at Rochester Institute of
Technology, Rochester, NY, September 5, 1978.

RIT is truly at the threshold of emerging as a distinctive
technological university with an international identity.
But many, including me, would wonder what [its] role
should be. Should we turn out technologists prepared
to be leaders and shapers of our burgeoning technological society? Or should we, as one [foundation executive]
sternly told me years ago, stick to training technicians
and "leave the hard questions about technology and society to the major universities."

The first RIT strength flows from Greater Rochester. A
renowned center of science and technology, laced with an
unusual artistic and cultural life, Rochester is the natural
home of an institute of technology. Its intellectual and
industrial composition makes of Rochester an international city.... As we know, the RIT-Rochester relationship
is one that requires continual revision and cultivation.

The second strength resides in RIT's authentic history. It
is a history of big leaps and big risks, challenges all. It had
served to make programs work that had failed elsewhere,
built a new campus, added upper divisional studies, and
welcomed NTID. Major changes have triggered upheav-
als from time to time. Yet the Institute never swerved
from its two central functions—career education and a
penchant for community educational service.

The third basic strength takes root in RIT's diversity of effort. This diversity enabled RIT to accommodate the swings and fads of higher education. A variety of professional curricula, an emphasis upon problem-solving, cooperative education, continuing education, and the blend, through NTID, of public with private, all help explain how diverse content and method have permeated RIT throughout.

VII

Rochester and RIT, Part 2

Personal Steps in a New RIT Chapter

EMPHASES AND VIEWPOINTS

SERVING RIT CHALLENGED me on how best to administer! Growing older and with more experience, I had learned that calling for change differs from striving to accomplish it. My foundation interest in social organization and administration came into fuller awareness and use. Slowing the pace, asking questions, involving others, formed a more dependable, albeit slower, process of change. There follows a series of projects, insights, and excerpts from my writings. Among them was my review of personal training and experience and what both were bringing to the surface for a consideration of new experiences. One among them responded to more understanding of certain foundation principles of academic administration. Such were explored in my chapter of a major book on applied anthropology. This collection of experiences, written by leaders of

American anthropology, was to honor Dr. Solon Kimball of Columbia University, who much earlier chaired my doctoral committee at Michigan State University.

Source: "Administrative Orientations from Anthropology: Thoughts of a College President." In Applied Anthropology in America, edited by Elizabeth M. Eddy and William L. Partridge. New York: Columbia University Press 1978/1987.

[An] interest in the interplay of microcosmic and macrocosmic projects becomes the centerpiece of the academic administrator whose way of looking at higher education is anthropological in nature. These two aspects, under the cultural view, eventually fall together. As they do, the administrator finds a way of viewing the academy in the holistic sense [that] is characteristic of the anthropological method. Moreover, this method embodies interests [that] veer to lateral rather than vertical channels of communication and to the ties between small and large systems. There is an emphasis upon working effectively within a given system of interpersonal relationships.... In the realm of personal outlook and style, one finds that applied anthropology offers much that is worthwhile.

The 1950s and the 1960s saw an extraordinary surge in the number of institutions and enrollments in higher education. Society had learned that it profits from higher education as much as does the college student. Community colleges in America were developed in that period on the basis of this awareness. They rode the wave of reform while adding some 1000 more in number in the 15 years after 1950. Thus the headiest adventure in the history of higher education exploded. Communities, private patrons, governments at all levels, all joined to accelerate the movement. Federal aid to education multiplied greatly in the 1960s. Professors perfected the skills for pursuing research grants and commuted regularly to Washington. Had not colleges and universities become the centers of societal development? It was almost true!

But new burdens would fall on academic institutions in a very short time. They were accommodating about half of all young people between the ages of eighteen and twenty-four. They inherited many of the tragic consequences of racism. They suffered with the anxiety of young people trying to make sense out of an adolescence that grew shorter as their schooling grew longer. Colleges bore the brunt of the experimentation with new lifestyles. And they could not ignore grievous issues, like the Indo-China War, which afflicted the American spirit. By the mid-1970s the signs seemed clear that the higher education boom in America was over: enrollments slowed with degrees in greater supply than jobs, costs climbed steeply upward, an occasional college folded, and signs appeared that the public prestige of academic institutions was beginning to sag.

These events and the predictions for the 1980s and beyond challenged every academic institution. They challenged RIT! Yet the One Hundred Fiftieth Anniversary Capital Campaign of the late 1970s was well under way with an introductory goal of $42 million. Happily, the diversity and uniqueness of the Institute's programs gave reasonable assurance of sufficient enrollments. But the lagging proportion of endowment value to income received from student tuitions posed a stubborn problem. Another issue grew: the Institute's tradition of serving the employed part-time evening student would be challenged. With softening enrollments of traditional students, other institutions developed an added interest in the nontraditional student. The Institute, long the major center for the part-time student in metropolitan Rochester, faced strong competition!

In the context of a dynamic of change in the composition of student bodies, a new factor loomed. With the movement through life of America's "baby boom" generation, and its nearly eighty million members, it seemed clear that a retired learning cadre was on its way to ask support from continuing education. This movement would become ever more entangled in the outreach and continuing education resources of college and universities, the rapid transformation of an industrial into a knowledge-centered society, and the rise of electronic networks capable of extraordinary speed and cost reductions for transmitting and sharing knowledge.

Source: "Negotiating the Retirement Rite." My preface to *Students of the Third Age,* Richard B. Fischer, Mark L. Blazey, and Henry T. Lipman, eds. (New York: Macmillan, 1992).

> The university may provide the campus as a new haunt where older people can initiate and locate a chapter [that] features learning as a major component of creative leisure. Moreover, the campus lends itself as a base (and support station) from which elderly people are able to launch service project forays in the local community [that], with encouragement, turn into useful research and community services. It is not impossible to imagine, as elder learners and retirees may grow in number, position, and influence on a campus, that suitable residential options nearby may be designed and provided them.... Citizens of maturity possess more discretionary time, and this may be devoted to the achievement of university objectives. They also bring to the campus a myriad of contacts with the wider world.

Greater Rochester was and is distinguished by a large number of competent people who were attracted to its educational, cultural, economic and scientific institutions. In 1977, with the leadership of the Institute's board of trustees; Richard H. Eisenhart, its chair and one of long standing with the Bausch and Lomb Company; William S. Allen, a major officer with the Eastman Kodak Company; and Loma Allen, civic leader and assistant to the president; joined with others to propose an institute capable of recognizing the lifelong learning interests of talented Rochesterians. This organization, in essence, recognized the desires of retired individuals in Greater Rochester, associated them with RIT, and gave encouragement and support of specific teaching, investigational and service projects they desired to pursue. Following a review protocol, some twenty-five Fellows would be appointed for specified terms, work on their projects, and meet voluntarily and monthly to discuss and learn from each other.

Termed the RIT Institute of Fellows, its members continued projects of merit (some works published) and of importance to both RIT and the community. One early example was developed by one of the founders. William Allen spent more than a decade in writing, testing and producing twenty-five bulletins and related training aids for the teaching of economics in elementary schools; he also demonstrated his methods as a volunteer teacher in Rochester pilot schools and others throughout New York. Also, following the Institute of Fellows, a more instructional unit unfolded and, during the administration of M. Richard Rose, my successor as president, the Rochester Athenaeum for Senior Learners emerged. Later, this invention became one of the pioneer institutions in the nationwide movement of Osher Lifelong Learning Institutes in American universities.

With widening visions of the electronic future, the 1970s at RIT linked several elements for lifelong learning. The Institute's computer capability was strengthened, as well as related academic curricula and organization. What eventually became the College of Applied Science and Engineering, with large enrollments in computer science and engineering, resulted from earlier and new units in the 1970s such as the, Engineering Technology and the "Institute College." Meanwhile, continuing and off-campus education achieved additional maturity and recognition. Inevitably, the advancing revolution in electronic capacity multiplied educational opportunity at ever greater distances from American sources and would extend more widely, even worldwide.

To forge that linkage quickly befitted an institution whose origins lay in technology and continuing education. To lead this effort in the mid-1970s, Dr. Harold Alford became dean of Continuing Education. While associated with Princeton University, Alford was identified with the innovative frontiers of continuing education and, especially, with the rise of residential learning centers on university campuses and elsewhere. Although his tenure at RIT was brief, Alford, conversant with the electronic revolution in information and communication, helped RIT unite its embryonic resources and activate "distance learning," even before this term appeared in the vocabulary. He led the design of RIT distance learning and introduced it to the southern tier of New York counties. In turn, RIT readiness for the future grew with new production and distribution facilities. More and more members of the faculty were prepared to use them. In these ways, the ground was prepared at RIT for the explosion in online and distance learning. These initiatives widened the vision of new social forces that would come to envelope all colleges and universities. Knowledge had become investment capital, and moved directly and quickly into the work plans of both industry and university. With the importance of continuing higher education assured, new partnerships between universities, corporations, and governmental agencies grew in importance.

Karl Mannheim, a perceptive student of social change in early twentieth-century circles, advanced his classic concept of Principia Media. By this, he meant those institutions or functions capable of special leverage in complex societies. Mannheim believed that once these levers are identified, their skillful combination and use can bring rapid and constructive change. My stay at RIT strove to emphasize four such "media"— education, occupation, technology, and citizenship—and the linkage between them as principal levers of the knowledge society. What the relationship between such levers involves and how to balance them on the academic work table became increasingly important.

Other questions also became ever more important. What new forms of educational partnerships in metropolitan scale were needed, those capable of wedding the public schools, universities, industries, and public and private agencies? How might an imaginatively redesigned school become the center of the urban neighborhood, reminiscent of how the farm family and local groups, including one-room schools, provided the glue for a partnership of rural advances? Reflecting privately on such questions and visions increased my desire to retire from administration and return to a professorship.

NEW PROJECTS AND REFLECTIONS

WITH ALMOST A decade of service at RIT, my thinking turned to issues geared to national and international realms: the globalization of business, the impact of technology upon education, and, increasingly, the proper balance between learning for employment and learning for citizenship. This included the challenge of how best to improve both the outreach to our own country and globally. Papers prepared as addresses to meetings and for publication turned in such directions, especially to how universities might best design and practice innovative ways of serving society in a globalizing world. Such presentations as in the two below are samples of a growing personal interest in the consequences of society's regard for technology as the fundamental arbiter of progress.

Source: "Educational Practice and Industrial Custom." Lecture published in *Proceedings of the Invitational Conference on Continuing Education, Manpower Policy and Lifelong Learning* (Leesburg, VA: National Advisory Council on Extension and Continuing Education, Leesburg, VA, January 10, 1977).

[But] now both education and industry confront an update of the criticism once leveled at the Industrial Revolution, when the factory system was damned for either destroying traditional values or for alienating and dehumanizing workers. A new critique has risen to charge that the technological society shapes and eventually dominates the institutions of life according to its own ends, among them both education and industry.

Source: "With the Hope of Doing Better." Lecture delivered at the Annual Conference of the North Carolina Adult Education Association, October 1, 1975.

We need today a new "hardware of citizenship," to collect, analyze, store, retrieve, share, and above all, communicate civic opinion…. One day soon, perhaps, adult educators will join the executives and the generals and seize some of the leadership of the media culture. We may see then how close we are to "citizen action and communication centers" in each community, rather as we think now of the post office, to provide person to person linkage, sharing a feedback at local, state, regional, and national levels. Otherwise, we shall lose citizen interest and competence for wise utilization and assessment of technologic employment.

The months of early to late 1978 witnessed a busy period of helping the Institute move forward. This meant tying up loose ends. After a review of options for a leave of absence in 1979, generously granted by RIT's board, Francena and I accepted an opportunity to be scholars-in-residence at George Washington University for part of that year. We would also spend a third of our time on three major projects as senior program consultants of the W. K. Kellogg Foundation. The first was to assist the Foundation with developing a landmark project on leadership development in the United States and internationally, a project designed to celebrate the Foundation's Fiftieth Anniversary. The second would prepare a report on how the Foundation might best initiate projects in sub-Saharan Africa. The third promised a challenging project of employing the last half of 1979 to evaluate the several programs of the Foundation in Latin America.

Our first stay in Washington during 1966–1968 had involved us with challenges emerging in both urban and international environments. The years in the RIT presidency gave maturity to such themes. This second Washington residence promised an opportunity to assess our respective interests arising in twelve academic institutions as students, teachers, planners, administrators, or trustees. During the 1979 leave of absence, Francena and I would take up goals springing from such involvements. Also of paramount importance was framing the direction of our forthcoming academic lives at RIT.

For this new adventure, numerous persons, in and out of RIT, helped us to develop such interests in significant ways. There are too many to name them all, but special note must be taken of nearly a decade of support by the RIT board of trustees, even for initiatives that seemed beyond RIT's traditional linkages to the business and industrial sectors. Board members recognized and trusted two rural sociologists and aided them to become immersed in a dynamic metropolitan community. Our gratitude went especially to key members of the trustees who helped enhance this learning: they also became supervisors, supporters, colleagues, and friends. Especially to be acknowledged are Arthur Stern and Richard Eisenhart, both of whom chaired the board during my tenure as president. They were splendid trustees, and stood close by me throughout my term of service, ever ready to help at any moment. Ritter and Hettie Shumway, vice chairman and trustee respectively, served similarly throughout our years in Rochester. They helped connect Francena and me to the rich cultural resources of Greater Rochester. Kent Damon, steady as a financial vice chairman of the board, was a giant in his impact. Having gained experience in public universities, I had moments of uncertainty in the early years at RIT lest I turned out to be improperly fitted for a private institution. But such persons, and many more, helped me across that chasm, never chastising me, even when it may have been deserved. Moreover, RIT's faculty and administrative officers, and many relevant leaders of the larger community, all expressed a general understanding and approval of forthcoming changes in our RIT responsibilities and life patterns.

So, off we went to Washington to arrive on January 2, 1979, for an intense period of study as visiting scholars at George Washington University. Francena turned to updating her interests in the American family, including the rising interest at that time in women's studies. My major emphasis would feature careful study of the social gains and unexpected consequences of science and technology. Our efforts on behalf of the W. K. Kellogg Foundation also began: this meant pondering the Foundation's interest in developing national and international leadership, the forthcoming Foundation projects in Latin America, and those to be initiated in Africa. Joining such initiatives would be that of devising our plans for teaching when back on campus in Rochester. We planned to return there in June, move into a newly purchased house in nearby Rush, NY, and organize our reports from the Washington studies. We would then depart for Latin America in early fall for the balance of 1979 and perhaps a month or two in early 1980.

While we were not strangers to Washington and Latin America, as earlier chapters indicate, a year to pursue these goals formed into a memorable period. With an apartment in the Georgetown area, and a nearby walking track (to satisfy our inclinations for steady exercise) and bus stops nearby, we were enabled to plan a private and professional schedule in Washington for daily periods of study, meetings, and consultations. These were centered largely at George Washington University (and our offices there), the nearby World Bank, and at the US Department of Agriculture. As members of Washington's historic Cosmos Club, we also found a useful place for meetings and dining with friends and colleagues. Time was also regularly reserved for visits to museums and landmarks not possible in our earlier days of more demanding claims on time and energy.

With notebooks filled, we returned to Rochester. After filing official reports to our sponsors, we made plans to leave in September for Latin America. Surprisingly, however, an additional project appeared during that busy summer period! Francena and I were asked to represent the International Council of Adult Education at the United Nations Conference on Science and Technology for Development to be held in Vienna for ten days in July. At this Conference (UNCSTD) we joined some seventeen hundred other nongovernmental representatives to meet in conjunction with the official delegates of UN member nations. Our summary report of that conference would go to the International Council on Adult Education and be published in late 1979. We attempted in it to portray the indispensable importance of adult and continuing education to the global challenge of social and economic development.

Source: "UN Conference on Science and Technology: Significance for Adult Education." *Convergence* 12 (1979).

UNCSTD provided a wide-ranging, global discussion, an international grammar (e.g., "The New International Economic Order") and countless reports and analyses [that] nations, disciplines, professions, and other organizations developed as part of the preparatory process.

The repeated references to the constraints of development acknowledged that development goes nowhere without popular understanding and participation; adaptation of technology to site-specific situations; the linkages of delivery systems to local institutions, including small holders; the disparities in dual economies (elite enclaves versus the traditional sectors); the importance of local, rural, and indigenous industry; and the critical need of local capacities for innovation and entrepreneurship.

We departed in September 1979 for the Latin America assignments, an unforgettable journey. We visited six nations to review the efforts fueled by Kellogg Foundation grants: Brazil, Colombia, Costa Rica, Dominican Republic, Guatemala, and Mexico. However, the highlight of the entire professional adventure was the month that introduced it, for it was then that we deliberately exposed ourselves to basic issues facing underdeveloped regions! We attempted this in Teresina, the capital city of the Brazilian state of Piaui, and the surrounding region. The purpose was to immerse ourselves in a large area of great developmental need and then strive to comprehend the challenges to social and economic development. The month also provided an unforgettable way to gain practice with the Spanish and Portuguese languages. From this introduction, we moved to the respective nations for the remaining months of our stay. Therein, the tasks were taken up largely with visits to major community sites of the projects: interviews were undertaken with their leaders on how Kellogg Foundation projects had affected youth and other populations.

A NEW CHAPTER AT RIT

HOME IN JANUARY 1980, the full weight of new responsibilities fell upon us. Francena continued as a professor of sociology in the Department of Social

Sciences. My professorship would be in a newly formed Department of Science, Technology, and Society (STS), also part of the College of Liberal Arts. We were assigned adjacent offices, along with one for a research/ assistant, all in the Liberal Arts building, a site happily but a few steps from the library. So, what we both had in mind in 1979–1980, teaching and scholarly effort, became a reality! What would the two of us, together, make of it? Added to this was the task of relating our lives together to important changes in our own family.

Throughout the 1970s, Francena served busily and effectively as wife and partner in the duties of the RIT presidency. She also built strenuous chapters otherwise: teaching with major reference to the American family and civic service in a medley of local endeavors. She managed to mingle these often-competing missions without complaint. Relevant recognition came her way from a grateful community; for example, she received an honorary doctorate by Nazareth College for overall civic and professional contributions.

Francena's son by a former marriage, Michael Nolan, entered college, married, completed graduate study for his doctorate at The Pennsylvania State University, and became the father of our first grandson, Christopher. My daughter Paula followed a similar pattern; she married, prepared herself as a counselor, and became the mother of sons Ryan and Evan. Her husband pursued medical training and entered practice as a physician in West Virginia.

Francena and I were both especially called to share a major concern with the continuing chronic and insoluble health challenge of my son, Thomas. In 1973, at the age eighteen, Tom had been diagnosed with a rare kidney disease. He carried on bravely, obtained his degree from the New York College of Forestry and Environmental Science in Syracuse, and re-turned to Rochester. Unable to take up his college major in forestry and environmental fields because of his health challenges, he developed an Internet business with rare books and glassware in Rochester.

As this new chapter began in our personal and professional lives, we were encouraged and supported by many faculty colleagues and RIT trustees and officers, especially by the new president, Dr. Richard Rose, who came from the same post at Alfred University. We received his warm welcome as he accepted and assured us his support of our intended efforts in the College of Liberal Arts. He also requested that we continue work on certain key projects, especially those directly relating RIT to the larger community.

Interest and support came also from the trustees who welcomed our return, and, especially, Bruce Bates and Thomas Gosnell, outstanding civic leaders who chaired the RIT board in that era. Two deans of the College of Liberal Arts, productive friends and colleagues in former years, continued support of our efforts, respectively Sister Mary Sullivan and Stanley McKenzie. As stalwart leaders in helping the Rochester Institute of Technology become what it is today, their colleagueship greatly helped us shape the next thirteen years of our lives and form a stimulating chapter. Still another partner of special note in the transition was Louise Carrese. She became a vital part of the new chapter as a research and administrative associate and, in years following, took up other vital RIT assignments.

But establishing the new roles in teaching and scholarship was also challenged by projects that had been generated by our stay in Washington. Some sprang from evolving scholarly interests, especially in the international realm. One of early importance was to chair a working committee on international agricultural research organization (Study Team 14) of the World Food and Nutrition Study, an overview sponsored by the National Research Council of the National Academy of Sciences. Another was to assist the staff of the US President's Council for International Scientific and Technological Cooperation. However, the aim of this project, to create an "International Center for Technological Cooperation" in the federal establishment was ill-fated, a disappointing outcome due partly to the resistance of other federal entities.

Once back at RIT in a new role, and given such related projects, it seemed proper to introduce the new chapter by joining the intellectual

fruits of the leave of absence with a key component of our professional careers: the international spread of technology to improve the quantity and quality of agricultural production. Of global interest at that time
was the technical revolution in breeding and spreading high-yield varieties of wheat and rice throughout the world. These innovative steps were
coming to be known as "The Green Revolution." A major paper on this
global enterprise was presented to a campus-wide RIT Faculty Research
Symposium in the year of our return. Happily, the sponsors chose the paper for a financial award sufficient to develop visuals enabling classroom
and public presentations of its findings.

Source: "Softworld vs. Hardworld: Contemporary Contrasts of the
Green Revolution." Paper presented at the Rochester Institute
of Technology Faculty Research Symposium, Rochester, NY,
September 2, 1980.

Does technology outrun human institutions? In the
short-term at least, technology often takes the lead. But
accommodation is eventually made, however painful,
or new institutions are fashioned. It is the lag [that]
proves troublesome. However, in the end, it seems
incorrect to assign the blame to technology! Rather, is
there not some human flaw [that] finds us willing to
take the gain from technology but unwilling to pay the
full (and often hidden) cost of its discovery and utilization?... Failures in human will and judgment lead to the
ultimate irony of our technologic age: that so much of
the abundant fruit of modern science and technology
is used up in the social chaos [that] may result as unexpected consequence.

Thus did the studies in Washington link our early and later interests. Under the umbrella of the Science, Technology, and Society Program in the College of Liberal Arts, my teaching focus grew to emphasize the "social consequences of technology." Courses centered on this theme also led to one on "science and technology policy." Soon to follow was a course oriented to natural resources in global context, "Face of the Land." Such courses expanded over the years and examined the interplays between the natural landscape, technology, policy-making, and social organization. In this connection, with an interest in Benton MacKaye, famed pioneer in regional land-use planning in the early twentieth century, Francena joined me for a fall semester at Dartmouth College to work together on his professional papers.

Still another international connection emerged in the transition to new assignments, one linked closely to adult and continuing education. Canadian J. Roby Kidd, an internationally famed adult educator, invited me in the early 1970s to assist the advancement of the International Council for Adult Education. As founder of the council, headquartered in Toronto, Kidd toiled until his untimely death to promote the growth of adult education on a world basis, and to foster collaboration among its leaders. My service on the council's board, and as its North American Vice President in 1972–1974, strengthened both interests and acquaintances in comparative adult education. Many internationally known adult educators in the developing countries were activists for popular democracy. Reading their works, notably Brazilian Paulo Freire's *Pedagogy of the Oppressed*, and Ivan Illich's *Deschooling Society*, heightened my concern for the civic power of the poor in developing nations. [10] The uses of science and technology seem often to outrun or ignore certain costs to human affairs, for example, that of ignoring and thus weakening civic life.

---

10 Freire, Paolo. *Pedagogy of the Oppressed*, trans. Myra Bergman Ramos (New York: Continuum, 1970); Ivan Illich. *Deschooling Society* (New York: Harper and Row, 1971).

Source: "Adult Education, Science, and Technology." Paper presented at the Working Session on Adult Education, International Aid and Poverty, Washington, DC, June 2–3, 1980.

> A somewhat curious paradigm is not infrequently found associated with the flows of science and technology. New knowledge is received first by a small group at the center, as likely as not to acquire the values embodied in the knowledge. The knowledge then flows through mechanisms of research and development, which are also oriented to the center. These features limit the participation of farmers and craftsmen in the applications of science and technology; they also inhibit the creative fusion of tacit and traditional knowledge with that which has arrived from elsewhere. To increase and free the flow of information is a process whose basic elements should command the attention of the adult educator.

The 1980s unfolded as a happy and stimulating chapter. A limited schedule of teaching (on the payroll until age sixty-seven and thereafter as a volunteer) made for a flexible existence. Our office spaces remained for thirteen years as the longest unbroken work location in our careers. A former president of an institution cannot escape certain social and other formalities of relationship. But those years garnered a friendly and ever more informal colleagueship about the campus, especially the welcome extended and sustained by the faculty of the College of Liberal Arts. Community tasks continued, importantly among them as board member of the Rochester Gas and Electric Corporation and board chair of Rochester's Center for Environmental Information. Overall, my participation in the Science, Technology, and Society Program of RIT served to combine and integrate interests of some fifty years in my career line.

Both campus and off-campus assignments continued to be undergirded by continuing efforts with the W. K. Kellogg Foundation. Francena and I continued an association with the longtime president of the Foundation, Dr. Russell G. Mawby. As I mentioned in earlier chapters, he was among my most influential mentors in adult and continuing education. After our helping form the program principles of the Foundation's Leadership Development Program during our Washington leave, Mawby invited Francena and me to co-chair the advisory committee for the initial class of forty Kellogg Fellows, selected for a period of three years of study, individual project development, and distinctively organized workshops. This effort initiated eighteen such classes and some one thousand national and international Fellows in the next twenty years. The Fellowship program, once completed under the auspice of the Foundation, would continue privately in Denver as the Kellogg Fellows Leadership Alliance, an international center of consultation that invites and applies the talents and skills of the former Fellows.

Of special note in this effort, and an example of the program's impact upon youthful leaders in early stages of their professional work, is Dr. James Votruba. As a member of the initial class of Kellogg Fellows, and one whom we were privileged to advise, Votruba went on to a continuing professional career in disciplines and positions rather similar to our own. He served in major leadership positions in national higher education associations, provost positions in the State University of New York and Michigan State University, a teacher in the Harvard Education Institutes for new college and university presidents, and as president of Northern Kentucky University. Votruba's writings and practices speak to major policy tensions in continuing education—for example, how best to distribute its leadership and related pedagogic responsibilities throughout the university. Votruba's insight and impact in such matters have been widely applied and tested, and includes the editorship of a well-known book on the subject, one to which he invited me to contribute.

Source: "Strengthening the University Continuing Education Mission." In *New Directions for Continuing Education*, edited by James C. Votruba. New York: Jossey-Bass, 1981.

> Three principles come to mind: (1) continuing education needs its own organization, budget, and personnel, to include, if possible, its own faculty core, whether housed together or dispersed, (2) joint appointments should be developed so that university-wide links may be forged; and (3) once such a dependable identity is assured, other departments should be encouraged to mount programs of continuing education (and the personnel to conduct them) within some reasonable plan of coordination.

At the turn into the 1980s, the importance of continuing lifelong education to business and industry seemed forever assured. No better example than RIT seemed possible when weighing the legitimacy of university outreach. Not only that, two sweeping changes validated the field even further: critical challenges of global competition calling for industrial change and reorganization, and knowledge itself as the rapidly rising foundation of innovation and sustainability. On every side, a new information and knowledge revolution was exploding and being acclaimed. No matter the sponsor, the place of lifelong continuous learning was here to stay!

Sensing that the field had achieved national policy importance, the W. K. Kellogg Foundation, in the mid-1980s, also supported the National University Continuing Education Association in establishing a Commission on Continuing Higher Education Leadership. The project aimed for a national dialogue between leaders of industrial and professional sectors with those representing adult continuing education. The commission was called upon to discern the directions of the field and lay a basis for strengthening the training of its leaders. I was asked to be a member.

This exercise sparked much enthusiasm, as the commission members came to sense that human learning was moving evermore quickly beyond the perimeters of schools and colleges. New technologies and institutions, and new sponsors, would see that the process continues. No longer would lifelong learning on a part-time basis be the stepchild of educational institutions. No sector would surpass business and industry with heralding its importance. We were elated with this evident breakthrough. In an era of transition, however, might we not restrict the mission of education by focusing too greatly on economic interests?

This began to grow in my mind at RIT in the 1970s: a steady weakening of the historic concern of American education for citizenship. An early paper was prepared for the 1984 Rosalind K. Loring Lecture on Continuing Education at the University of Southern California. I decided to enlarge on the need of adult educators to help achieve a better balance between the economic and civic paradigms of American education. Another soon followed at Michigan's Oakland University to propose similar solutions. Both presentations more than hinted at the need to review human learning in relation to local and global civic challenges.

Source: "Academic Leadership and the Civic Culture." Lecture delivered at the University of Southern California, Los Angeles, CA, April 9, 1984.

How best might higher education shape its influence... for orienting the electronic media to social learning? Public television can scarcely be thought of as standing on steady ground. Information and telecommunication technologies are merging, shrinking the globe still further. Indeed, a new telecommunications era—the convergence of multiple channels of cable television, satellites, and databanks—points either to greater fragmentation of the nation or to the possibility of a newly interactive process of governance. International corporations, the bankers, and the military system are drawing those exploding changes into their own innovations. But the promise of this new era appears far from centered on the planning tables of the very system that stimulated its technologies in the first place.

Source: "Serving the Civic Culture." Lecture delivered at the Twenty-fifth Anniversary of the Public Service Seminar, Oakland University, Rochester, MI, October 8, 1984.

The main body of citizens is unaware of how the theorem—"knowledge is power"—is at work in today's world. On one day, having an energy policy is of high priority, but on the next, it is quietly stalemated. Military hardware is proposed, designed, and produced with little public understanding and reaction. Problems [that] groups, regions, and nations share are commonly met with division rather than cooperation: need one do more than mention water allocations, acid rain, global warming, hunger and malnutrition, encroachment of deserts, toxic waste storage, natural resource depletion?

Such events and projects, with the analysis and writing they stimulated, evolved in relation to our professorial roles. These stimulated opportunities for continuing to serve in the global domain. Among them, two stand out and will be long remembered: in 1983, they challenged Francena and me to explore the outreach functions of the Catholic University of

Santiago in the Dominican Republic, and in 1988, the Agricultural and Industrial Institute (the American Farm School) in Thessaloniki, Greece. The former studies analyzed the impacts of an academic center in the mountain region bordering Haiti. The second project examined the role of an extraordinary institution in light of promised impact throughout Eastern Europe.

PUZZLES AND DECISIONS

WITHIN THE ACTIVITIES in adult and continuing education (perceived in an even larger framework of university outreach to society) I engaged in activities, carefully planned implemented, that did not function well, if at all! However, perhaps these disappointments led to greater insight, humility, and the wisdom to strengthen future decisions. Given the emphasis on the outreach functions of the present account, two Rochester events come to mind. The first dealt with the Urbanarium mentioned earlier. The other case refers to an unforgettable experience in the late 1980s with Rochester's entry into the "drug wars" that were so often front and center in the national news.

Soon after our return to RIT in early 1980, the board and staff of the Urbanarium requested my service as chair of an Interim Planning Committee. The aim was to evaluate this history and anticipate the future of the unit. An Interim Planning Report was completed in early 1981 that addressed the history of the Urbanarium, its major efforts in the past decade, its financial prospects, and its methods of governance and administration. Other more pointed findings cited how its name had remained a puzzle to many and would likely need to be changed. Following foundation support, securing sufficient local funds for its efforts had grown difficult. Its mission to advance collaboration in urban contexts remained difficult to define, given other agencies with competing intentions. Moreover, a tension had grown between respective advocates for "social" improvement and those given to "economic" development.

Source: "Urbanarium's Interim Planning Report." Report prepared for Urbanarium Inc., Rochester, NY, January, 1981.

> [T]he loss of traditional integrative institutions in community life (isolated political parties and leaders of locally based firms, family and kinship groups, well positioned religious and welfare associations), will require creative new institutions that will stand on the side of total community concern rather than on mounting clashes of special interest. With the major problems of community life growing more general and cross-cutting, yet the solutions to them increasingly specific, the resulting tensions between problems and solutions demand that more thought be given organizations which work to create community cooperation.

In the end, in a move that disappointed many, the board decided to phase out the Urbanarium in 1982. Its efforts had scored significant and lasting accomplishments, however, including the formation of central technical police services, forty cooperating agencies joining to reduce youth unemployment, a comprehensive business plan of investment in tourist expansion, the conduct of a continuing Issues Management Institute for community leaders, and the formation of Greater Rochester Citizens for Action involving over four hundred volunteers and thirty work teams.

On the whole, perhaps the greatest gift of the Urbanarium's rather short life was to help stimulate a new group of younger community leaders. As Rochester's *Times-Union* newspaper editorialized on August 10, 1982, "No other organization has worked so hard to find leadership in every corner of the community, and to train it for problem-solving.... [It] is likely that the Urbanarium will have to be re-invented."

If the Urbanarium is remembered as a disappointing outcome of an idea of the sixth president of RIT, another, also as a professor at work, was a project providing leadership for greater Rochester's entry into the American policy of fashioning "drug wars." This feature of the late 1980s continued, placing in its local and national records a history as complex in outcomes as they are in number.

In the summer of 1989, I was asked by Rochester's mayor and deputy mayor, Thomas Ryan and Christopher Lindley, respectively, to undertake a metropolitan-wide task of the substance-abuse challenge. They proposed to establish a metropolitan commission of some forty citizens to address the challenge of illegal drug abuse. These city officials asked me to serve as the chair of a commission called Greater Rochester Fights Back (GRFB). The assignment was to prepare a proposal for private foundation support, immediately form the commission, develop an office, establish a secretariat, and launch a program. While my role was a volunteer one, the tasks would surely demand full time. It required familiarity with the urban landscape, from "inner city" to city-at-large and the whole metropolitan region.

This assignment lasted for two rather uncertain years. The GRFB grew into a vibrant body of able and devoted members. A program was put in place that mobilized a variety of institutions and special agencies. GRFB quickly became a metropolitan center to recognize and react to the trends and impacts of drug addiction. Its mission would continue on the Rochester scene, though eventually in different forms. Importantly, a lasting project emerging from its deliberations was the founding of one of the earliest "metropolitan drug courts." Such courts set out to enable creative legal reviews and solutions other than jail time for many charged with misdemeanors and crimes of abusing or otherwise dealing with illegal drugs.

But difficulties for the GRFB emerged not long after its inception. These centered on the not-unusual snags of modern urban life: the conflict of special interests, whether personal, political, cultural or ideological. The national importance of the "drug war" at the turn into the 1990s created an arena in which individual, organizational, and political aspirations could be met for some and lost for others. The conflict between "either/ or" seemed everpresent, emerging behind the outward face and agenda of GRFB—for example, between urban or suburban emphasis, private or public intervention, prevention or punishment, mass media or participatory "on the ground" approaches in the neighborhoods.

My own outlook cleared with time and generated moments of conflict and tension. In my view, drug abuse was a tenacious problem growing out of disorganization in urban and suburban life. While believing that media exhortations helped people refrain from drug abuse, equally important to me was to intervene positively, on the one hand, in those urban neighborhoods where life was challenged by poverty and disorganization, and, on the other, to improve the functions of legal and criminal justice systems. My interest on drug prevention for individuals joined with a renaissance of urban neighborhoods built upon growing participation of their residents.

I had agreed with the mayor and deputy mayor to hold the job for two years. When the two-year period neared completion in the summer of 1991, with my fatigue and other tensions as above mounting (and likely showing!), I asked to be relieved of the post and depart GRFB. The experience was among the most complex of those in a career of many field-oriented projects. I value it to the present day, not only for the personal challenge it provided, but, more importantly, for a better understanding of the road ahead for enhancing urban and suburban institutions to strengthen effective and humane objectives and methods.

Of course, as with the Urbanarium, the project kindled further interest in civic society and culture. Importantly, I also made new friends. In addition to the mayor and deputy mayor, a working partnership grew with police officials. Deputy Mayor Christopher Lindley, a public servant of rare compassion and intellectuality, continued as a close friend and one given to challenging me intellectually. The same may be said for William Johnson, then president of Rochester's Urban League, who later became Rochester's first African American mayor, and an RIT professor of political science.

Greater Rochester Fights Back, together with the ill-fated journey of the Urbanarium, enabled me to better appreciate how attempting change through "social and administrative technologies" does not come easily or quickly, sometimes not at all! Even the most creative and well financed initiatives, whether public or private, are but a structural overlay and unsustainable without a foundation of the values of collaboration and thus geared to solving issues no matter the variety and intensity of disagreement. Indeed, the years as the sixth RIT president and then those following in professorial and community serving roles, all joined to help me develop a disciplined overview of the RIT chapter then nearing twenty-five years in length.

At such moments, as surely in most careers, I seem compelled to review such contours, events, crises, victories, and moments of confusion and despair, as one attempts to install a common vision in a large and complicated community. With such a review, various circumstances and good fortune come to mind. Such is the case for 1992–1993 as it unfolded as our final year at RIT. To be sure, return after return to such recollections would be made in the years following. Again and again, a question has repeated itself and still awaits resolution: "What was the dominant feature in RIT's culture while I was serving as the sixth president?"

That question has endured throughout the years following the close of our RIT chapter. Despite happy adjustments and worthy challenges to follow elsewhere, RIT and greater Rochester remained as "home." Members of the faculties, trustees, Rochester citizens and leaders, and vibrant corporations and associations remained undiminished in our memories, thus joining the earlier and similar remembrances that lingered from the West Virginia experience. They and many others not possible to include herein, formed a context (to a couple challenged to serve in several shorter chapters) that gave us a sense of lasting stability infused with affection, purpose, and commitment.

But as time sorted out and mellowed such reflections, the thought grew that perhaps the most tenacious RIT memory of the RIT years dealt with the five vice presidents who served with me. Their arrival and some aspects of their duties have been referred to earlier, but their distinctive qualities—especially those that united them into a vibrant team—have yet to be described. They formed a working group at a most uncertain moment in the long history of RIT. My striving in those years without such companions would have built upon thin ice! Therefore, no more fitting way seems proper than to salute these five men as I bring to a close the RIT and Rochester chapters.

The late Dr. Todd Bullard served through the 1970s and beyond as provost and academic vice president. His rare capacities for strategic planning and decision-making informed all Institute operations: among his strengths was seeing that operations were planned and executed on time. He was a splendid listener! He had an immense knowledge of academic life and the historical, social, and political principles upon which it rests. His capacities included a never-failing drive toward common purposes, along with the creative use of humorous anecdote. This made him an impressive master at overcoming irrelevance and time-wasting and sending off adversaries with cleared minds and smiling faces.

James Buchholz served importantly as vice president for business and finance. Having experienced similar duty in other institutions and the American Council on Education, he possessed a seasoned and competent knowledge on how to size up problems in need of proper blends of academic and fiscal goals. He seemed always ready with alternative courses of action when the need for them burst suddenly upon the conference table. Given to concise statements of principle and plan, his standing in good stead led to quickened repayments of campus debt, securing adjacent properties, teaching fiscal realities to academic colleagues, and grooming Jon Prime as his successor.

The late Alfred Davis, a legendary figure in the history of RIT, continued with me in what he had so well done with Mark Ellingson: sharing the wisdom of many years at the Institute, a capacity shaped by the countless tasks asked of him on behalf of both the Institute and Rochester. He gave to both, and without relief, with a demeanor quiet, steady, and wrapped in an infallible memory. His affection for RIT continued in retirement: finding prospective givers, assisting a major development office to grow from what once was Al Davis only, and to support RIT with his own means. An example of this is the origin of Margaret's House for Child Care and Development in memory of his wife.

Dr. Robert Frisina, as first RIT vice president and director of the National Technical Institute for the Deaf, was also first on site on behalf of that institution-within-an-institution. As the dean of Graduate Studies at Gallaudet University, he brought with him an international reputation in audiology, not only to the founding of NTID, but also a rare administrative capacity. He built national and international respect into the new post, making possible such campus morale as to clarify NTID's own mission as well as its place within RIT. Thus he would lead locally, nationally, and internationally, and help develop his successor, Dr. William Castle. In due course, he returned to critically important research and writing.

Dr. Fred Smith, as vice president for Student Life, came in 1970 from Oakland University. Given the new campus, Fred's assignment was instantly complex! Competent and hardworking, with a clear and dependable character, and a natural builder of community, he was admired by students and faculty alike. At the same time, he served in an equally challenging deanship, for Complementary Education, which charged him to lead the whole of RIT in becoming a "learning community." Such capacities would be long lived at RIT: along that way, his early associate in student affairs, Dr. Thomas Plough, became RIT's provost and Fred Smith would serve as RIT's vice president and secretary of the board of trustees.

WINDING DOWN

SUCH EXPERIENCES AND reviews, arising in the early 1990s, affected and were affected by our family life. Given this, and having reached our mid-seventies in age, we began to reflect on what might be best for the future. Not surprisingly, the matter of retirement became more weighted in our conversations. Moreover, the more intimate aspects of our family life were changing, even dramatically. Two of our children, and three grandchildren, had moved to Columbia, Missouri. The underlying events in this regard now follow, a saga of academically involved people, in terms of change, residence, and collective expressions of professional service. This mixture of experiences would send us to a new place and efforts with a transformed family.

When Francena and I married in 1966, she was the dean of Home Economics at the University of Connecticut. Her son by a former marriage, Michael Nolan, having completed his doctorate in rural sociology at The Pennsylvania State University, moved to a new post at the University of Missouri (MU) in 1971 with his wife, Jeanne (also a rural sociologist), and infant son, Christopher. Michael's stay at MU encompassed a distinguished career as professor of rural sociology; chair of the department in that field; associate dean for international projects in the College of Agriculture, Food, and Natural Resources; and director of the latter's Division of Applied Social Sciences. Our visits with him and his family from 1971 onward further enlarged our acquaintance with Columbia and MU (the first public university west of the Mississippi River) and the state of Missouri.

My daughter, Paula (whose mother and my wife died, as noted before), received degrees in sociology and counseling from West Virginia University in the late 1960s. She married a fellow student, Blair Thrush, who became a practicing physician of notable achievements. They and their two sons, Ryan and Evan, lived many years in Morgantown and then Charleston, West Virginia. Paula, in those locations and elsewhere, served professionally as a psychologist and counselor, with much of her efforts devoted to students and other youth. The union of Paula and Blair established itself distinctively in professional and civic duties. They also helped sustain our affection for West Virginia and Appalachian culture, and the evolution of West Virginia University.

This story became a saga in the 1980s with the divorces of both Paula and Michael from their respective spouses. They eventually married each other, and anchored their lives and those of the three involved children in Columbia, Missouri. Not unnaturally, our interest grew in joining them, despite our genuine sense of Rochester as home and our earlier intentions to remain there. So it came to pass that we decided to move to Columbia in the early part of 1993. Our changed and growing family recognized that they counted for much in this move and supported the decision with enthusiasm. Son Thomas, while endorsing the good sense of our move, decided to remain in Rochester. We moved to Columbia in the spring of 1993.

As our final months at RIT unfolded, they grew ever more poignant. Dr. Albert J. Simone arrived in 1992 from the presidency of the University of Hawaii to become RIT's eighth president; he began fifteen years of exceptional leadership in the post. As had his predecessor, Dr. Richard Rose, he immediately stretched out a friendly hand to Francena and me. Both leaders also welcomed me into discussions among the three of us, including how our respective emphases connected and underpinned the promise of RIT. We three marveled together on what Mark and Marcia Ellingson had accomplished in developing RIT during their long service past.

The years, friends, and colleagues, among so many unnamed others, had made RIT an imaginative and vigorous workplace. The Greater Rochester blend of professional, industrial, and cultural institutions had introduced us to a great number of persons and families of remarkable capacities. All provided a crucible of experience and learning, and example after example, for guiding the maturation of our intellectual and cultural lives. Such growth was sure to aid in finding and accepting relevant activities associated with the University of Missouri and the Columbia community. As graduates and former workers on behalf of state and land-grant universities, we would arrive at still another such site with new learning, experience and priority interests, and especially those following:

...Responding to the importance of combining formal leaning with practical application and human service.

...Pondering and acting upon the challenges ahead that spring from both cosmopolitan and global systems.

...Achieving a better balance of economic and civic values throughout the whole of American education.

With such principles in mind, and given the format of "events" and "excerpts" employed throughout this work, perhaps a fitting close to the Rochester experience is the paragraph completing my address at the Seventy-Fourth Annual Conference of the National University Continuing Education Association. This excerpt was chosen later by the Association to close its comprehensive history of adult and continuing education in America from 1915–1990.

Source: "Long on Management, Short on Soul: A Critical Look at Continuing Higher Education Today." In *Expanding Access to Knowledge*, edited by Rae Wahl Rohfeld, 219–226. Washington, DC: National University Continuing Education Association, 1990.

For all its grandeur in scale and investment, American education is failing to educate the people about education. Widespread confusion prevails over what is expected of schools and of their reform. Despite the rhetoric, teaching is accorded low status. But the problem underneath such issues—whether in or out of education—is the failure to make learning more meaningful and enduring to our vocation of making public judgments. This is the problem that we must take up as we enter the twenty-first century, and overturn the warning of Nietzsche when he said, "The advancement of learning at the expense of man is the most pernicious thing in the world."... Continuing education is daily in touch with human interests and needs, and with the sources of a vital literature. Continuing education was born of the desire to build the public process; should it now direct its enterprises to restore that process? Finally, continuing education can look to what is now a proud profession...and to be reminded that the twenty-first-century task herein mentioned will not get far without a great measure of "soul."

VIII

$\mathcal{M}$ISSOURI $\mathcal{A}$ND $\mathcal{M}$U

$\mathcal{A}$DVANCING A $\mathcal{C}$ULTURE OF $\mathcal{P}$EACE

THIS ACCOUNT, BRIDGING *Campus and Community*, began with the transformative move in 1928 of my parental family and me to a small West Virginia farm. Building on early boyhood influences, this career journey moved through seven major chapters. This eighth chapter embraces a move to Columbia, Missouri, in August 1993, with steps for added interests and partial retirement. The move was also shaped by the family transformation described at the close of the previous chapter.

The University of Missouri-Columbia (MU) figured early in my professional life. My senior faculty advisor at West Virginia University, Dr. John Longwell, became dean of the College of Agriculture at MU in the early 1940s. We met again in 1948 when Michigan State University sent me to a Columbia workshop where delegates from state and land-grant universities pondered the promise of television for public universities. A major paper (cited earlier) was presented in the mid-1950s to an MU Cooperative Extension Service Conference. The MU Press published my centennial address (also cited earlier) on American agricultural colleges. This paper was presented to the 1961 Centennial Conference of the National Association of State Universities and Land-Grant Colleges.

C. Brice Ratchford also enriched my family connections to MU. From 1959 to his death in 1998, Ratchford held several MU posts: MU Director of the Missouri Cooperative Extension Service, dean of Extension, vice president for Outreach, and president of the four-campus system of the University of Missouri (1970–1976). He then served MU as professor of agricultural economics and leader of international development projects.

In earlier years, as respective directors of Cooperative Extension Services in North Carolina and Michigan, Ratchford and I joined in common projects. One is of special note. After my chairing the earlier-cited National Commission on the Scope of Cooperative Extension in the 1950s, Ratchford soon led Missouri's—the first ever—implementation of it, a pace-setting event in that dynamic period of agrarian transition. That period also experienced quickening support of universities by the federal government and private foundations; rapid gains in college enrollments; and, with technology-induced efficiencies, the rapid displacement of rural workers and their movement to cities and changes in occupation.

Relevant experiences of a personal and family nature would also be taking place. As described in the close of the previous chapter, the move to Columbia was stimulated by the new centering there of our family. However, a few years later, we were rocked by a deeply felt family loss. My son, Thomas, had attended the New York State College of Forestry and Environmental Science, graduating in 1977. While a high school student, he had been diagnosed with a rare cystic disease. When that led to kidney failure in 1978, Thomas altered his career by launching an Internet business of marketing rare books and glassware. He continued his Rochester residence and Internet business after Francena and I moved to Missouri. Then, after years of chronic health challenges, a sudden downturn came in 2005. A year later, on top of the long challenge of kidney ailments, Thomas died from an unconquerable onslaught of cancer.

A NEW BEGINNING

A NEW IDENTITY for life in Columbia began to form before the actual move! Professional MU acquaintances urged that I serve as an adjunct professor of rural sociology, despite years of assignments in other fields, such as applied anthropology, international education, urban development, continuing education, and educational administration. This linkage seemed a positive way to add service in the new location. Another gesture sealed the matter: in recognition of diverse applications of rural sociology, an MU recommendation led by one of the field's esteemed practitioners, Dr. Daryl Hobbs, brought to Francena and me (as the first couple) the 1995 Distinguished Service Award of the Rural Sociological Society.

The initial link to rural sociology also animated early participation in the Division of Applied Social Sciences in the College of Agriculture, Food, and Natural Resources. This included participation in an MU project of identifying unique niches of MU scholarly competence. Thus, the door opened to MU's capacities in public policy and to my mounting interest in the nature of civic cultures. A further opportunity arose in 1994–95, this to chair a committee reviewing the outreach programs of the College's Applied Social Sciences Division.

Source: *Report on Outreach Findings and Recommendations for the Applied Social Sciences Division.* Columbia, MO: College of Agriculture, Food, and Natural Resources, University of Missouri-Columbia, February, 1995.

Public Policy is growing as a sharper focus in the Division. We believe that the several centers and institutes for public policy in the university gain much by creative attention to the importance of leadership for public policy. Few would deny that competence and leadership are needed in a day when the public process is rather stranded and less effective in contrast to how the nation's educational strength and the outpouring of science-based knowledge have focused increasingly on transforming the economic process. Helping people learn how to use knowledge in choosing and evaluating public policies is looming as a compelling challenge for all land-grant universities.

Another project of interest was the service of Francena and me as official evaluators of the National Capstone Symposium on University Outreach. This conference was held at Michigan State University, October 22–24, 1995, and sponsored by the National Association of State Universities and Land-Grant Colleges. The experience, not unlike that under way at the University of Missouri-Columbia, provided a further view of how the land-grant and state universities were preparing to enter the twenty-first century.

Throughout the 1980s and into the next decade, my interests turned increasingly to changes emerging in universities. One strand was the concern with how public universities might best "engage" with both national and international societies. A "paradigm shift" seemed under way on how academe serves society. Also of importance to such changes was the rapid rise of technologic/electronic advances in human communication. Francena and I wrote the Epilogue and an overall evaluation for the subsequent Summary of the National Capstone Symposium:

Source: Miller, Paul A., and Francena L. Miller, Epilogue to *Fulfilling Higher Education's Covenant with Society: The Emerging Outreach Agenda*, 151–157. Edited by Lorilee R. Sandmann. East Lansing, MI: Michigan State University, 1996; Washington, DC: National Association of State Universities and Land-Grant Colleges, 1996.

No institution, and especially the university, is excused from attending a social process that seeks a better balance of emphasis on economic and civic cultures; helps people reconcile the conflicting values of equality and freedom; becomes a stronger helpmate to those engaged in voluntary action; assists people to understand and cope with the turbulence and complexities of contemporary problem-solving; and expands and serves participation in an information revolution rooted in technologies spawned by academe.

These early activities in our return to a state and land-grant university helped refresh memories about such institutions, especially their efforts related to pubic communication and service. Of special importance was our sense that public colleges and universities were risking a drop in public esteem. Citizens, patrons, and state legislatures appeared less enamored of them. Concerns over costs were rising more rapidly than felt benefits.

During the Rochester stay of twenty-five years in private higher education, admirable gains had come to the global food system. The public land-grant institutions were its significant leaders. But also to be noted were related problems: the accelerating exodus of rural people from local to metropolitan areas; a shift of political focus from rural to urban issues, the heightened inflow of immigrants, both legal and illegal, especially from Latin America; and the transfer of portions of rural poverty into urban poverty. Those left behind in many non-metropolitan communities would also face declining services, uncertain employment, and levels of living. I discussed this in my keynote address for the inauguration of Thomas R. Plough—former vice president for student affairs and provost at RIT—as the twelfth president of North Dakota State University.

Source: "Why Are We Here?" Keynote address delivered at the inauguration of Thomas R. Plough as president of North Dakota State University, Fargo, ND, April 26, 1996.

How will we respond to new forms of interdisciplinary collaboration within and among universities? Have we confronted the puzzles of fitting increasingly specialized solutions to increasingly generalized and interdependent problems? Have we put too much emphasis on technical power and too little on moral responsibility in its use?

Research related to non-metropolitan life suggests that it is in a "silent crisis"; in the least, scenarios of what non-metropolitan America needs are in order.... [This] would bring knowledge to policy formation for improving cultural and economic viability, and deliver human services of higher quality. Universities must be the meeting grounds where the past, present and future complexities of non-metropolitan America will be fully explored and addressed.

No question challenges an educator more (and, for so long, me) than what is education for and how one puts it to use. Plato and Aristotle debated the question, especially how to connect mind and soul. St. Thomas Aquinas kept the question in mind when he foresaw how European cathedrals might create civic schools to serve the secular needs of medieval cities; these would, in turn, evolve into such early universities as Paris, Bologna, Oxford, and Cambridge. The same tension carried on at Harvard's founding in 1636, in the liberal arts colleges, and in the land-grant colleges of the nineteenth century, and community colleges in the twentieth century.

Whatever the emphasis, however, universities have been long held accountable. Such was exacted by king, lord, papacy, or court, or by city councils overseeing the early civic universities of Europe. Responding to this accountability challenged the academy for more than a thousand years. Nor have American universities, despite the pragmatism of their public charters, escaped this challenge. They have felt the unease attached to "public service." Public needs overlap with public problems and can lead from confusion to controversy. One case in point includes the roles taken by universities when connected as an addition to America's "military-industrial complex," the memorable exclamation of President Eisenhower. Moreover, public interests do not absorb easily into collegial organizations where specialized knowledge and departments may reign autonomously.

Further tensions spring from unexpected consequences! A personal reflection provides a case example of how such consequences have arisen when new knowledge is created, communicated, and applied to food production through pervasive technical systems. This refers to one of the greatest accomplishments in human history: America's extraordinary gains in efficiencies, varieties, qualities, and quantities of food production. But there were also unexpected issues: immigrants (legal or otherwise) in search of farm employment; the growing presence of corporate farms, the exodus of displaced people

in search of a better life, the impoverishment of many
left behind, the weakening of family and community
institutions, and the appearance of exurban and exclusively gated communities oriented to the security of
those favored by class, status and wealth.

While this illustration transpired over much of the twentieth century, an exploding information revolution in
the new twenty-first century now multiplies unexpected
consequences: they ramify throughout the global setting and remain difficult to identify, define, comprehend
and confront. They also require solutions [that] require
attention over long periods, duties requiring collaboration beyond the willingness, capacity and patience of
nation-states. Overcoming such impediments falls upon
today's world as uncertainty arises over how to mobilize
the political ideas and informed participation of citizens.

Source: "Adult Education's Mislaid Mission." Lecture delivered at the
Annual National Conference of the American Association
for Adult and Continuing Education. Also published in *Adult
Education Quarterly* 46, no. 1 (1995): 43–52.

[Glancing across two centuries] suggests the long and
inexorable shift that education in general has made, one
encouraged and demanded by constituents and supporters alike, from education for citizenship to preparing
people for occupational success. Adult and continuing
education legitimized itself more and more by veering in
the same direction. One may observe how difficult it has
been, once innovative projects in civic education have

been introduced, to sustain them, salvage them when they falter, fashion them into a lasting movement, and balance them with the necessity and the importance of adult education to the world of work Political orientations throughout the world edge toward democratic practice. But democratic civil society depends broadly upon the will, the understanding, and responses of citizens. These citizens must now face the gap between technological and institutional innovation.

NEW BLENDS OF OLD INTERESTS

As THIS ACCOUNT records previously, the international sphere appeared to mingle with my interests in adult and continuing education: military service that brought in several areas of the world; chairing a commission to form the Colombian Institute of Agricultural Education; concern with African projects while at WVU; a major emphasis on international education while assistant secretary of the US Department of Health, Education, and Welfare; board member and North American vice president of the International Council for Adult Education; board member of the American Farm School in Greece (and, with Francena, taking up certain planning tasks therein); and, also with Francena, both serving as senior program consultants of the W. K. Kellogg Foundation. Continuing adult education strengthened as the mainstay of our professional interests, and stimulated even more by my being elected to the 1995 class of inductees into the International Adult and Continuing Education Hall of Fame.

These professional interests responded to the upswing of a new period in international affairs, and what appeared as an epochal challenge. Included were those tremors in the scaffolds supporting the "modern era" of some five hundred years: weakening boundary maintenance and authority of nation-states, challenges to capitalist production and markets, a weakening stature of middle class families as sustainers of democracy and capitalism, troubling problems of public schooling, the mounting challenges of immigration, and, importantly, the implications of the electronic technologies for enlarging and sustaining democratic practice.

A mingling of orientations found its way to new MU colleagues with mutual interests in the rise of global influence. Especially among them were Dr. Daryl Hobbs (mentioned previously); John Galliher, a sociologist and director of the Peace Studies Program (PSP) in the MU College of Arts and Sciences; William Wickersham, veteran professor and analyst as well as a national presence in America's peace movements; Parker Rossman, a former Yale University professor and Internet pioneer; Uel Blank, economist and president of MU's Friends of Peace Studies, an MU support group; and from the civic world, Charles Atkins, a noted community leader in the peace fields.

From these and other colleagues came an invitation to join the board of directors of the Peace Studies Program [PSP], and, soon after, its executive committee. An initial response to this welcome was my paper for a PSP informal journal. Its theme in the fall issue of 2000 was Strategies for Peace in the Twenty-First Century. Major attention was given the remarkable growth of international nongovernmental organizations, commonly referred to as INGOs. As the twenty-first century opened, they numbered some twenty-five thousand! Their branches and local chapters throughout the world were producing growing numbers of actors in global civil society.

Source: "INGOs in the Search for Peace: Civic Parameters and Questions." *Peace Talk* 7 (Fall 2000).

International NGOs (INGOs) aid in collaboratively exploring human interchange as the scaffold upon which to promote peaceful conflict resolution in every corner of society. To learn and practice creative interchange [a concept of theologian and philosopher Henry Nelson

Wieman] describes the role of listening with disciplined attention, grasping the outlook of the other, muting special interests at least temporarily, imaging options for the common good, recognizing the likely need of compromise, and exiting the exchange with more understanding of the other participants, even when agreement is elusive or even unreachable.

[INGOs need to stand with] nation-states as the latter are challenged by declines of sovereignty, and help them strive to promote human security. Such organizations, evermore numerous, can promote a cosmopolitan citizenship [that] in turn comprehends, enlarges, and aids in sustaining a global civil society. Global civil society and the INGOs can help stimulate a cosmopolitan citizenry to enlarge, comprehend, promote, and sustain human security.

Earlier Vietnam War tensions and consequences stimulated many universities to prepare students and citizens as leaders in building cultures of peace. The University of Missouri, and especially its home campus in Columbia, is an example. Stalwart members of both the campus and civil communities joined to organize and sustain a Peace Studies Program (PSP). Mainly sponsored by the College of Arts and Science, the PSP installed courses leading to undergraduate and graduate degrees, conferences, speakers and, eventually, a journal to encourage scholarly and civic endeavors.

Also coming into this mix of new experiences were those of volunteer assistance to constructing a new building for Columbia's Unitarian Universalist Church. The long commitment of Unitarians to human rights (e.g., extensive support of anti-slavery and women's suffrage movements in the nineteenth century) includes the peaceful resolution of conflict. My belief strengthened that the peaceful resolution of violent conflict cannot be achieved without collaboration among the various forms of religious faith and educational institutions, and, in turn, cooperative efforts between these two vital groups. This collaboration seems necessary for shaping civil societies that can resist war and violence by fashioning rigorous and continuing dialogue in search of common ground.

To explore modes of cooperation among the various religious groups and doctrines grew as a fitting project of PSP's major support group, the Friends of Peace Studies. I was asked to prepare a paper addressed to the question of how, in a given community, the faith and education groups might best collaborate in fashioning dialogue capable of fostering peaceful resolution of conflict.

Source: "Establishing a Faith and Education Collaborative for Advancing a Culture of Peace." Paper prepared for the Peace Studies Program, University of Missouri-Columbia, Columbia, MO, October 7, 2002.

The Collaborative would explore how communities of faith and learning might join to help people understand and pursue steps toward non-violent resolution of conflict no matter where or how experienced…. While many transformations are likely to emerge as the new century evolves, none surpass the call for a transformation in citizenship and a civic agenda centered on a search for peace amid the new ambiguities of war: uncertain enemies, locations, victories and rules of engagement.

Military, economic, and political capacities have made the United States the world's superpower. Should not this position enable our nation to discover, choose, and

> apply artful leadership for peace rather than the least artful option of pre-emptive lethal force? To aid our nation in understanding and making such choices in the decades to come, no other can take the place of religious and educational institutions!

Further amended and adopted, this paper provided an opportunity to establish the Columbia Faith and Education Collaborative for advancing a culture of peace. The first community-wide conference was conducted in December 2002 to explore the mission and define next steps. Representing only Christian groups at the outset, attendees at the initial conference began wide-ranging discussions of possible approaches, including the urgent need to grow evermore inclusive in membership. These ranged from initial efforts centered on youth, training programs for conducting dialogue and listening groups, exploring what is meant by "advancing a culture of peace," and, importantly, discovering and testing the teachable dynamics of dialogic behavior.

These hopes and related questions continued throughout three annual community conferences sponsored by the Columbia Faith and Education Collaborative. By the third conference, such interests as above were sufficiently elevated as to center the agenda. Of importance was the presence of an international team on dialogic processes from the national office of the Community of Christ denomination. With such aid, the third community conference explored the question, "What is meant by a culture of peace, global citizenship, and peaceful conflict resolution?" I was asked to present a paper responding to such queries.

Source: "An Update on the Columbia Faith and Education Collaborative & Brief Reflections on Advancing a Culture of Peace." Paper presented to the Peace Studies Program, University of Missouri-Columbia, Columbia, MO, January 31, 2004.

[A] new scenario is rising! With the extraordinary reductions of cost and distance brought about by the ongoing communications revolution, individuals, organizations, and institutions in society grow more interactive. Thus cultural homogeneity is challenged by growth of new and more numerous reflexivities: particular cultures, despite possible resistances, may become less stable and sustaining in their influence. Culture changes more quickly as people discover and use new experiences, practices, and solutions.

Moreover, the communications revolution makes culture more fluid, open, and reflexive; nation-state diplomacy weakens in favor of coalitions; civil society and social capital underlying democracy are being rediscovered; the Armageddon prospects of nuclear armaments enlarge and stimulate new constituencies for peace as well as fractious splits in civic publics; and global support systems of thousands of non-governmental organizations are networking their way toward the peace-making side of international struggles.

A widening commitment grew among a growing number of participants in the Columbia Faith and Education Collaborative for advancing a culture of peace. Despite the sluggish and limited participation of faith groups at the outset, their interests and participations grew in the fourth and fifth community conferences. Representatives of Protestant Christianity had peopled the initial conferences. However, by the fifth conference, conducted in early 2007, came a substantial growth of representatives from the Jewish, Islamic, and Buddhist faiths, along with an increase from the Catholic community.

This growth of interested participants was to great extent shaped by a steering committee with two devoted and skillful chairpersons from the faith and education communities—the Reverend Otto Steinhaus and Dr. Uel Blank, respectively. Under their leadership, interest turned soon to conducting training institutes to advance dialogic and listening skills. Manuals for instruction and practice were developed after the third conference, under the steady leadership of Kakie Love and Fran Reynolds. A Columbia city agency advanced both interest and financial support to enhance such training. For the fourth and fifth community-wide conferences, members of the steering committee consulted with members and leaders of the respective faith groups. Throughout the Collaborative's development, issues and options tested the academic community, principally MU in the Columbia pilot project. Not surprisingly, when we turned to the university as a collaborating partner in such a venture, we had to be prepared to interpret outreach roles in the emerging global era. My part and interest in the Collaborative, rather backstopped by the experiences and ideas outlined throughout Bridging Campus and Community, had occasion to be critically shared from time to time.

Source: "Citizenship for the Global Era." Paper presented to a community-wide conference of leaders in the Columbia faith and educational communities, Columbia, MO, February 23, 2003.

Three examples indicate the unintended consequences of putting nature's principles to work for humankind. The first is evermore lethal weapons. This consequence of modern technology threatens the very existence of humankind. The good news is that an awareness of this danger is moving through the global community.

The second of technology's unintended consequences reminds us that there are limits to the finite resources of the planet: a new moral code is in order that will lead us to act against our lopsided abuses of the natural world. Twenty percent of the world population consumes some 75 percent of the world's resources....

The third consequence is the strengthening power of humankind to design its own evolution. To this point Edward O. Wilson [in *Concilience*, Vanguard, 1999], one of the world's foremost biologists, comments, "The prospect of a volitional evolution—a species deciding what to do about its own heredity...will represent the most profound and ethical choices of humanity."

WIDENING INTERESTS

AS DISCUSSIONS WIDENED on a culture of peace, additional but related subjects appeared. Some concerned activities in a wider university context. Among them were present civic challenges: the declines in civic participation in the intermediate institutions of democratic practice (e.g., those of family, kinship, schools, and religious forums); the growing educational emphasis on employment and consumerism and a lessoning interest in civic competence and participation; a distancing clerisy of professional elites (politicians, intellectuals, and journalistic commentators) evermore influencing angry polarizations of civic views and potentials; the legacy of endogenous militarization of governance, production, and education that resulted from continuing wars, cold and hot, through 75 percent of the twentieth century; the build-up of global systems to blur nation-state boundaries, policies, and programs; and the crises in human security emerging from global climate change, lurking shortages in petroleum, new and stubborn forms of terrorism, and the threatening presence and spread of weapons of mass destruction.

Such influences produce and sustain troublesome divisions in the most practiced of democracies. This sense, in America, was enlarged with such military excursions as those in Vietnam, Iraq, and Afghanistan. Throughout grew more puzzles of installing democratic practices in differing political cultures and religious histories. And, as humankind is experiencing, there is no singular model of democratic philosophy and accompanying institutions susceptible to easy transference to potential practitioners.

Several clusters of values underwrite definitions of democracy and entangle and confuse what components are essential: all are likely present at the same time but bear different emphases. One cluster is the sum of the formal and recognizable array of political institutions, for example constitutions, voting, legislative bodies, political parties, freedoms of speech, full access to information and education and relevant research and information. A second cluster forms from the cultural attitudes and philosophies supportive of independence and individual freedom and welcomes diverse identities and wide ranges of tolerance. Another perspective emerges from the tension between freedom and equality and urges that justice govern the distribution of financial and other rewards.

Given such conceptual elements in democratic practice, there is also the nature of receptivity in the nations to which the chief principles are to be transferred. Must certain of the major components in democratic practice be already present in the recipient nation, a seedbed to nurture a new or stronger venture in democratic behavior? Does the essential history of the recipient offer promise to such an implantation? What factors bear upon the length of the gestation period? What disruptions may be expected and what supports by others are available?

Accompanying such steps of the Collaborative was that of a new professional journal, *Peace Studies Review*, to invite and stimulate interest in collaboration for advancing a culture of peace. This project gained much from the leadership of Dr. Charles Cowger and Dr. Daryl Hobbs, two distinguished faculty members of MU, and both pioneers in devising scholarly and other efforts for peaceful resolution of conflict. Under their leadership, the first edition appeared in the spring of 2005. I was invited to submit a paper, and did so. Thus was I enabled to reflect upon the organizing theme of UNESCO at its 1997 Declaration Conference in Hamburg: "Adult Education becomes More than a Right: It is the Key to the Twenty-First Century":

Source: "Civic Learning in the Search for Peace: Notes on a Balance Lost." *Peace Studies Review* 1, no. 1 (2005): 35–44.

> Local life and global action are no longer distinct. Each intervenes in the other, although abstractly until action emerges and takes root in somebody's community. To understand these connections draws upon the best knowledge and experience of all educational institutions. As universities help define and lead people, communities and whole societies along a new civic pathway, it is likely to be loaded with obstacles. Policies, decisions, and actions will be as complex and volatile as the forces compounded by globalization.

> [We must learn] that another hazard is the pull toward choosing solutions [that] are short-term, sudden, and drastic. When the aims are those of peace and justice, a healthy skepticism of dramatic and messianic goals must hold sway, lest the eventual result stimulates more

violence, misery, and destruction. [Isaiah Berlin, in *The Crooked Timber of Humanity*, wrote that] "revolutions, wars, assassinations, extreme measures may…be required… but we must always be aware, never forget, that they may be mistaken, that certainty about the effect of such measures invariably leads to avoidable suffering of the innocent."

Such a broadening of interest in how to place studies of peace, and leading further into other regions of university life, widens the space for new ideas and fresh thinking. One example is represented in the inherent tensions that may spring up on campus when programs and actions take direction on achieving cultures of peace. The subject, especially in the years after the terrorist attacks on US soil on September 11, 2001, was heightened generally on academic campuses, though not to the extent experienced in the Vietnam War era. Nevertheless, the MU chancellor, Dr. Brady Deaton, devoted one of his "Chancellor's Global Issue Forums" to a contemporary appraisal of academic freedom in American universities following the "9/11" attacks, and invited my response.

Source: "Reflections on the Theme." Remarks at the University of Missouri Chancellor's Global Issues Forum, September 28, 2006.

By means of a linkage of the overall theme of this Forum to issues of academic freedom in America since 9-11, this question: Why is controversy surrounding academic freedom so moderate at this critical time? I am moved to take note of global militarism; social disorganization; growing casualties of our uniformed men and women and of countless innocent adults and children; new technology increasingly designed to more efficiently kill and maim more citizens than soldiers; the growing and already strong membership of research universities in the military-industrial complex; the increasingly accurate methods for reducing community infrastructures to rubble in minutes but requiring years and billions to replace; widespread polarization of views rooted in hatred; and the growing sentiment around the globe that our nation is unilaterally failing what might be more rapidly and strategically advanced, that is, to lead in building a system of heightened global sovereignty, collaboration and responsibility.

As pointed out from the outset of *Bridging Campus and Community*, adult and continuing education has served as an organizing principle. However, in an academic career extending across some seventy years, this emphasis played out amid the other functions related to campus life and learning. Still present was the idea of an entire community choosing to join in both practice and support of university-like values and endeavors. The same notions carried on in Columbia, also a community of such values and practices. Columbia finds three academic institutions closely located to each other in its metropolitan center: the University of Missouri-Columbia (MU), which serves more than thirty thousand students; Stephens College, the first women's college west of the Mississippi River (and adjacent to the MU campus); and Columbia College noted for "distance learning" centers in the United States and elsewhere.

In such a context, the theme of *Bridging Campus and Community* is clearly present! Of special interest was the approaching retirement of the "baby boom" generation, almost eighty million in number, and likely the most highly educated and financially secure US generation. As part of the adult education genre was the fast expanding subfield of organized lifelong learning. Support of this expansion also came with the added emphasis upon lifelong learning especially tailored to older people. First was the creation of an MU Lifelong Learning Institute under the direction of Dr. John Parker, long a leader in MU's Cooperative Extension Service. He would be followed by Dr. Lucille Salerno, a noted MU professor of Social Psychology, with the creation and her directorship of a newly established Osher Institute for Lifelong Learning. Both Francena and I became members of the respective advisory boards. And I activated my own courses for mature adult students in these institutes, concentrating on such works as those of Alexis de Tocqueville, Reinhold Niebuhr, and such moderns as Robert Nisbet.

Rather in a spirit of gratitude for taking part in such an unusual blend of academic, civic, and residential strengths in Columbia, I have included the following excerpt from a commencement address I gave at Columbia College:

Source: "So What's New?" Commencement address delivered at Columbia College, Columbia, MO, May 1998.

> The best that a college can guarantee is that you will navigate wisely and successfully through the years to come. The best it can do is equip you with the foundation for an adventure in continuous learning as unique technological and social revolutions keep coming over the horizon.... This zestful companionship with learning quietly gives a more accurate realization of one's own self, an intelligent capacity for citizenship, and an ethic for weaving your technical skills into the fabric of society. On that journey also is learned that there is a goodness only you can do, a brave word only you can speak, a personal witness only you can make. And no one can take your place!

The National Defense and Education Act of 1957 urged the advancement, in numbers and competence, of new vocations and professions. This emphasis grew persistent and seeped into schools, colleges, and universities. At the same time, changes were also evident in the civic order. Of special importance was the decline in civic participation, a trend affected in part by the rise of women in paid employment. Voter turnout in major elections lessened. Declines appeared in the number and membership of labor unions and in organizations of long importance to civic affairs, such as Parent and Teacher Associations and the League of Women Voters. Vocational interests as those in business and industry bonded more closely with science and technology, a linkage serving industrial productivity. All told, the conclusion grew apace that American education as a whole had turned to preparing people for the job markets with a lessening interest in preparing them to become thoughtful and active citizens. My view grew also to reconcile and temper this quickening trend toward careerism, not to make it an either/or challenge, but, rather, a search for a rebalancing of the career and civic emphases in American education.

Source: "Rebalancing Civic Education for the Global Future." Paper presented to the Gist Seminar, University of Missouri-Columbia, Columbia, MO, February 28, 2008.

The explosion of information technologies and World Wide Web innovations, those now in hand and others sweeping into our midst, all challenge the capacity to plan, organize, and maximize knowledge availability and utilization. Important questions arise: How do we know what we claim to know? What do we count as legitimate knowledge? Is technical rationality sufficient or too narrow for today's problems? What new learning formats and changing roles for learner and teacher may emerge and be adopted?

Today's major issues are global, cross-cutting and long term! This calls for models of interdisciplinary cooperation by professors. For students and other learners, more linkages are in order for both study and practice (as in cooperative education and service learning). Edward Wilson, a foremost scientist-writer, exclaims, "We are drowning in information while starving for wisdom.... How can we best organize in a world henceforth run by synthesizers, people able to put together the right information as the right time?"

Citizenship in democratic states is believed to take root in local places as the seats of intermediate and balancing institutions between market and government. But E-government and E-democracy now take up new and far-reaching expansions. Does this pull up the roots from a place? Is a form of global citizenship possible? Can the blogosphere take the place of neighborly visits on local porches?

FAMILY CHANGES AND OUTLOOKS

AS THE TWENTIETH century turned into the twenty-first century, our settled nature as a family, augmented by marriages and new professional positions for our three grandchildren, began to change. Eldest grandson Christopher would locate with Jenny and two children in Phoenix. Our grandson Ryan would locate in Montrose, Colorado, with Barbara and three children; and Evan and Jen would move from Baltimore to San Anselmo, California, with their two children. Given these circumstances, our own children, Michael and Paula Nolan, decided in 2010 to move from Columbia to Montrose, Colorado, and thus establish a more central location to all of the above. Given these circumstances, Francena and I elected to also relocate in Montrose and take up residence in a welcoming retirement center.

But tragedy struck again, as it had done near the close of my term as the president of West Virginia University and the sudden death of my first wife, Catherine. Throughout our forty-five years of marriage, Francena remained tuned to our relationship, the larger family, and a host of friends and associates. She remained a vigorous advocate and example of the qualities and practices of marriage and the family, specialties that centered her own academic career. Her devotion to health and exercise was widely recognized, especially by me. She was a member and continuous devotee of a Columbia women's athletic club, which energized our almost daily walks and hikes together. But she arose on an early July morning in 2010 to report intense pain. A quick trip to the University's Medical Hospital revealed that she suffered from a sudden and serious issue of the colon. Following an operation and a failed sequence of recovery, her death took place on July 9, 2010, at the age of 92; I was at her side.

Throughout our pleasant lives together in Columbia, and then our decision to move to Montrose, Francena and I carried on our own conversation about the state of human lives in today's world and also of the larger family…and of our own. Rarely would a day pass that our discussion failed to include our responses to local, national, and international reports and trends. Although prepared in similar fields, we had ultimately taken up special and different interests: Francena's pointing to the family and community and mine that had moved from rural life and its institutions to urban and global challenges.

We commonly smiled together over how all this had happened and endured as we would turn to our professional interests. Somewhere along in our almost a half century together, and with extensive global travel as a stimulant, our discussions turned again and again to how best might the academic outlook contribute more to achieving a world in which peaceful collaboration became a new and spreading practice! The imprint upon me of such discussions between husband and wife influenced greatly the next and final chapter of *Bridging Campus and Community*.

$\mathcal{A}$N $\mathcal{E}$PILOGUE

$\mathcal{G}$LANCING $\mathcal{B}$ACKWARD AND $\mathcal{T}$HINKING $\mathcal{F}$ORWARD

GLANCING BACKWARD

HOW JOURNEYS BEGIN and continue through twists in the road yields stories to be remembered and perhaps told. Just how the journey was made, whether planned or fortuitous, remains with the traveler and those who join. The previous chapters take root in the premise that universities serve well and rise in public esteem when they effectively interpret and communicate their teaching and scholarship—the advancement of knowledge—in ways that aid positive changes in human cultures. Other actors and agencies of change are also numerous and the serendipity of human events so widespread that direct cause-effect analyses are sure to promote more heat than light. However, the application of science to human need and preference locates universities near if not at the center of change in modern society. All the while, universities digest and learn from those occasions when technical methods yield solutions expected from their applications, and, similarly, when the outcomes are unexpected.

My journey enables backward views of such meanings and outcomes across more than ninety-seven years of life. Certain influences gave such views both shape and endurance. Some came early and lasted while others faded. Other influences appeared later. Such impacts emerge throughout the earlier pages and fall into several categories, chapters of a life one might say. A summary of them echoes throughout the crafting of the previous chapters. Such biographic accounts commonly sum up the earliest roots of family, schooling, and other events that shape and provide purpose to a pathway in life and how it was traveled—and then the turn to the consequences!

First, as outlined in the initial chapter are those persons who played important parts in my boyhood years, especially those spent in a valley with hills so close and steep that the sun disappears by midafternoon. My parents, siblings, teachers, church leaders, librarians, and county agricultural agents, helped me peer over those ridges and grow entranced by the wider world.

Second, with unforgettable teachers, colleagues, and sponsors, as noted heretofore, the college years and early employment added insight and purpose about the world beyond those ridges. And, by the luck of the draw, when assigned as a soldier to worldwide duty, a wider experience added a global awareness.

Third, whether by formal learning or experience or both, my participation in graduate study and later scholarship fashioned new ways of thinking about human culture. A number of scholars and teachers, individually and together, helped me understand and write of how human authority and influence relate to social planning and action.

Fourth, life and career pathways take form not alone by actual study and experiential learning. Unexpected experiences also appear to stimulate other turns in a life story, which brings to mind one of my colleague's metaphors that "one career may dig a single and perhaps lasting hole, while another digs several shallow ones."

Fifth, whatever the nature of the wider world, those who join in family and home stand at its center. It was my good fortune to be supported wonderfully by two marital partners for the sum of seventy years. As noted in the Preface, they helped me absorb and organize what I was learning both inside and outside the family cluster. And each partner in special ways served and grew as a prism for clarifying my visions of the wider world.

Sixth, this work emerged from years of participation with a special interest in the linkage of the university to society. My writings of the relationship, as sampled in the excerpts heretofore, attempt to draw lessons from that linkage. Moreover, other writers are cited and help this summary to be better rooted.

The theme of my intentions while engaged in academic tasks was to explore and advocate how universities help local societies solve problems. Indeed, this effort became the central plank in my platforms as they emerged throughout most of the twentieth century. How such a theme arose and grew is perhaps worth this sort of memoir, not because it is personal, for which I hope to be forgiven, but that it reviews how people take account of their standings as citizens.

Moreover, at the age of eleven, I learned that there was something called a university, this from the West Virginia State 4-H Leader, I. B. Boggs. More and equally lasting references came from Walter C. Gumbel, the county agricultural agent in my West Virginia County of Hancock. He served greatly as an early model and continued this influence through our steady communications and visits until his death some 65 years later.

At fifteen, I saw my first university campus, that of West Virginia University (WVU). Sighting across its major quadrangle, it was love at first sight! While my first college year was a successful and memorable one at West Virginia's Bethany College, that love affair with WVU was consummated in 1936 when I enrolled as a second-year student. I am grateful that although it would take many years, Bethany finally forgave my desertion by granting me an honorary doctorate and linking me to those Bethany graduates who carried that College's great influence into the wider world.

The years following as a WVU student were tumultuous ones! The Depression of the 1930s found most of us poor, even poorer once we got to the university. But nearby urban residential basements offered cheap rents and boardinghouses such bountiful meals that with sufficient ambition, you could manage on one good meal a day. Students in WVU's Agricultural College were rather like a family, although this also rather descriptive of the whole campus. We were served by devoted teachers and advisors, and, in my case, such unforgettable counselors as entomologist Dr. L. M. Peairs and agricultural chemist Dr. Robert Dustman. Also of memorable importance was Dr. Robert MacLachlan, chairman of biochemistry, who recruited me as a student assistant and a continuing donor of stomach bile for his research. He allowed me to don the proverbial white laboratory coat. This enticed me, in private moments, to preen before the instrument cabinet glass! These advisors, along with others, deepened what had been glimpsed at the age of fifteen—to work one day for a university.

While I worried that I lacked sufficient farm experience and seemed more given to theory than practice, Extension Director J. O. Knapp nevertheless dispatched me in 1939 to West Virginia's Ritchie County as an understudy of county agent Ben Morgan. A more adult life, a marriage, and a full county agricultural agent post in Nicholas County, West Virginia, would follow. WWII military service and graduate studies came next. Some sixteen years of training, seasoning, and unforgettable assignments followed under the guidance of the notable president of Michigan State University, John A. Hannah. It was there, finally, that I became a devotee of the land-grant system of colleges and universities. My public civic awareness grew evermore "populist" in nature. These still-forming views went with me when destiny intervened again in 1962 and brought me home to West Virginia and WVU as the latter's fifteenth president. I brought a central view: that educational opportunity releases the intelligence and creativity among all people, and all work is dignified and amenable to lifelong education. This emphasis grew as my chief interest and in time widened to include the capacities and institutions of citizenship.

It was also a time when the outreach of universities expanded rapidly from local neighborhoods and counties to other nations of the world. Conferences and workshops grew in abundance, as did exhibits and public lectures, art and musical performances, weekend colleges and media presentations. However, with all that coming to pass, no university can avoid questions, and none more critical than those of how best to provide specific educational services that enliven America's civic culture. Such new and even rekindled challenges now rise for higher education in general and for the land-grant and metropolitan institutions in particular.

First, with the golden age of higher education that followed in the decades after World War II, the need arose to rationalize the rapid expansion of physical, curricular, and administrative infrastructures that the good times afforded and to reconcile a tightening and stubborn public skepticism that educational costs have grown too high, priorities too confused, and performances to seek solutions too unclear.

Second, as universities moved to the front of the stage after Sputnik, federal agencies, private foundations, and other sources multiplied the funding opportunities in support of science-based projects. They were expected to provide not only more quick answers, but to learn anew that quick fixes may work no better for universities than for other entities.

Third, America has become a nation of agencies (and of their special interests). Each agency builds a client base for its service and competes with others for resources. Such "clientelization" invades the universities, as it does the sinews of democracy itself, making them appear as a giant collection of fragmented pursuits often given to disorganized and competitive searches for further expansion and funding. Thus, they grow long on singular project managements, but short on unified and collaborative efforts.

If such additional challenges fall especially on universities, other strains fall similarly on our nation as a whole. Disconnection among people, and a weakening of their obligations for each other, now borders on becoming a way of life. This may soon, if not already, threaten the civic cores of American culture. Surrounded by racial and ethnic tensions, domestic and community violence, disintegration of cities, the challenges of global competitive power, people, feeling left behind, risk hunching their shoulders and deciding, "I had better get mine; forget the rest!"

Vivid symptoms depict such disconnections and characterize what we expect the schools to do for our children. Indeed, a third of them risk failing in needed progress because our society is failing them. Certain of our work habits and related preparations have grown dubious in an era of rising global competition. The real story behind political debate over the gap between rich and poor is this: the well educated grow richer and the poorly educated grow poorer. Furthermore, while the universities have led the revolution in science and technology, they now face how best to reconcile those who create and apply science with those who would use it without regard for its underlying social failures of unexpected costs, as is indicated in the tension building over the worldwide collision of economics, geology, and the environment.

The universities need review their mission statements and take sight of likely new contours of social change and service as the twenty-first century moves on. Both education and practice might be joined and so implemented as to enable people to think, plan, and act collaboratively. We live today amid an avalanche of undifferentiated and unmediated changes in the arts of human communications: they must be better mastered and employed lest we are overcome by the skepticisms, anger, and consequential disagreements that respond to private and/or public nostrums. Our time is one of getting ourselves excited about problems but failing to see them through with long-term goals capable of timely amendments or changed altogether as new data become available. We aggravate public concern and ignore public ignorance, all at the same time, a dangerous combination in a supposedly free and democratic society.

A second guideline would have universities hone the utilization of knowledge into as full a discipline as they have done in creating and disseminating new knowledge. Land-grant institutions are especially strong in this regard. They help fuse indigenous knowledge of the people with experimental new learning accomplished elsewhere, whether at home or abroad. Product and process innovation in industry is much advanced, as well as its partnerships with academe, but we have not codified these learning experiences into models and practices that can be taught to rank-and-file citizens, nor taken sufficient steps to help such folk find, retrieve, and integrate knowledge to better understand and cope with particular situations

A CLASSIC EXAMPLE OF *INTERVENTION*

THE IDEA OF extending the university into the public domain was uniquely introduced with the early establishment of American *state* universities. A similar idea was further extended by the Morrill Act of 1862, introduced by Senator Justin Morrill of Vermont. This later legislation made possible the founding and development of a land-grant college or university in each of the states of the American union. They were founded to take up the chief aim of advancing the economic and social lives of farm people and, in due course, the lives of urban people as well.

A vast history and an equally vast literature developed to explain this meta-idea for an important phase of American higher education. Moreover, there emerged an outreach arm of these institutions for the creation and transmission of research and instruction, and to include unique forms of adult education and civic practice. These in turn became institutionalized, and transformed not only American agriculture and rural life, but also became modified and shared throughout the developing world. Moreover, greatly enhanced food production in the United States would eventually enable but 2 percent of America's people to produce not only the food and fiber needed by the American population, but also for large international exports as well. Norman Cousins, an early and noted editor of the weekly *The Saturday Review* once wrote that this achievement of creating and extending research, as developed by America's land-grant universities, exceeded all other scientific exploits since the Enlightenment period of world history!

The food production miracles reaped in the United States represent a stunning case of social and economic planning in the modern and globalizing age. These impacts were felt in two technological revolutions: the *first Green Revolution* was the transformation of American agricultural production itself; the second was the following adaptation of such American innovations in the tropical and other less-developed regions of the world. This latter effort first centered greatly on the global productions of wheat and rice, an advance often called the *second Green Revolution*. Thus joined were new varieties and new technologies, along with better irrigation and more effective applications of fertilizers, pesticides, herbicides, and methods of cultivation. This widening global interest also stimulated a chain of research and application centers throughout the world, invented to large extent and now supported by America's land-grant universities.

As this *second* Green Revolution evolved throughout the wider world, the first one in the United States reached maturity. Thanks to the collaborative efforts of the land-grant university system of outreach to farm people, one technological innovation after another mounted in America's food production and distribution systems. Related consequences and changes also came to the production structures and processes of the United States itself. For example, in the period of 1925 to 1950, the average annual gain in farm labor productivity was 3.3 percent; in 1950 to 1976, this annual gain would almost double to 6.0 percent. Man-hours required in agriculture dropped from some twenty-three billion in 1930 to 6.3 billion in 1980. In those same fifty years, rice and wheat yields per acre doubled and those of cotton tripled! Moreover, in 1930 to 1980, the economic payoff of these gains would hover between 100 to 110 percent per year!

Also well known in this twentieth-century agricultural revolution in America were dramatic changes in farm production, marketing systems, and other rural institutions. The US farm population declined from 30.5 million in 1930 to 8.5 million in 1980. There were some 6.5 million farms in 1920, 2.8 million in 1974, and 1.8 million in 2000. Human migration from farm to city accelerated as a distinctive theme in American life. For example, in the ten counties of the Mississippi Delta, a major cotton and corn area, mechanization grew linked to quickening reductions of African American farm laborers and sharecroppers. Farm labor requirements in 1940 to 1960 dropped in these counties from 170 million man-hours to little more than 13 million! Between 1915 and 1970, some six million African American farm workers migrated from southern states to seek new jobs and residences in northern industrial cities. Meanwhile, production shifts between regions increased as well as longer and longer marketing transports from farm to market.

By the close of the twentieth century, the US labor force employed directly in food production had dropped dramatically to some 2 percent of the whole! This number was not only sufficient to meet food and fiber consumption needs in the United States, but also to provide an expanding portion of such needs of the world as a whole. At the same time, moreover, farm population and related institutions rooted in rural America persistently declined. For example, the number of rural school districts dropped in the 1930–1980 period from 128,000 to 17,000. Other changes, many dramatic, followed: some 149,000 rural schools with a single teacher dropped in that same period to 1,500! Yet by the close of the twentieth century, and despite the drop in the US labor force engaged in food production, American agriculture provided not only sufficient food for consumption in the United States, but also for an expanding portion of the food and fiber used in the wider world.

This century-long production marvel of American agriculture played a major role and served as an example for the acceleration of a wider industrial revolution, not alone in the United States but also as a major force for similar developments in the world at large. Out of this expansion came the rise of what is now frequently termed the global era. Two major lessons emerged in this advance of spreading new technologies to the developing world.

The first lesson, as the rural case affirms, outlines the roles and results of science and technology at work in rural economic and social systems. Gains in farm production and underlying efficiencies increased greatly: more, better, and cheaper food; a cornucopia of consumer goods; reduced underemployment; new opportunities for more meaningful and productive work in the urban sector. And despite the gains being distributed unequally, the larger and more general welfare was better served. In short, the rural case produced a stunning example of the power of science and technology in revolutionizing the economic production of goods and services.

The second lesson refers to fundamental changes in the related cultural and civic systems embodied in rural life. The production and marketing gains accrued unequally among landowners and those who provide labor and other resources. Ever more technologic methodologies displaced hired workers and, in their place, an ever smaller number of farm owners as well. A more concentrated ownership of farmland and how it was to be used and managed would occur. Traditional work patterns and social roles in farm communities changed or even disappeared; in their place grew science-based technologies to advance both production and marketing.

HARDWORLD AND SOFTWORLD

THE HISTORIC EXAMPLE in the United States of applying the fruits of science and technology to the production and marketing of food and fiber played a key role of releasing workers to countless other endeavors. This seemed most fitting in an expanding urban era and its desires for economic development, human convenience, and improved human health.

With the food production marvels herein cited, it is also possible to trace certain outcomes in applying technology that seem imperatively positive on some fronts yet fail to prepare the users for possible yet unexpected circumstances. The example of the seeming miracles attached to the worldwide and major employment of technology for producing more food at less cost and more convenience also associates with another vivid story: one of paradoxical events and what has since become a more commonplace reference, that of unintended consequences. Thus, it is possible to envisage the results embodied in the unexpected interplay between the *hardworld* and the *softworld*; the former represents pervasive technical systems put to work, and the other is organized by and within relevant cultural systems of human values and beliefs.

Cultural systems reflect collective arrangements of customs that are commonly thought of as institutions. These in turn provide and shape the rules of behavior among formal and informal groups and organizations that are present in neighborhood, community, and society. Generating and using knowledge are embodied in both traditional societies and in the more formal roles and institutions of modern ones. Thus, specialization advances with the growth of institutions that generate new knowledge and implement it as newly innovative applications. As they have in agriculture, these innovations take the form of new science-based methods of production and specifically those that advance more productive plantings, cultivation, and marketing.

CONSEQUENCES OF SCIENCE AND TECHNOLOGY

THE PREVIOUS CHAPTERS charted my career experiences along a professional pathway of more than seventy years in the twentieth century. This period witnessed a variety of displacements and other changes in both rural and urban life. One of them is the change brought respectively to America's Deep South and urban Northern regions. New challenges arose with the reduction of need for southern farm workers, which the advances of technology bearing on the production of such crops as cotton and tobacco had made possible. To considerable extent, these workers were African Americans. Their displacement in the southern farming states prompted a growing proportion of them to seek new lives and jobs in the expanding northern and midwestern industrial cities. Once they arrived in such centers, however, these new pilgrims found no easy improvements in their lot. With continuing technical substitutions in farm production methods, ever greater numbers of rural workers were released to difficult challenges in urban life and employment. Traditional rural communities continued to weaken in population and earlier farm functions, while more technical production, marketing and transport methods grew steadily to foster urban, national and global food systems.

Looking backward on this twentieth century shift in focus from farming in rural America to an emphasis upon industrial endeavors in urban America, one finds it important to witness the remarkable spread of the power of science and technology. That the universities of America and beyond were key stimulators in this epochal century seems without doubt. As one who spent much of that century related to the land-grant colleges and universities, as a youth and adult, such a reflection is a stimulating one indeed!

But there is more! Overlapping and succeeding the surge in urbanization in twentieth-century America were other worldly engagements of the United States in the aftermath years of World War II. Included therein was an acceleration of successes with science, technology, and other improved industrial techniques. Such ambitions and development processes of the United States also migrated abroad, adjusted to new situations, and stimulated further migrations of workers from rural to urban centers in search of new lives and opportunities.

Along with expansions of *urbanization* are those involved in the spread of *globalization*. Economic, political, and other human systems were all affected, and ways of life challenged! The linkage of urbanization and globalization in the twenty-first century has impacted all our chief institutions. Accordingly, new challenges, affecting the world order as a whole, continue to appear. They will demand that reviews be made without cease of the implications cast by the spread of technology—for example, ecological strains upon the resources and climate of the Earth itself, and still others embedded in the demands and consequences that followed in social and political life.

As the nineteenth century closed and the twentieth century began, the impacts of urbanization and globalization began and then accelerated in all parts of the world and to great extent witnessed, as if the outcome of some sudden wave of a magic wand, the quickening and spreading applications of science and technology. Had not the seminal unit of human culture begun to unravel by the sheer impact of an emerging and mechanistic civilization? And with the growth of consumerist values underpinning human comforts, had there not come a disconnection of people from one another and from their institutions? Karl Mannheim warned in 1937 that despair would replace hope and optimism if social progress was expected from the advance of technology alone!

But what are such consequences, or perhaps we should think of them as costs, that seem so easy for humankind to overlook and ignore? What explains the haphazard attentions paid the evidences that attend the plans and actions of technocrats leading to the impacts of technologies upon the orders of nature itself—the consequences of crowded settlements in gigantic urbanized conglomerates; the basic resource and atmospheric challenges; the consequences of the human mania for evermore economic growth animated not only by human need but also by human greed—which in turn sparks acquisitive rivalry among civic habits of living in neighborly proximity?

> It is difficult to envisage any decent way of life without a wholesale reversal of the powerful trends—technological, philosophical, economic—that began in the 18th century: the phenomenal expansion of human population, the secular trend toward centralization, the hectic pace of obsolescence, the spread of auto mobilization and air travel, the growth of mass media, the increasing mobility and uniformity; all such forces will have to go into reverse if such commonly voiced aspirations as variety, order, intimacy, conservation, care, margin, space, ease and openness, are ever to be realized. (Mishan 1971, 64) [11]

THINKING FORWARD

A DISTINCTIVE SET of relationships and impacts, those of the American land-grant colleges and universities, holds an important place in contemporary life—and in mine, as the past chapters and this final one may suggest. However, this is not to undervalue the importance of the several other types of academic institutions that serve to foster social, economic, and civic advancements. Whatever the orientation of the site, the connection of campus and community has not been without measures of tension! One such tension rests between headwork and handwork. John Dewey wrote of the linkage of experience and society. Others have called for

---

11   Mishan, E. J. "On Making the Future Safe for Mankind." In *Selected Readings on Economic Growth in Relation to Population Increase, Natural Resources Availability, Environmental Quality Control, and Energy Needs*, 2 vols. Washington, DC: US Government Printing Office, 1971.

more unity of theory and practice. Van Wyck Brooks saw culture as often at odds with utility.

Such tensions came ever more to mind with my retirement and acceptance of an adjunct professorship at the University of Missouri-Columbia. My interests also grew on the state of the peace movement, as did those related to the nature of education and practice for citizenship. Such pursuits joined to produce the idea of preparing a memoir. The organizing principle of the long previous period had been adult continuing education, an emphasis also related to Cooperative Extension Service work and to such special assignments as those of many years with the W. K. Kellogg Foundation in collaboration with its then-president, Dr. Russell G. Mawby.

Along such a route, moreover, additional and relevant influences emerged: they have also influenced the composition of this memoir, and special reference is made to three of them.

The first is *The Civic Arts Review*. Published by the Arneson Institute for Practical Politics and Public Affairs at Ohio Wesleyan University, this journal also serves in a working partnership with the Charles F. Kettering Foundation. The journal also presents a wide variety of updated and online presentations that track the continuing evolution of American democracy and its civic foundations and the outlooks and skills contained therein. I remain both indebted to and tardy with good thoughts and words for this journal. Its regular editions have helped shape my approach to both this memoir and to this chapter of summary in particular.

Another organized source with a direct bearing upon this effort is the Charles W. Kettering Foundation. Organized in 1927, the Foundation elected active participation and scholarship with a major focus on advancing understanding of democratic citizenship. The Foundation cooperates with academic and other institutions and emphasizes meanings and methods to be developed and employed with the interaction of citizens in their community institutions. From this long and successful venture comes both a wide and penetrating examination of the architecture of civic culture in its varied cultural and economic settings.

For many years have I gained from the colleagueship and friendship of Dr. James C. Votruba, president emeritus and now professor at Northern Kentucky University. His career and participation have related to many aspects of American higher education through his institutional and national assignments. He has become a noted leader in taking up the quest on how to plan, organize, and guide the modern university into a natural and stable form of public engagement. Dr. Votruba is one of three authors, with Carole A. Beere and Gail W. Wells, of *Becoming an Engaged Campus: A Practical Guide for Institutionalizing Public Engagement.* [12] This work is perhaps the most comprehensive body of workable concepts and procedures yet developed for defining, planning, and achieving a lasting university-wide model of public engagement, one that embraces the entire university.

When higher education is viewed as a whole, it is clear that it has moved inexorably to preparing youth to join the nation's economic life. From colleges and universities flows a tide of entrants into the labor force with the credentials necessary to take their places within established divisions of occupation and profession. Thus has higher education strengthened evermore to become a critically important component in society's system of production and marketing, one that requires workers who have appropriate and continually updated knowledge and skills. They should also possess a sense of self-worth and personal agency along with the desire to improve their well-being and advance themselves in pursuit of their own ends. Citizenship in the global era came especially to my attention when returning to teaching after serving some thirty years mainly in administration. I joined younger colleagues, then forming a new Department of Science, Technology, and Society. With a measure of exposure to international

---

12 Beere, Carole A., James C. Votruba, and Gail W. Wells. *Becoming an Engaged Campus: A Practical Guide for Institutionalizing Public Engagement* (New York: John Wiley & Sons, 2011).

projects, I reminded the students that global dynamics would ever more shape both their vocational and civic competences and, indeed, their lives.

But the students refused to accept my observations! Little of such interest appeared in their conversations and writings. Some grew brave, took note of my accessibility, and reminded me that they were in college to prepare for a good job; in short, "cut out the global stuff!" Their parents, they said, faced by mounting costs of entering a college or university, had not sent them off to "learn of Bangladesh!" The experience was unsettling! Globalization was casting a picture of market expansion throughout the world. How would democratic states be helpful in shaping this expansion? And would democratic states be able to reconcile discernible economic, cultural, and ecological conflicts? But I would mellow with respect to the youthful indifference, and wonder how the civic mentalities of their elders, and of me, might be better organized!

So I turned to a review of the matter: first to Horace Mann, the principal founder of the idea of free and compulsory public school education in America in early nineteenth-century America. He urged the development of citizens as its leading aim. Moreover, higher education, offered early in church sponsored colleges, gave initial emphasis to moral character as an important plank in the foundation of citizenship. Early adult education centered on civic learning, with Benjamin Franklin, among others, creating philosophical societies, local lyceums, literary associations, and civic forums. Still later, President Theodore Roosevelt's Progressive movement would connect civic values and science in a national effort to enhance local communities. Many other writers and leaders worried over this linkage of citizenship to vocational and other aspects of life. Max Weber, the noted German scholar, sought the balance between science and human intuition. And the notable American journalist, Walter Lippmann, even questioned that sufficient civic competence could be achieved and strengthened in a large and dynamic industrial democracy.

Arriving later are the 1988 insights of Robert Nisbet in his *The Present Age: Progress and Anarchy in Modern America*. [13] Therein he treated, in an unforgettable manner, the "prominence of war in American life since 1914... the staggering rise of the American military establishment since World War II...the Leviathan-like presence of the national government in the affairs of states, towns, and cities...the number of Americans who seem only loosely attached to such groups and values as kinship, community, and property, and whose lives are so plainly governed by the cash nexus."

The shift of academic America to an ever-stronger emphasis on education for occupational careers began in earnest after World War I. The Great Depression expanded this trend, one that would gather more momentum after World War II and the return of a great number of veterans to further study under the so-called "GI Bill." This trend was further advanced by the National Defense Education Act of 1957. The aid from such major enactments greatly increased the numbers of those ready to serve in occupations and professions needed for the technological expansion then leaping forward. Thus also grew an era centered increasingly on electronic communications as a core communicative and cultural emphasis.

Simultaneous with these policy and academic moves came stronger interests in taking up occupational posts, this at the expense of declining participation of citizens in civic organizations. The number of such latter participants has declined by at least a fourth since 1995. Voter turnout in major elections declined similarly. Even more dramatic drops came in labor union membership and in organizations that deal specifically with civic affairs, e.g., such as parent-teacher groups and female voters among others.

Meanwhile, a growing emphasis on vocational and professional training at the expense of the liberal arts component grew steadily in emphasis, and especially in those fields geared to science and technology in relation

---

13   Nisbet, Robert A. *The Present Age: Progress and Anarchy in Modern America* (New York: HarperCollins Publishers, 1988).

to industrial organization and administration. Of special note was the growth in employments involved with the "military and industrial complex." Robert Nisbet added more insight by calling attention to what he termed the "the rust of progress." By this he meant those underlying issues (e.g. the hidden social and economic costs) that can build up from technologies employed to seemingly advance the well-being of populations.

THE RUST OF PROGRESS

AT THIS MOMENT of writing a summary, looking backward and thinking forward on the roles of universities, a review of contemporary literature leaves me with a medley of both positive and negative trends. Academic institutions confront the intersection of issues and solutions that range from those that appear to shape the human future as well as those that suggest a looming catastrophe in the Earth's future capacities. The dilemma grows in part from the delayed and/or hidden costs that mount in the mass employment of technology to advance levels of living and production.

To cite one report on the opportunities gained from science and technological development, but also the unintended possibilities when achieving them, is an important study that scans the world of 2025 from the vantage point of 2005: a product of the Center for Strategic and International Studies and directed by Eric R. Peterson. [14] Throughout this treatment a key theme is advanced: "In the new era before us, we face an even more pronounced promise and hyper-peril—a period in which we have the opportunity of achieving even more exciting opportunities, and a period in which we face even more threatening dangers!" Following,

---

14   Peterson, Erik R. *Seven Revolutions: Looking Out to the Year 2025* (Washington, DC: Global Strategy Institute at the Center for Strategic and International Studies, 2006). See also http://csis.org/program/seven-revolutions

and greatly abbreviated, are selected items from the report's seven "revolutions" now under way.

1. *Population*—By 2025, the world's population will rise to approximately 7.8 billion and will stabilize in 2050 at around 9.0 billion. Hyper-urbanization will increase from the current 48 percent to some 60 percent of the world's population.

2. *Resource Management*—Resource management will need to help increase food requirements and require advances in biotechnology sufficient to advance movements similar to those accomplished in the "green revolutions."

3. *Technology*—Technological innovation and diffusion will also likely advance computation speeds, especially in molecular and quantum computing, in our workplaces and homes and "even in our bodies."

4. *Information and Knowledge*—Information and knowledge flows, reduced time lags in communication [will all serve] to foster the "weightless economy"—in which knowledge and know-how assume ever more significant positions relative to the material world.

5. *Economics*—Global economic integration will increase. The "advances in technology have not only increased the scope, speed, and efficiency of business operations worldwide. ...[T]he challenges to continued economic development remain tremendous.... A staggering 2.8 billion people live on less than $2 a day; in fact, 1.2 billion live on less that $1 a day, and evidence suggests that these income gaps are widening not closing."

6. *Security*—Also changing will be the nature and mode of conduct. Coming steadily into view after the asymmetric terrorist attack of September 11, 2001, are the spreading national interests in nuclear weapons as well as others that enable mass attack (e.g., radioactive, biological, and chemical in nature), and yet to come those making cyber-warfare a new reality.

7. *Governance*—The above circumstances "will severely test the capacity of all kinds of organizational structures, from nongovernmental organizations (NGOs) to corporations and to international organizations and national governments." Their leaders are increasingly captive to short-term and urgent demands at the expense of long-term strategic outlook and action. As one historic example of the complexity, hundreds of NGOs cooperated, largely on site, to advance the US presence in Iraq and Afghanistan.

In the background of such global challenges, both positive and problematic, of the forthcoming gains and issues attending the applications of science and technology, is also the reporting on the health of planet itself, especially the current pressures now challenging the environment. One of the more important documents on this subject is Lester R. Brown's book entitled *World on the Edge: How to Prevent Environmental and Economic Collapse.* [15] A professional acquaintance in my Washington period, Brown went on to a distinguished career as the founder and leader of the Earth Policy Institute. In that capacity, he has shaped a steady output of important documents that analyze the issues and propose solutions for some of the most critical aspects of the human future. In his opening chapter of *World on the Edge*, Brown wrote the following:

> Although we live in a highly urbanized, technologically advanced society, we are as dependent on the earth's natural support systems as the Sumerians and Mayans were. If we continue with business as usual, civilization's collapse is no longer a matter of whether but what and when. We now have an economy that is destroying its natural support systems, one that has put us on a decline and collapse path. We are dangerously close to the edge." (Brown 2011, 10)

---

15   Brown, Lester R. *World on the Edge: How to Prevent Environmental and Economic Collapse* (Washington, DC: Earthscan LLC, 2011).

CHALLENGES IN THE AMERICAN
ACADEMIC SPHERE

THROUGHOUT THE PRIVATE and public realms of higher education in America is also the sense of a mounting crisis! Whatever this term will turn out to mean is still uncertain, for a long history in the academic form must be taken into account. In short, this form, which unfolded throughout most of our history as a nation, is being challenged. Such reviews cover such items as the place of the "department" as the home of academic disciplines, and the historic rise of science and technology as major themes of American practice for industrializing both agriculture and manufacturing. And while *bureaucratization* resulted from such mission themes remains widespread, the new cultural context now demands an information era with *collaboration* as a special challenge.

American academe is now sorting out its own past accomplishments. Its pathway of significant responses now confronts several emerging pressures, if not crises, on gaining and continuing both private and public support of higher education: the rapid rise of online learning; the dropping of the United States from its first rank to that of twelfth among the nations with reference to the proportion of twenty-five to thirty-four year olds with college degrees; the trillion-dollar debt possessed by American college students; the persistent rises in tuition; housing and other student costs which now bring rapid and new strains to both public and private funding. In the long and short of these matters, the overall sense now extant in the academic world is one of nervousness over the present roles of US college and university missions, practices and costs. And looming ever more important as well, are the nature, sources and competitive costs of higher education in an ever more electronically organized world.

Thus, new forces and options grow in strength and now bear down upon the historic evolution of American higher education: the exploding communications revolution, increasingly sponsored by electronic-geared innovation and communication, now joins with the slippage in state and federal funding and the turn to supporting students rather than institutions; an expanding vision of continuous lifelong learning more free of set times, places and expectations; and related pressures on how intellectual capital in universities is distributed, organized and administered. Questions have arisen that now radically ponder if college attendance should be resolutely centered on four years; if faculties should be organized mainly by departments; if professors should necessarily have a doctorate; and if students should be held to a single major.

Other changes have widened the influences upon decisions made with regard to academic tenure, promotion, and monetary reward. The measure of entrepreneurship required to successfully obtain grants made one a member in the grant-making and receiving fraternity, this breeding a loyalty sufficiently strong to dilute that once given to the home institution. Provincial ties eroded further as new specialties blossomed and one's own scholarship linked better to scholars similarly engaged at centers other than one's own. These additional and external loyalties took on an enthusiasm and a measure of impatience with local duties.

Equally important changes grew in general university operation. Growth in numbers of students and their housing and other facilities, larger and more numerous streams of funding, including the inflow of research grants, student aid and other services, and such functions as intercollegiate athletics, were met with a weakening interest and involvement of faculty, a widening void filled by a build-up at the administrative center. Portions of these new and added operations filtered to department chairs at the very time when the scope of their authority was weakening. Meanwhile, the basis of departments as the home of academic disciplines grew more complex when called upon for long-term academic planning to enhance interdisciplinary effort. Moreover, the administrative centers of the research-oriented university, challenged with promised declines in financial support from the several public sources, find it more difficult to creatively address the expectations of the teaching and research departments.

Growing also in the face of such forces now being released in higher education are the pressures and competition of online learning. They now begin to openly challenge the conventional modes of colleges and universities. One is startled by the likes of Stuart Butler's "The Coming Higher-Ed Revolution" and Nathan Harden's "The End of the University as We Know It"—articles whose themes now appear in ever greater number and impact. [16] Such captions come among other exclamations now rising in the academic lexicon: "the college classroom is about to go virtual"; "the live lecture will be replaced by the streaming video"; and these along with such inventions as Massive Open Online Courses (MOOCS), now being revealed and put online by esteemed universities.

The foregoing chapters are organized about the chief theme of my career, one that extended for more than seventy years with a lead interest in *continuing adult education*. Thus I came to believe that the heartbeat of a genuine democracy beats but partially in government and market, but also in the overlap of what people believe and do as participants individually and together in their homes, workplaces and communities. At its best, primary citizenship is nurtured in families, schools, churches, labor unions, and in a host of voluntary associations. People also initiate and sustain charitable and other public works. However, as one noted observer after another has commented: we have steadily increased vocational knowledge at the expense of the various civic forms. The full sense upon which civil society depends cannot be achieved by politics or economics alone: continuous civic learning, participation, and work are all essential. To this end, three collaborative steps for adult continuing education are proposed.

---

16 Butler, Stuart, "The Coming Higher-Ed Revolution," *National Affairs* 10 (2012): 22-40; Nathan Harden, "The End of the University as We Know It," *Higher Ed* (January/February 2013): 55–62.

1. **Strengthening the Social Covenant**—One task is to seek greater understanding of the institutions of civil society and their part in social, economic, and political development. We must strive to foster understanding of the social *contract*, by which problems may be transferred to political centers for solutions, yet honor the social *covenant* that is based on a common identity, a social bond, and the coordinate values of civic commitment and moral obligation. Such qualities are not given; they must be achieved, developed and practiced.

2. **Restoring the Importance of Place**—A second task would help people understand how and why national and global institutions must be linked to local institutions if they are to function effectively for the long term. While the future will be in part shaped at the appropriate levels of institutional compass, it must eventually take hold and be understood in the places where people live. Special notice needs to taken of such linkages so as to secure civic understanding that is rooted, legitimate, and effective.

3. **Achieving the Self-Guiding Society**—Another task would employ citizens' participatory action research in building what Charles Lindblom defines as a "self-guiding society," in contrast to a "science-driven society." The former is one that tolerates less than a grand and final outcome but instead may accept lesser solutions that can be more easily defined and grasped. Such a process anticipates continuing study and planning to progressively comprehend more complex problems and *relevantly* and *continually* define ultimate and workable solutions.

THE NEW CHALLENGES: RECONCILING THE URBAN AND GLOBAL MIX

THE ORGANIZING PRINCIPLE of *Bridging Campus and Community* attempts to fashion a memoir of a career especially given to the outreach functions of universities. As summarized above, for many years that emphasis turned to rural settings and paid special attention to continuing adult education. This experience essentially began in 1929 when I was but twelve years of age. The occasion was my joining a 4-H rural youth club in my native state of West Virginia. Some half of the years to follow went to emphases that mainly featured the advance of rural population and the missions of the land-grant colleges and universities. This earlier period gave several opportunities to serve these outward facing institutions of higher education and take part, first, in their rise in serving rural populations and, next, their widening applications in the world at large.

As noted earlier, the applications of science and technology in the production of food and fiber not only transformed American rural culture in the twentieth century: such adoptions and adaptations continue to be evermore employed throughout the world. As also explained earlier, this revolution, as a consequence of the global transfers of American models, is influencing the remaking of rural life on a global basis, as has already been accomplished in the United States. Accordingly, in addition to the enormous gains of global importance, there are two major consequences to human life and institutions: the *urbanization of human life* and a *weakening of its civic foundations.*

1. **Urbanization: Issues for Response**—Rampant urbanization on a world scale has risen to challenge all human institutions, colleges, and universities among them. Metropolitan cities are increasingly filled with policy puzzles and degrees of urban disorganization. This is not to exclaim that educational and other urban services have failed. Conferences and workshops, exhibits and lectures, art and musical performances, weekend retreats, evening and distance learning projects, and the active efforts by leaders of continuing adult education and other fields of interest, all are evident. Despite such gains, however, urbanism on a world scale now

challenges most of its centers (e.g. public confusion fueling political conflict and voter apathy, and social breaches which provoke anger and conflict and find slippery footing in family, school, and other neighborhood institutions). Metropolitan communities are filled with intricate webs of private and public agencies. Each agency provides special services, builds client bases, and defends its claims for resources and acceptance. Agency networks make the city a receiver and contributor in still larger systems, but they do not normally create visions of the whole nor take account of shared concerns. Indeed, narrowly focused agencies may prosper while the common civic enterprise weakens!

2. **Civic Culture and Technical Competence**—Metropolitan universities, along with their various outreach divisions and interests, have evidenced a renewed concern with the meanings and technologies of public service. In response to these signals, the thesis herein is that the urban metropolitan university might well strengthen its role in helping students better confront the meanings and tools of civic life. This combination might also strengthen what is learned in the student's "major" and what might well enrich it by the greater understanding and practice of citizenship. Such a carefully developed participatory mode of civic learning, to include relevant participation of the student off the campus, might be advanced to provide a creative way to link the technical and civic categories. This step might borrow from the practice in some universities of Cooperative Education conducted in collaboration with the business and industrial worlds. With movement on such a matter, the academic major of the student would also relate to the student's community participation and interest. Such might well build a creative linkage of campus and community with a strengthening of both and, as well, introduce the student to some measure of on-site duties and skills of civic life.

Karl Manheim, a perceptive analyst of social change, used the phrase *Principia Media* to identify those functions capable of special leverage in urban society. He believed that once those functions were identified, the skillful use of these levers would contribute to constructive change. Using this principle seems especially fitting for university approaches. Another famed scholar, Ortega y Gassett, in his *Mission of the University*, wrote, "The university must intervene as the university in current affairs, treating the great themes of the day from its own point of view: cultural, professional, and scientific.... The university must stand for serenity in the midst of frenzy, for seriousness of purpose and the grasp of the intellect in the face of frivolity and unashamed stupidity."

EDUCATION AND INDUSTRIAL PRACTICE

AS THE HISTORY of business and industry unfolds, both have been more and more revealed as the partners of colleges and universities. Indeed, the preparation in colleges and universities of students for promised occupations has so expanded that a serious concern has arisen for an overemphasis on job preparation in the missions of our colleges and universities. Academic institutions may also react in a manner that stops short of a true working partnership with public schooling, business/industry, and government. Whatever the nature of such collaboration, workers should be assured attention as social beings that desire to play stronger roles in family and neighborhood.

Enriching the meaning of work leads to greater productivity and fuller lifestyles. Yet employment itself appears problematic for some if not many in American society. Americans hold employment as a fundamental measure of self-esteem. For those who desire meaningful work but find it withheld, and for those who are under and unemployed, the American dream seems far off indeed! Over the social agenda dealing with human work hangs a special shadow: the plight of unemployed youth in the central cities. Fully a fourth and perhaps even more of America's youth risk joining an underclass with little hope of taking up the responsibilities of employment and gaining the privileges of an active and positive citizenship. How to help these youth on to a pathway to mature adulthood and meaningful careers as both workers and citizens contains a critically important cry for cooperation among education, business, governmental leaders, and respective facilitating systems?

EDUCATION AND GLOBAL CHALLENGES

WHAT THE GLOBAL challenge is becoming will enlarge the space and impact of the world's systems of higher education. The major issues are ever larger and clearer for America: to help build an understanding of its role to help resolve and learn from global conflict; help reduce if not eradicate terrorism, including the seedbeds of human misery in its connection; work steadily to prevent the spread of (or achieve the outright abandonment of) modern military weaponry now ominously waiting in the wings; foster efforts to strengthen social and economic justice in those areas ignored by the major nations in the Cold War period; reconcile the multiplying demands upon the Earth's climatic, resource, and energy foundations now being made by rich and poor nations alike; and prepare for mass immigrations of people across nation-state boundaries, a force now exploding in the early years of the twenty-first century.

Global issues cross-cut countless fields of knowledge, many social, political and economic fields of endeavor, and with the not-unusual presence of conflicted policies and sponsors. They also link up with the background presence of some 195 nation-states, such bodies as the United Nations and its many agencies, and a considerable number of regional governance entities. Some thirty thousand INGOs exist worldwide with countless branches and offices. As economic, political, and communicative functions grow more numerous, interactive, and global, such expanding policy and action systems will in no small way face increasing demands for more reconciliation and cooperation.

The World Wide Web is in process of revolutionizing the customary efforts of American colleges and universities. Even before the contemporary partnerships of major universities, there were earlier steps to greatly widen the Internet system and add and multiply creative models to extend online opportunities (e.g., the University of Michigan, MIT, and Harvard University, among other universities). And as noted above, such pioneering with new models as a consequence of electronic innovations is still under way and shows no signs of abating. Moreover, with the horizon of possibilities being thus stretched ever more, it is not surprising that the implications of urbanity in the various world systems would arise and create a search for workable American models capable of contributing to both them and their global connections.

As examples of past planning, I cite two pieces of proposed Congressional legislation during the Lyndon B. Johnson presidency. While serving as the assistant secretary for Education in the Department of Health, Education and Welfare, I chaired a budget planning subcommittee for global programs in 1968–1969. One, the International Education Act of 1966, gained passage through the outgoing session of Congress, only to be abandoned when it failed to receive appropriations from the incoming session. A later recommendation, the Urban-Grant Act of 1968, was proposed. Reminiscent of the longstanding land-grant college and university movement, both the title and mission were modeled by the Morrill Act of 1862, which provided for the establishment of a land-grant college or university in each of the states, and by which this entire work, *Bridging Campus and Community*, is largely referenced. The Urban-Grant Act of 1968 proposed that an established university be selected in a major metropolitan community in each of the fifty states. Such a proposal reflected the view that such institutions would attempt in urban centers what the land-grant universities were continuing to accomplish in rural settings.

However, the overall circumstances of that period occasioned the failure of Congress to act upon the measure.

THE GLOBAL CHALLENGE OF CIVIC COMPETENCE IN AN URBANIZING WORLD

WITH THE TWENTY-FIRST century as the organizing focus, UNESCO convened a World Conference on Higher Education in Paris in October 1998. Among the recommendations made there was the Hamburg Declaration. This enactment had been urged earlier, in July 1997, at the UNESCO International Conference of Adult Education:

> Adult Education [is the] key to the twenty-first century: It is a powerful concept for fostering ecologically sustainable development and the building of a world in which violent conflict is replaced by dialogue and a culture of peace based on justice. Adult learning through life implies rethinking of content to reflect such factors as age, gender equality, disability, language, culture, and economic disparities. [17]

Glancing backward through the strands of this work, *Bridging Campus and Community*, one may note that the steady concern is about a question: How strategically apt are American universities with balancing education for citizenship and education for preparing students vocationally? As the earlier chapters have suggested, urbanism and globalism have joined to form a greater and more complicated emphasis on careerism than on citizenship. Later leaders worked to balance the linkages between citizenship and vocation. John Dewey gave citizenship a major emphasis. Yet Walter

---

17   http://www.unesco.org/education/uie/confintea/declaeng.htm

Lippmann, the noted American journalist, would even question that citizen competence could be achieved in a large and dynamic democracy.

So, if not now, when?

The twenty-first century turned the United States to a war footing even sooner than did the twentieth century! The "new terrorism" did not become widely apparent to Americans until the still unbelievable attack on the US soil on September 11, 2001. The US "War on Terrorism" was born then, and in its wake followed a global debate on its strategies and consequences. All of humankind would again confront that crucial question of Western philosophy: Do the values of specific cultures so outweigh universal values that war cannot cease its reign over peace?

Much of the content advanced in this professional memoir springs from the historical responses of the land-grant colleges and universities. My organizing principle was to sum up that model of outreach of academic institutions at work in rural America and its philosophy and method now at work throughout the world. This special dynamic is briefly summarized in Chapters I and II, and examined in more detail throughout the balance of this book. But in this final chapter, more attention is given to the academic institutions of *urban* America. Moreover, my approach herein partly updates pieces of my article published as "A View from the Center: The Future of Continuing Education in Metropolitan Universities," *Metropolitan Universities* 3, no. 2 (1992): 17–25.

As the United States grows increasingly urban, as does the entire world, the cities become increasingly the dominant residential mode. As the rural sector experienced the steady decline of its population, those of the urban sector rapidly increased. Whereas the rural sector experienced the relevantly specific design of a university in the public land-grant form, the cities founded institutions and often termed them as "metropolitan," whether public or private. The outreach and civic functions of universities are likely to be refashioned for urban populations by both the land-grant and metropolitan institutions. At least a quarter of

America's youth are at risk of being subsumed by an underclass with little hope of advancement through the responsibilities and the privileges of an active and positive citizenship. And no group or location is exempt from such misadventures of youth as dropping out of school, teenage pregnancy, and substance abuse. Also taking their toll are oppressive poverty, racial discrimination, and a work force that many urban youth are not prepared to enter.

The complexities and unintended consequences of the present urbanizing, globalizing, and electronic age, which now challenge civic cultures the world over, urge a restoration of positive citizenship. Whether public or private, metropolitan universities should assess these stirrings and grow evermore as major leaders in shaping the vision and goals of their respective areas. Continuing adult learning and its outreach instruments should especially seize upon those initiatives that are especially suited to university missions. Colleges and universities need to plan and conduct events that single out and advance the aims of community planning, advance understanding and practice of primary citizenship, and take steps to heighten science literacy in general and the use of tested knowledge for solving problems in particular.

Academic institutions must be independent in their service as both helpmates and benevolent critics of society. But by their developing practice of collaboration, they can serve the larger aim as beacons, even models, of public discourse, hope, and achievement. Moreover, by seizing the potentials of worldwide communications embodied in television, databanks, computers, and satellites, higher education can promote a widening discourse on the common good, and ensure that the human community is informed by the full range of intellectual, artistic, and cultural experience. And, given the vision, the will, and self-confidence, colleges and universities, in cooperation with a great number of related institutions, may do more to aid the urbanizing community to fashion a civic capacity ever more strong and relevant.

A POSTSCRIPT

As I REVIEW the whole of *Bridging Campus and Community*, in many respects the central chapter is that focused on my presidency at West Virginia University. I grew up as a 4-H boy under WVU's influence, acquired there my undergraduate degree, my first professional position, and eventually became its fifteenth president. My stays for earlier and longer tenures in central positions at Michigan State University and the Rochester Institute of Technology introduced me to both rural and urban societies, and to some of the ways by which relevant civic cultures might be sustained and strengthened.

In this regard, I did not seek nor apply for any of the posts enumerated in these pages and throughout my career. Among them, the requests for my consideration of the two university presidencies were first refused: these and all the other cited employment situations came first from the initiations of others rather than from me. Clarifying this point enables me, with equal candor, to draft these concluding notions.

The personal and professional circumstances that led to my "somewhat abrupt end" from the West Virginia post, the death of a beloved first wife, and a later and second great marriage, influenced that departure. Moreover, the new and waiting post in Washington, DC, and among those established to help advance American education both nationally and globally, carried its own challenge and attraction, especially when made at the request of John Gardner, one of the greatest American educators of the entire twentieth Century. But the poignancy of departing the WVU post would never diminish, a sentiment expressed in the last words of the WVU chapter heretofore: "These would remain my people!"

My background of graduate study and administrative duties at MSU had prepared me to help define and move forward a comprehensive plan of MSU's Cooperative Extension Service effort in statewide development. And it was to this kind of experience that my service as the fifteenth WVU president turned. Such a plan would have a university be among the chief leaders, perhaps even the coordinating spirit, for helping launch and renew a capacity for spirited *statewide collaboration*. This facilitating ethic would be that of working relationships based on deeply shared, uniquely designed, and imaginatively employed capacities for statewide goal-setting, priorities, participation, collaboration, and achievement.

As my time in life extends more and more into the retirement years, albeit relatively active ones, my interests remain, as the later chapters suggest, on how best to perceive civic affairs in American communities for an urbanizing and globalizing twenty-first century. Accordingly, as excerpts from some of my writings along the course of a lifetime are scattered throughout the preceding chapters, so have I chosen brief excerpts from an earlier article of mine that attempts to capture key challenges if not principles that might aid the collaboration of lay and professional participants at work in the civic order.

Source: "Adult Education's Mislaid Mission." My Lecture delivered at the Annual National Conference of the American Association for Adult and Continuing Education. Also published in *Adult Education Quarterly* 46, no. 1 (1995): 43–52.

The Erosion of Civic Culture

People are less given to positive assessments of America: how the good life has come to a high proportion of its citizens; the international example of its governance; the spirit and degree of charitable giving; and the personal liberties and range of opportunities [that] continue to make America the new home of immigrants from everywhere.... But such verities also lose against the fears of walking on one's own street, and against the surge of violent crime and destabilized families.... Global trade is good but not if it risks jobs at home.... Healthcare for all is seen as a national priority, but not if one's own care seems threatened. Such fears and contradictions in civil society not only undermine confidence of people in government but also in the worth of their participation in civic affairs. (44)

The Public Process

Enrichment of concept and language enables people to become more effective in deliberative civic dialogue. Such also makes it possible for people to identify and create the physical and social spaces in which the dialogue may occur on a regular basis. (49)

The Common Good

Two clusters of values overlap in the American psyche. On one side are those [that] see the citizen as basically the bearer of individual rights, and the other is found in the sharing of life's commitment and common visions and plans for the future. The central question is: how shall we best live our lives together? (49)

Voluntary Action

Too commonly, [agency] training defines the needs and skills desired by the particular agency and overemphasizes agency loyalty and effectiveness. In the bargain, the trainees risk becoming followers rather than leaders. This *clientelization* of citizens may also result unintentionally when the stress on human caring, however laudable as a value and an agency spirit, can instill a dependency in both the client and the volunteer. Thus the rise of community- centered leaders from the ranks of volunteers is reduced. (50)

Professional Education

New definitions of what is meant by a "problem" are emerging [that] take into account that problems must be repeatedly redefined, since they exist amid change, uncertainty, and complexity. Problems are not "out there" waiting to be solved; rather, they become what both the professional and the client define them to be. Thus, the client and the professional partner join for a continuous adaptation of solutions. (50)

Science Education

As civic behavior broadens to incorporate the primary citizenship of family, neighborhood, and associational life, and becomes more decentralized in the effects of its action, and more strongly challenges professional autonomy, using knowledge—whether informal and tacit or formal and scientific—will grow as the mainstay of civic practice. Similar to the earlier influence of Progressivism on citizenship, an informed utilization of knowledge should strengthen civic practice and cast it in a new light. (51)

Epilogue

Citizens must now face the gap between technological and institutional innovation, a crisis in urban governance, high rates of more violent crime, the jeopardy of losing a high proportion of youth as productive citizens, the stubbornness of racial and ethnic polarization, and, as mysterious as it is persistent, the spread of cynicism about public life and its leaders. Something resembling a civic entropy now knocks at the gate. (51)